Names I Can't
Remember

Welcome Home
Doug Bergman

Foreword

You've seen them, the Vietnam Vets who gather at the Vietnam Wall. They pause at the top of the incline for a moment, as if gathering the courage to walk down to the wall... to travel back to that time and place that is forever locked in a chamber of the soul.

They stand in front of the wall, looking at the names. The veteran who reaches up to put his hand on the name of a man who died in his arms in a stinking rice paddy, half a world away and half a life ago, may look to some like a graying, bulging, innocuous, next-door neighbor. But the reflection the veteran is seeing, is that of a helmeted, flak vest wearing, M-16 rifle carrying, young man whose "thousand-yard-stare" eyes have seen far too much death.

Doug Bergman is one of those men, and his book is a gripping, gut-wrenching story that forces the reader to confront the scars that war left. If you are a veteran, be prepared to be jerked back to a time and place that, if you are honest with yourself, is the watershed of your life. If you are not a veteran, if perchance you can't even remember America's most divisive era since the Civil War, then reading this will give you a post-graduate understanding of the turmoil that gnaws, to this day, at the soul of all of us who served.

"God would let me forget the names but force me to grow old with memories," Doug Bergman writes. And in this magnificent book, he forces you to share those memories with him.

—Robert Vaughan
Author, *Brandywine's War*

What's being said:

"Brilliant grasp of words."   —Lee Davis Willoughby

"Beautiful descriptions."   —K.C. McKenna

"Gripping."   —In-country combat vet

"... the prose is passionate ... has a surreal quality ....", I think this book will reach an important and significant audience... "
—Colin Harrison, VP Senior Editor

"Gut-wrenching."   —In-country combat vet

"Magnificent book."   —In-country combat vet

"A modern cross between from Here to Eternity, Catch-22, and Naked and the Dead."   —Patricia Matthews

"It's a powerful piece of writing. Your graphic language and the images it forms will stay with me for a long time. "
—Noel L. Parsons

"What a harrowing and overwhelming journey! Not only to have lived it, but to write it in such a compelling and graphically poetic manner. My congratulations and respect."
—Kent Broadhurst, writer, Movie/TV star

"I would give my eye teeth to string together words like you do."
—Jonathon Scofield

"Exceptional talent."   —Paula Fairman

"...a post-graduate understanding of hte turmoil that gnaws, to this day, at the soul of all of us who served."   —In-country combat vet

"...a... story that forces the reader to confront the scars that war left."
—In-country combat vet

"Wild... unruly... the poetry of your prose is so evocative of existential angst, desperation, trauma, and coming face-to-face at any moment with ruination and death. I've seen many books about the horrors of Vietnam, none of them more compelling than yours."
—Donald S. Ellis,

"the story was intriguing." —Peter Lynch, Editor

"...writing is quite captivating;" —B. Dove, Agent

"He tells a strong story," —Tracy Carns, Publishing Director

"Very descriptive and visual." —Jo Ann, Editor/Agent bon vivant

"... it's delightful," —Debbie Luica, Agent

"You do have a wild, Kerouac way with words ... with your storm of emotion and experiences ..." —Charlotte Gusay, Agent

"There is a lot of energy and excitement in the writing... In fact it reminded me of the beats..." —Matthew McGowan, Agent

"Dough Bergman ... Dear Mr. Berman ... Upon careful review the editorial staff at Four Seasons ..." —Frank Hudak, Publisher

"Dear Mr. Berman..." —3 times

"Thanks for sending me *Names I Can't Remember* by *Lawrence Henry Bank*..." —Doug Grad, Senior Editor

"There were many fascinating passages. But ultimately it was way beyond me." —Marlene Conner Lynch, Agent

"For me, at least, the beat-esque voice was so conspicious that it kept me more distant from the narrative than I wanted to be." —Mark Roy

"This is certainly an unusual story and I found the writing to be quite quirky and interesting." —Abby Vietor, Publisher

"...the prose is passionate ... has a surreal quality that doesnt correspond to my own views on literature and warfare."
—Colin Harrison, Publisher

"... you did an excellent job of evoking the intensity of the time and settings," —Mark S. Roy, Publisher

"... writes with great emotional detail and outpouring. His use of assonance and consonance certainly does create a poetic and even spoken word feel." —William J. Thomas, Publisher

"A little too 'blue' for my tastes."
—Unnamed Agent with broom up ass view
of war as fair, kind and polite.

Names
I Can't
Remember

An
"Assassin"
Confesses

douglas r. bergman

Warrior Group
New York

"Instructions for Search" © Francine M. Storey is used by permission. Poem © Mariah Hochhauser used by permission. "Boxer" by Simon & Garfunkle used by permission

Every person, place, and happening is real and true. Zelda the bag lady is the one character that is a compilation of the many homeless people I met at and since that time. My alcoholic inner voice, conscience and God character are shown here in a few did they happen chats, drunk imaginings and the Cat Man, a real person. They all are based on Jim Lipka who has the bushy beard, wore the floppy leather hat, fringed leather vest, smoked that god-awful Latikia in an ornate ivory Meerschaum pipe and had Mees the cat around his shoulders. Conversations are not exact duplicates of thirty year old events. In the interest of humor, drama, the meaning of the book and times, artistic license has been taken in reconstructing conversations of long ago and the imagined outcomes for the coffeehouse gang. So Ma, while I stretched the truth a tad (our birds and bees talk) everything is true to the emotions and events of the moment.

10 9 8 7 6 5 4 3 2 1   05 06 07

ISBN 0-97-59177-0-6
First printing

Library Cataloging-in-Publication data is available on file.

Published by:
     The Warrior Group
     Jack Butreau, Editor
     47–28 Francis Lewis Blvd.
     Bayside, NY 11361-3046
     WarriorBooks@aol.com
     www.namesicantremember.com
     http://vietvet.infopsyc.com/visit/px/n-p/htm

Printed in the United States of America

I Owe You

In the beginning and always, I thank the master of survival and my mentor, with the biggest heart, thickest hide, and the toughest broad I know, Ma.

Jim Lipka, you read my first crumpled pages so many years ago, said 'You wrote this? Keep doing it.' Thanks for making me believe I could write.

Kathy Kaltech, thanks for 'giving a shit if I lived or died.' I didn't.

I thank Denise Sodaro, my editor, for her craft, honesty, and pushing me deeper to the point of being a pain in the ass. I detested every agony in doing this book. You made me face them all and turned avoidance into crafted stories.

Also by Douglas R. Bergman:

Books:

Montrose Harbor
No One Applauds in the Suburbs
Radical Ice-Cream blue Rag Café and (ssshhh) Demolition Society

Plays:

Eyes
Castle on the Moon
X-51 Incident
The Decision
Poets, Pimps, and Poker Players

It was my privilege and honor...

...to have served with these known members of A Co. 2/327th "No Slack" Infantry 101st Airborne Division "Air Fucking Mobile—All the Way." I salute you all. Forgetting your names saved me a few tears at the Low Black Slab. Be sure that I remember every face and that what we shared has been in my heart and mind every breath of my life. You have made me laugh. You have made me cry. I have cherished each joyous and painful moment. If you recognize yourself in these pages, please get in touch. I would like to finally put the faces and memories to a name, shake your hand, and cry like a baby on your shoulder. Thank you. I have never forgotten you. Welcome Home!

William "Doc" Acree
Rex Andrea
John A. Ansell, Jr.
James W. Arms
Raymond E. Benson
Joe K. Berry
Reiner W. Bierowski
Gary Bills
Edward Bova
Marion D. Calvert
Paul D. Caramella
Hilliard Carter
Thomas D. Catlin
Charlie Cato
Theodore J. Chason
Charles T. McCorkle
Dennis W. Malewski
Bruce A. Masters
Raymond G. Mendibles
Nick Mihalic
Dan Mingo
Rich Montgomery
Fabiani
Willie Farmer, Jr.
Jim Faust
Barry W. Fox
Thomas M. Murray
Tom Furgeson
Gerald L. Parsons
Michael Guest
David Pitts

Marion "Mouse" Hammond
John H. Harding
Joe (Dave) Henslee
Joseph J. Hernandez, Jr.
Daniel R. Hickman
Richard Hinton
James H. Johnson
Ronald J. Jones
John Keeney
Paul E. Labrecque, Jr.
Phillip D. LaFramboise
Eugene S. Lee
Benjamin F. Liddell III
Thomas J. Locastro Jr.
Richard Luttrell
"Yankee Jim" Simchera
Donald D. Streicher
Norman W. Tarpley
Arthur J. Turkstra
Paul E. Vallely
Dave Walz
John F. Ward
Patrick T. Mooney
Lester L. Moore
Eugene M. Moppert
Alton B. Munn
Charley Fraley
Pat Noonan
Eduardo Gonzalez-Droz
Freddie Pitner
Michael R. Hall

Richard W. Powell, Jr.
Cruz Ramirez
Larry Redmond
Eugene F. Robinson
Theodore Rodgers
Richard Rodrigues
Paul D. Rodrigues
Rick Salazar
George Santaguida
William A. Sawyer
Ed Schlappi
Ray Sellers
Frank Seeman
Dennis Sheridan
John Coleman
William F. Collier
Leland R. Cottin
Edward J. Cox
Floyd C. Denson
Dave Dresser
Earl Erwin, Jr.
Peter "Wailing Wop"
Ken Williamson
Wayne Willingham
Terry Wren
Michael J. Francis
Ron Nagy
Roy D. Cierke
Gerald F. Pelzmann
Eli Haggins
George R. Pope

Instructions For Search

point your hands like a compass to down
and dive off the edge of madagascar
into the tea-warm indian ocean

as the fathoms widen before you
in a blue-green peacock's tail
elongate yourself like an eel
round and flat at the same time
then move your arms in great arcs
and descend along the path of broken sunlight

swim carefully through the hypnotizing seaweed
over the ragged battlements of tulip-colored corals
until at last, you pass
the ironwork of the continent
and you are below the world.

here where the sun is repulsed
by the fist of pressure
blind fish like beggars
wait for alms
and the sea is a buddha
silent and dark

no progression
no regression
fullness   flatness of tides
the eye in the throat beats the time
when the pupil is ready
the teacher arrives
          wait
for the coelacanth
fish of rounded gills and lobed fins
400 million years old
last inhabitant of the devonian sea

if he approaches
          unseen
          unheard
ask him

how did you survive?

Francine M. Storey   © 1991 Pau 1 465 197

Produced in the verse-drama, Surviving The Barbed Wire Cradle, Cubiculo Theatre, NYC, NY 1976. Winner
of the Dylan Thomas Poetry Prize, 1980, New School, NYC, NY. Publishd in The Art and Craft of Poetry by
Daisy Aldan, 1980, HMS Bounty 1997. Quoted in Marine Ecology Progress Series, Inter Research, Volume
161.1-15 12/31/97 by Dr. Hans Fricke of the Max Planck Institute, Seewiesen, West Germany. Featured in
the films, Instructions for Search and A Fish Out of Time, Producer Jerome F. Hamlin, Third Wave Media.

Bath in hall SRO, 1985

Prologue

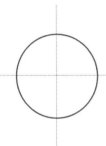

January 1985

"Rage buys a lot of survival."

What a gaudy life it's been. In the empty field of weeds out back of my drunken youth, every fear and failure magically became a dragon slain and kingdom conquered for the damsel of my dreams. I was stealing what I guarded in Vegas to pay for the pilgrimage back to my gimme' gotta' get church of the High Holy Temptation and Dazzleland; Man-love me hate me jes lemme know it-hattan. Charming BS that I fell off the wagon and am suicidal got me in a Vet Hospital psych ward. Sights and sounds that booze isn't hiding are causing Vietnam War flashbacks. I stroll the locked ward with a hard-on smile. Punk survivor lies get me free food and a bed with nuts, heroes and junkies.

"Wham!" backfires the truck outside.

"Enemy attack! Artillery fire for effect!" I scream at an Army radio in my empty hand while trembling in a corner.

"Who the fuck are you?" I yell to the empty doorway.

"Answers," says the bearded man in a leather hat, fringed vest, meerschaum pipe and a cat on his shoulder.

"Remember," Mees purrs. "If he has the guts."

"NO! I'm hungry, so very hungry for popcorn and tea."

Killer legs and South Pole smirk nurse says nothing sauntering off. She glances back to see me drooling at her swaying two hands-full ass. Desperately, I hang on to a cheap metal chip that means I have been sober for a year. Homeless, I need this time to find an apartment and job like the ones I drank my way out of.

Everything I see and hear in this warrior graveyard of the living is a haze of fear, anxiety and confusion. I'm an angry punk yanking a locked ward door keeping me from escaping. Cage and confinement beat me to my knees.

"Break your load into small parts so you are stronger. Carry it many familiar miles. Faith is a journey not a destination," smiles the bloody but still bearded Baha'i.

"Let me out!" I scream at an empty chair.

"You signed in," Nurse Santofuro sighs. She catches and cradles the warrior defiantly standing on festering stumps. The pill she pops numbs the feeling of fingernails gouging her palm bloody. Rage buys a lot of survival.

Staggering to my door, I gasp. It's my chicken bone sculpture of a winged warrior with a hard-on.

"Oh-lee-anna. Oh lee, Oh lee, anna!" I hum, drooling.

"What's that?" Santuforo asks, writing in my file.

"Awn-lee thang that'll drop quicker than hillbillies, niggers, er spics is'in Second Lieutenants. Hi y'all, Lieutenant."

"What's its name?" I demand, fixated on the bones.

"Who's name?" the nurse asks, scribbling furiously.

"That guy there!" I shout pointing to the empty hall.

"Flies feed on jellied dead dink eyes, Sir!"

"Can't you hear any of them!?"

"Hear who where?" she says, trying to calm me.

There's no escape from my cage for work the system con artists, emotionally whacked vets and psychotics on the way to lifelong confinement. The narrow hallway is sparkling tile and battleship gray cinderblock. Its scent is antiseptic, Thorazine and piss. The day room is always a cloud of cigarette smoke. TV babble and drooling warriors yell at ghosts but talk to no one. The security-glass enclosed nurse's station is where we beg for meds and get ignored at any hour.

"What's wrong?" Santofuro asks, writing.

"How should I know! Isn't that your job?"

I bump into a drooling ex-POW. The clinking medals on his robe are bravery bombs in my head. I fall and coward crawl, covering my ears to quiet the screams I alone hear.

"Saddle-up!" yells the pot-belly Sarge. Safeties click off by kids come thee killers to this lock and load cry of Beethovan's da da da dum dirge lullaby for baby-faced assassins.

"Jesus Christ. What have I gotten myself into?"

I run and get my patient report on me that I typed and head to the conference room. Stumbling on, I open my eyes and lurch. The pay phone offers me a mint julep.

"Bet the pig!" yowls the kid there and gone.

I crawl along the wall and look back. Nothing.

"I love's dem mens when dey needs me," cackles the black whore holding her nipple out to me and fading away.

I rise and grab the bitch's knees. My arms are empty.

"Resign your commission for the good of the service!" howls the skinny major, spitting disgust in my face.

"No!" I yell, wiping nothing off my dry face.

I yank open the conference room door, rush in, slam it behind me and gasp for air. Inside is my experimental pill pusher treatment team waiting for me to bleed on cue. Survival is reading about the stranger he/me from my third person report while they talk as if I'm not there to hear the joking insults.

"He's the behavioral disorder gook hater, the smiling psychotic or the sociopath gook lover?"

"Ah, 3491. Bagman... Boogyman?

"Y'all got mah store bought teeth, L T?" cackles the Asian woman doctor in the nun's habit.

Unable to breathe, I blink and look again. The Asian woman doctor in the white lab coat smiles. I run out. Safe in my room, I'm trembling, looking at the helicopter pad fifty feet from my barred window.

Chopper rumble and dragon fly eyes shiver me. I begin to sweat and cry, backing into a corner.

Crawling in the stream, I thrash my head high to see the sun one last glorious time. Massive why eyes is all I see. Their savage disgust rapes me and I crumble in the hot shower fully clothed drenched in shoulda coulda.

"What the hell is wrong?" I whimper. No one answers.

I manage to tumble into the counselor's room.

"How do you feel today, Doug?" he asks, innocuously.

"Save me!" Blam! Brains.

My Hiroshima guilt babble detonates.

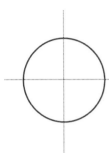

Popcorn and Hot Tea

FEBRUARY 1968

"Memories are feasts for the starving."

High School Graduation, 1967

At eighteen I was a drunk and a thief who stole tomorrow's hope with promises I hocked yesterday. I was a junkie hooked on dreams, not paychecks with suicide notes on the back, and I had survived a week without a fix.

In the barren front room of a vacated parsonage, I shivered by a dying fire of twigs and cardboard. A dim orange glow filled the empty room with faint shadows and little heat. Reaching from under a newspaper blanket, I stuck a finger in the bone-dry vodka pint I'd stolen. Desperate for a precious last drop, I licked that damp finger as if it were the last water at the only Sahara oasis.

My cold turkey and February tremors got worse, heartbeat by hopeless hour. Doing useless things slowly killed time. I hummed to the beat of my chattering teeth. Fingers gnawed raw from nerves and hunger, combed tangled, sandy hair unwashed for days. My sea blue eyes flooded with desperate loneliness. The addict in me jumped at the enemies in the shadows, and the starving boy in me stuck fingers in ears to silence a growling belly craving my own musky stench. The man in me froze but inched closer to a useless fire of embers and anguish. Smoky air was a lip-smacking banquet of desperation.

Encased in crumpled paper, I searched the lifeless rooms I'd roamed an hour ago. Perhaps some forgotten warmth, some morsel of forgiveness or scrap of dignity had magically appeared while I was gone. In each, I yelled at the ghosts of blame that devoured my soul. I laughed looking in the bathroom mirror. Its reflections of wasted youth all looked like me. The wandering burned off enough panic to survive one more hour. Quaking in angry, heaving sobs, near the gasping fire, the stubborn rebel in me refused to give up. They were the tears of a clench-fisted man surviving in a bowl of shit learning to like the taste.

When my yowling belly demanded relief, I ate my nightly feast of popcorn and hot tea stolen from the unlocked cabinet in the church kitchen across the street. Dead coals were intimidated back to life with desperate breaths. I made the meal like a manic junkie fucking his arm with a needle while cops banged at the door. A mangled pot full of spoiled kernels leapt into the fire after I cursed the tea water. The burnt kernels that stuck to the bottom of the pot were the best. They tasted like creamy, thick gravy over butter soft turkey that strained belts and put you to sleep. I tasted each morsel with the slow, delicious passion of endless foreplay, for memories are feasts to the starving.

The carpet in the wood-grained, paneled living room was the only comfort in the empty house awaiting the new minister. The departing family had left it spotless and utterly empty of anything I could use. I could hear the faint echoes of their gentle joy. They put a mask of a weak smile on my face. In the narrow off-white hall were the dust shadows of treasures that once hung there. I listened to my father knows best ghosts.

Names I Can't Remember

"Dear, we have to take Mother's gift," said the minister's wife in a summer dress.

"Ceramic fish? They look like a vacation shirt on a dad-blasted Methodist trying to look cool."

"Earnest, such language in a minister's house for Christ's sake? Oh my! That's what I get for marrying a bingo player."

In the kitchen, I collapsed on the cold floor of lifeless light tan linoleum stamped to look like bricks. The cabinets were cheap pine stained to resemble rich cherry. The counter was ugly speckled Formica bubbled here and there. The God-awful wallpaper an homage to dime store plastic flowers that had exploded at a cheap funeral. Rust footprints from the metal legs of kitchen chairs had been scoured away. I swore I heard a toaster pop and could smell the delectable aroma while the minister scraped his toast and cursed Episcopalians. I pounded the floor in frustration. Stumbling out of the kitchen, I stopped abruptly at the door. I ran my trembling fingers tenderly over the growth marks carved in the wood and strained to hear the negotiations.

"Hmph. Two inches in six months," beamed the proud father at his gangly teen.

"Big enough for a...a— Honda scooter?" he eked out.

"Damned Episcopalians with all that TV and Rock-and-Roll. Your son wants to talk to you, Mother!"

I smashed the abandoned clock hanging over the door. Less than ten minutes had passed. My nights were filled with wandering and the immediate panic known only to the homeless. Watching the moonrise, I paced and worried about where I'd live next. The gift of a few days here from a youth minister risking his job would soon run out and I would have to leave.

There was no going home. Dad told me it was time to go. Man to man, I agreed despite being taller and a hundred pounds heavier. Although she was seldom there, coming home when I damn well pleased had broken my mother's heart. I was kicked out of an apartment I shared with other troubled boys while finishing high school.

Shoulders slumped by emotional exhaustion, I stared out the picture window at midnight. My gaze fixed on the occasional passing of a weaving car full of horn blasting teenagers on Graceland Avenue. At one, I cried for my next booze and toilet paper. At two, the ghostly laments of the owls signaled the beginning of the hunt. At four, I shuddered by the dead fire and tried to sleep. Awake, I dreamed of a bed and hot meal.

When sunrise finally came, my goose-bumped skin stopped shaking. At the picture window, I watched the sky fill with calm. The threatening sky of velvet black streaked with soulful emerald blue and vibrant gold warmed me. There they were. I could see them now. Their silent might quieted my fears.

"Good morning trees. I made it through the night."

I greeted each sunrise with a defiant smile. Sunshine was a reward for beating the demons this time. The trees were my friends. I waved to Abraham, the oldest, wisest, and the most scared. Could I make it like he did?

> Beyond the trees, the battle fires blazed,
> Body bags and empty graves waiting.
> Graceland poets sang joyously,
> Bozo's Circus tickets had finally come.
> In Abraham's restful shadow,
> Prom dates were sealed with stolen kisses.
> At the horizon of the sixties sun afar,
> Rose armies of bloody arms
> Through the haze of hemp and hate.
> Daddy daddy tell me true,
> Freedom's just your red, white and blue?
> On Graceland echoed what father knew best,
> Fading sermons do as I unto you,
> Mop haired prophets beating
> Love me do koo koo ka choo.
> Graceland's wise trees weeping
> For the last suburb sheep about to die.
> Mom's little helpers scream our world's free.
> The death rush reveals a bloody line,

War's not hell it's just the truth,
Each tribe must come to see and sigh.
Every child of any rainbow grew old
In the next mangled flesh line and lie,
Freedom's only free and peaceful
Near Graceland's wise fat trees,
No purchase required, comes with batteries.

The cathedral tall Elm and Maple trees swayed with the slow dignity and quiet confidence of survivors. They danced with the wind in the sensual flow of a Vienna Waltz played in a wise symphony of many years. Their thick and countless limbs, covered in soothing, jade green leaves created the tranquil tunnel below. Their mighty presence added the last pinch of innocence to a sixties recipe of rage. They fed me a weeping wisp of carnival cotton candy, sang my last lullabies and read final fairytales. In this quiet suburb outside Chicago, Graceland Avenue was the last sumptuous meal of youth and I blindly ate my fill.

The first draft lottery would soon be drawn. The papers that kept me warm were full of the news. A pundit quipped about the panic that struck students with rotten grades. Student draft deferments required good grades. His column bannered the birth of the A+ term paper business. That page kept an armpit warm. I cracked a smile when Charlie Brown asked Snoopy to deliver a Valentine to the little red-haired girl. Snoopy complained he didn't date redheads. One report was about seniors canceling backpack travel plans for grad school safety from the draft. Another interviewed kids with blue-collar dreams, whose previous worst worry was that their Pop would be the boss at the plant, who now had plans for junior college. Editorials under my ass asked how many poet chess players would sacrifice their rebels' virginity in a violent bloody underground. I was reading about auditions for a kid theatre touring company. Sixty a week!

My travel section pillow sold tickets to Canada. A column satirized them as failing student escape visas for solitary confinement in squalid rooms filled with old snapshots, paranoia and coded letters from shattered parents. Other columns screamed love of country. More lamented lives, home down payments and factory seniority traded for junior college lectures on sitcoms. I skipped that column. I scanned booze ads.

The editorials warming my shoulders complained about the stampede of punks with criminal records and fathers that wrote fat checks for conscientious objector lawyers and Peace Corps applications. Leaders demanded an end to the immorality, while politics made relatives rich civilian contractors.

All I gave a damn about was Zelda, the bag lady, coming up the walk. She always had coffee and sympathy for the other stray dogs. I opened the door and waved.

"I'm guess'n you'd like a slug of this coffee," she said in a gruff voice that made a gravel truck sound like a French maid.

She watched me slop the coffee even when I tried with two hands. Inches from my mouth, it stalled and jiggled too much to sip. This gruff woman who scowled and dressed in stinky layers steadied the cup to my lips and fed me like it was mother's milk.

"What's wrong with all this?" I asked.

"You're a tad young to have shakes that bad, Sgt. Pepper. Before yah get skunked, drink all the water you can. Morning too. You won't ache so God damn bad and maybe get a cup to yer yap. Slower, sonny. Let yer gut untie. I don't give a twit if ya' tremble or shoot gutter water in your veins. I mind the waste of good coffee. You enough a drunk to know to drink java with the thick, old-time mugs? Guess not. Weight steadies shakes. Or ice coffee in a glass with a straw. Fooled the last mister with that fer years," she laughed through her toothless smile while brushing my hair back softly.

I sat beside her on the stoop. One drunk learned from another who'd survived. "Thirty years a professor with a Masters and I have no idea how it started. One day I noticed I drank more sherry and graded fewer papers. When the last mister died, I packed a few shopping bags, bought sherry, headed out and never looked back. There ain't no answers, punk. The only truth was that damn telegram "The President regrets to inform you your—," she said, stopped cold by the memory that hurt too much to say out loud.

I handed her a last scrap of tissue. She refused to let me see her wipe the tears away..

"Not yer fault. Thanks. He'd a died in a knife fight or jail if not there. That damn brother...," she said stopping again.

I put my arm around her. Silently and with much hesitation, she leaned into it.

"You damn fools don't see it. Kids, soldiers, and parents too, fighting the same damn war in different uniforms woven with the same regret," she cried into my shoulder.

I didn't have the heart to ask about the brother she was yelling at. The tears were all I needed to know about a tough, drunk sister driven to the street.

"My name is...," I tried, but she stopped me.

"I don't mind faces. Names hurt too much," she said with a prophetic sigh and shaking her head.

Scuffling away, she threw me the paper. Hidden, squatting behind a tree, I used it to wipe my ass in Zelda's honor. I imagined her smiling far off, knowing a fellow drunk emptied himself of one truth. It wasn't an immoral war, just the dump of the day. I was at peace until the hunger of a new day started. I was free and living by my wits. The trees were friends and relief until the hungry cold lonely after sundown when the panic began.

At the curve in Graceland Avenue headed to the center of town was Abraham. He bore the scars of ancient weather and dual-carbed muscle cars fueled with beer. His gnarled trunk was covered with elephant hide bark. It took two sets of arms to circle him. The crusty bark was three inches thick and flowed along the trunk like slender streams with deep caverns of time between them. At the knot scar healed with tar just beyond reach was once a mighty limb as thick as a man. It was severed by a 57 Chevy that lost the drag race. Three feet lower was the two-foot square deep gash to the heartwood from a Mustang whose driver was copping a feel.

A hundred feet above this four-lane street were the towering boughs draped in a lush layer of calming, pale green leaves. They shut out the rat-race rhythms of life. The only sounds beneath them were the comforting rustling of the leaves and the creaking limbs that gently taught the wisdom of compromising with the wind. The noise of the commuter trains two blocks away was silenced. The 60's hurricane was a 50's breeze of gentility here. God made Graceland Avenue a quiet zone. Its smooth four-lane blacktop was a bumpy country garden path.

On this and the other streets were the old homes built when Des Plaines was farmland, a mere watermelon seed spit from Chicago. Brick or wood, they all had large porches or stoops. Bold sky evenings drifted lazily to velvet black nights on swings while enjoying lemonade sugared with gossip, waving to passing neighbors headed to the Sugar Bowl for homemade candy or ice dream, and enjoying a gentle breeze pungent with the aroma of backyard charred beef. Each large family home was three or four stories high. In the dormers, pimpled kids scribbled hope in diaries. The lawns were large, plush green carpets where every game was more important than any score. Sidewalks were wide enough to pass without interrupting a hop-scotch championship. Graceland was clogged with gossips the night widow Hundley was seen on her porch swing with widower Apple-baum, with nary an inch between them.

On the corner at Laurel was the one story main library where a cloth flag was raised and saluted each day. I'd wondered why they didn't use a plastic one they could leave out and wash with a hose. Plastic or cloth would be the same freedom, just easier. I'd lived a punk's life and hadn't learned that one you expect, the other you fight, even die for.

Lining the surrounding streets were the shops of merchants I knew by first name and played penny poker with. Downtown had everything: Sam's small Jewel grocery store, Mrs. Dres-den's gift shop, old man Griswald's movie theatre, Kazinski's Tru-Value hardware etcetera and son. Saturday and Sunday break-fast at the Mandas' family Greek diner, in the heart of downtown, was tradition for great food and gossip about how immigrants could make better flapjacks and home fries than Grandma.

Names I Can't Remember

Downtown fought the malls, called shopping centers then, with charm. Storeowners stood in doorways and asked how the wedding went. There were a lot of weddings in '68 after the lottery. January strangers married in February and brought baby home to the dorm in June; the Lottery Loser Lovers. Downtown gave out free smiles and fed your parking meter for no charge. They gave out balloons to kids so parents wouldn't need one to mark the car in the shopping center parking lot desert.

Fast food joints had come to the outskirts of town but weren't doing well. From them, you bought any form of mom's faster food minus any taste, smile or stroke to the cheek. Downtown was the blanket no boogieman shopping center could get under. Graceland Avenue was an artery pumping gentility into our hearts. When shopping centers made me feel like an orphan, Downtown was mom holding out milk and cookies.

Graceland's trees shaded the prayer at the First Church of Christ Congregational Church in the center of the block. The church was as non-sectarian and as liberal as it could get. That's like being Episcopalian without admitting it. The church had the audacity to marry divorced or pregnant couples, ignore what people did in the bedroom and allow young people to give sermons. Elders flinched. God smiled.

The church sanctuary stood six stories tall. Most of that was the bell tower. Walls were built of red brick. The tower, stairs, border decorations and impish gargoyles were carved from gray granite speckled with color. On the street side towered the two-story stained glass window. It mesmerized and confused. The many images were a perfect Reader's Digest account of the whole damn Bible, Eden to Armageddon. A peaked roof was topped by a bell tower that rang the hour and half-hour. In all of downtown, no one gave a hoot if their "Timex took a licking but kept on ticking." They checked Dad's gold pocket-watch with their ears. The L shaped church bordered a lawn with a tall shady Maple in the center. Its only scars were hearts with two sets of initials inside.

Another door beneath the main stairs, led to the basement community room used mainly for Sunday school. On Saturdays, it was the youth group's teen coffeehouse. I was part of its in group. Our ideas pointed the masses to their time clocks in Hell where they kept up with the Joneses while we ran things. We were going to change the world, whether the world liked it or not.

The white bread, suburban rebels dreaming the free love revolution in song and word at the coffeehouse were crap to me. I liked the place because it was noise that filled the lonely that booze never could. My rebellion was watering my parent's booze, pissing on Ma's paint-by-numbers dog, stealing money from the till at work and falling into line with all the other sheep in powder blue Levis and bleeding madras shirts. I got B grades because A's took work. I told a rigid teacher to go to hell on the final, and proudly waved the paper slashed with a red F. I ran away to Malibu, but returned broke. I did plays rather than football because physical pain sucked. I buzzed the school on my Honda and puked my guts out at parties to ovations of silent shock, jokes and disgust.

None of it mattered. I'd survived another lonely hungry night, had coffee with street queen Zelda and taken a great dump. It was Friday, one more day to survive until tomorrow's coffeehouse. I walked over to my silent best friend and sat. With a pencil stub and stained paper, dream junkie me hid in Abraham's peaceful shade and shot up.

> Three meals a day and a soft warm bed,
> God please help me from one so free.
> In a house stripped bare wall to wall,
> Just fireplace embers on cold shiver nights.
> I toss and turn on a frigid floor near a useless fire.
>
> Lost in dreams and drunken free,
> Unholy three I myself and me
> Gorging stolen popcorn and hot tea.
>
> Thank you David for letting me stay.

Yes, I know I must soon be gone.
Where shall I go,
What do I do with all this free?
He's not there to hear the plea.

Just glowing coals and shadow wall dances
Belly growls and cold turkey yellow pee.
At graduation the rebels met
To dance the defiant drunken spree,
Chopper, Fat Butt, Tom, Phil and me.

Life now ours to flower power shower
A world with what I wondered,
The white bread rebels we.
Who gives a fuck I 80 proof bellow
In a chemical chorus so Mellow Yellow

When ma yells dinner in three.
The rebels call lulls you to slumber
Under cotton and wool so warm.
Yet where do I go now eighteen?
I took the shove from the nest with glee.

Lost in dreams and drunken free
Unholy three I myself and me
Gorging stolen popcorn and hot tea.

Mop heads; Goo & the Toes Jams.

Names I Can't Remember

The Radical Ice-Cream Blue Rag Café and (ssshhh) Demolition Society

FEBRUARY 29, 1968

"In 1968, kids bartered dreams for beds and burgers and were never seen again. If we hadn't gambled our lives to beat the boredom with a joint of lonely, maybe we could have finished being young."

I t was a room with the personality of cold oatmeal. With checkered cloth, discarded Chianti bottles covered in candle wax and bold images of flower power, kids turned a jackass into a lean, jet-black stallion and galloped it out of loneliness and confusion. In a plain church basement coffee house, I found family and friends that screamed every fear never shared with any parent. That room asked how I felt and listened. It never yelled jerk at me when I said I didn't know. It talked with me, not down at me. It was all the encouragement and hugs home never had.

A warm morning sun and soothing rustle of Abraham's leaves calmed my night shivers and drunk's tremors. With a sigh, I crossed Graceland Avenue. Coffee house was a day off but I had to see the room that made me feel more safe than home.

At a street level door framed by ivy, I looked through a small, wired glass window down the steps into the empty space. Large windows and dull gray floor tile defined the empty space. Shaker plain shelves and cabinets on each wall held boxes of Sunday school stuff. There were stacks of wood grained, Formica-topped folding tables, and steel chairs that outlasted Moses' aching ass. White bread rebels would pay fifty cents for munchies, get their hands stamped and shake the world making promises they'd never keep. They were going into politics. I imagined their voices.

"If you all burn bras, the principal caves," said the king with a three-hair beard and moon crater acne.

"Far out! I dig. Why can't class officers just raise a 'We Refuse' banner? Babes, just get 'it' up before eleven, my curfew," said the warrior queen slyly stroking his thigh.

"Me, raise a banner, risk my slot at Northwestern? Doll, they don't draft burnt bras," said the next class president, too busy counting votes to catch her bold invitation.

"Dance 'till dawn, Babes. Miss curfew! At sunrise, I have that home plate that you've wanted to slide into."

"Miss curfew? Get grounded? You nuts? I just got my license!" said the bell-bottomed idiot destined to die a virgin. Doll slammed his hand in her back pocket.

Suburban coffee house rebels shattered commandments with the courage of a four-lipped ass kisser. Our sins were weed that might be spice, a six-pack stale it had been hidden so long, and sexual rebellion quashed by your aunts make-up to cover a hickie. When an anarchist held match to flag, he got an ovation of cotton candy apathy.

Leaning on the door, I relived my first night there. Face hidden by

Names I Can't Remember

my jacket, I took a swig from the pop bottle full of whiskey stolen from my folks' bar. Lazily, I stuck out my hand to get stamped. Maybe this dump would fill time between my complaining and drinking.

The chick stamping hands watched me drink. She had dyed to death blond hair. Her face was scarred by knife fight acne she barely survived. Her rusty blade voice slashed me low and cold with jagged honesty. I almost dropped my 80 proof guts.

"Some of us like it when you come in our mouth. Ask. It beats that crap," she said with a grin that signaled I've been there.

Chopper stamped my hand saying, "It's great in there. Avoid the idiots afraid to take a drag of freedom. Breathe. Thinking is a great buzz," she cracked as I grimace walking in. I guess showing fear made you a regular.

Anxiously, I looked at the desert room that would be an oasis of cocky smiles tomorrow. A February sun blazed through the windows. Like columns of might angled to the walls, golden shafts full of swirling dust angels gave the room a warm glow. My first night, I wandered through a noisy crowd and my jaw dropped. Kids spoke out-loud! Most shocking, chaperones listened. I heard excited debates, not mom and dad lectures. The music of laughter and thrust and parry of repressed ideas was deafening. Shared cider fired blazing dialogues. I didn't see anyone scribbling horrible angst poetry in a notebook, as I did at home alone in my room.

Two singers got on the tiny stage to get their agonies healed with lights and applause. I twirled a chair and sat with my chin in my hands on the backrest. The skinny blond had ironed flat hair and jeans hanging on her hips. The guy looked like a hairball refugee from some soup line. With their eyes on each other they swayed defiantly, played angrily, and moaned familiar whispers fucking their egos silly with a scratchy-voice opera of rebellion.

> Three TVs blare at vacant eyes
> Alone he sets aspirin in two neat rows
> On pages full of angry cries
> Stained by whiskey wishes

Gulps their affection running across the floor
To tell his buddy that lives next door

Empty rooms scream all his fears
Starving by a fridge full of affection.
In whiskey wild fire hazy years
Blazing holes in a charred black heart,
Desperate but can't fill the lonely
Anymore with fringed flowers only
So he lies alone
And coughs in his room

Blinding lights and applause kept me out of their cocoon. With heads thrown back and mouths wide open, they wailed. She couldn't carry a tune if it was welded to her ass. His playing made fingernails on a blackboard sound like Mozart. Later, his guitar committed suicide. I devoured every note. It was a feast of emotion for the starving. I secretly guzzled whiskey and grinned. The healing from their poetry of attention got me drunk on ideas. I wanted to die in this wino heaven. My friends ran the joint. I could get drunk on bastard amber, masturbate in public, and be paid applause.

Here was my escape from working parents, babysitting siblings that cut into a nonexistent sex and social life, fridge full of what's on your mind and I love you. Folks that worked so many nights and weekends would barely miss me. Their hate of any place I loved made it instantly cool. It didn't clink in Dad's glass of Seagrams. Ma would hate it because it wasn't on her list or oven door diatribe about cooking the dinner she'd started. Her hate grew worse with every scotch after she got home.

A youth minister oversaw the coffeehouse. He never took a parish. He said why in his ordination sermon, "Too many come to church once a week to fill their spiritual gas tank and think they can sin the week away until they run out of God." Dave gave us space to express, fail, and get his nudges of guidance, not judgment. Some got more because he was human and needed company. It was hard making peace between parents and pimpled prophets. We knocked on the window to his basement apartment after hours. Then we elite explained Sergeant Pepper and planned revolution. French kisses, beer and occasional joints made Dave nervous, but he allowed them and sometimes indulged. We were smart asses too anxious to be old. We knew what Koo-koo-ka-choo really meant. Euphoric ideas, loud mouths, and a desire to change the world bound us together. We would lead an army of individuals wearing the same tie-dyed T-shirts and patched bell-bottoms. Every generation revolts against conformity wearing the same rebellion.

Before each coffeehouse, the inner circle gathered. Tables were set randomly. Sunday school room dividers were covered in butcher paper. The space was carved into nooks and the tiny stage was set in an alcove. Coffee can lights were hung over the stage. Paint was mixed based on who smoked or swigged what when Dave wasn't looking, or just let me get away with it.

Dave looked at the mess and scratched his bald spot. "What's the blue? Could it be..."

"Angst," said the longhaired boy emphatically, while hiding his bag of grass in the chips.

"Ah. I see the struggle to find God. The blue is deep belief battling the organized religions that spilled more blood than any soldier. I never did figure out how killing people because my god is better than your god made sense to people that believed in God. Politicians and popes need votes. God likes quiet and private faith. It's your rebellion reality blue because—"

"Because we ran out of green," said the teen with a vacant stare.

"And the royal magenta is?" Dave asked, his voice trailing off.

"Who's asking?" said the couple in a constant embrace.

"Ah hah. When it's your parents?" Dave asked, winking.

"Folks and kids fighting evil together," answered the couple in a monotone and trying not to giggle.

"And if it is your friends asking?" inquired the youth minister grimacing and know what was coming.

"Us in the most cosmic sixty-nine ever," giggled Dandelion and

Free Wind stroking each other's ass.

Dividers were scrawled with giant words in rebellious black. Stolen from everyone, they meant little to any. 60's poets were take out Chinese for the soul: the cute phrases tasted great but didn't last and meant nothing. We wrote crap like McKuen's Listen to the Warm because to cure the acne of our souls we knew you win revolutions with ideas that taste good not bullets.

Our rickety stage was a great ego throne. It was the Globe Theatre for disgusting renditions of Beckett, Ferlengetti, Brautigan and all the rotten poetry we wrote. The audience always gave ovations. Youth thinks guts is brilliant and stupid is talent. The Barbie and Ken record player blared Dylan, Peter Paul and Mary, and the Beatles. It made us Bobby McGee free, feelin' faded like our jeans, and busted flat in Baton Rouge despite curfew daydreams.

Coffee and cider flowed freely from seven to the curfew at ten. It was a break from boring arguments at home. Was this Topo Gigio's fifteenth or sixteenth time on Ed Sullivan? Who broke Hoss's heart? Did Ward solve Beaver's latest crisis?

Reverend Dave served the last milk and cookies in a Camelot coronation for wannabe queens and kings. Dave knew what we ate the rest of the week. Families would pick half-heartedly at food in aluminum trays. In separate rooms, three TVs would blare Cronkite's deadly menu, "And that's the way it is." The nation's dessert was the same each night. We choked on bodies in rice fields too many would soon slog through.

The janitor once lived in Dave's small apartment. Appliances looked like toys in a blah mini-kitchen. The living room was two old mattress couches and a bookcase of bricks and wood. The only cool thing was the bedroom window that opened to the street level parking lot. That's where our secret after hours knocks gained us entrance.

Scotty smiled and rolled his revolution one joint at a time. He was tall and had mop head blond hair askew. His grin started in a peaceful heart. There was a bit of a hiss in his speech. A front tooth had been broken to a point.

"Stop staring, Bergie. It's checkmate," he said holding EZ-Wider rolling papers and stifling a yawn.

"Again? After fifty losses, I gotta' be doing something right," I said defensively pounding a fist on my leg.

"You are. You lose slower. Pay more attention to the next move, not the one you're making. You might get me to think about the game," he said with a snicker.

Dave was watching us while sipping beer. He gave Scotty the parental frown to put the joint away. Scotty complied with his usual shucks sigh and eyebrow wink.

"Two EZ-Widers burn slow and save precious cargo for all," he said, dramatically while acting the motions.

Dave gulped his beer and peered over the rim of his glasses sporting a foam moustache. "Save the charming BS for the judge. You still going to read your poetry at the convention rally in Grant Park?" he asked Scotty in a concerned tone.

"Yes," Scotty replied, defiantly.

"Don't!" Dave pleaded. "I saw more than God in seminary. Do you honestly think Daley will let hippies ruin his convention?" Dave asked, ominously, shaking his head.

Scotty argued, "He let political goons stuff JFK's ballot boxes. He won't try anything with all the cameras running. Besides, the police will be there with dogs!"

Dave had just put Jefferson Airplane on his stereo. No one bothered to listen to Gracie Slick as she moaned the truth, "The White Knight was talking backwards and the Red Queen lost her head. Remember what the door mouse said. Feed your head."

I gave up on Scotty and chess and went to Dave's fridge for a beer. I signaled a refill run with a wave of my empty can. Chopper belched in the affirmative with a sisterly smile to remind me I was too many ahead of them. Her bitch with balls honesty shocked everyone. She didn't give a damn what the world thought of her. Judy was her name but Chopper fit her image. Her coffee grinder on overdrive voice in-timidated at a distance. She was short, chunky and had an in your face attitude only stupid me messed with.

"Hey Chopper, why pour all that crap on your head just because

Tom likes blond hair. Some guys love necking with natural red heads," I cracked with a smart-ass grin.

The gang backed away, giggling. Dave gave me the sign of the cross with a laugh. Her lawn mower glare never chewed my face off until then. Chopper slowly rose. With a strong swift move, she lowered her jeans a bit and rammed my face in her crotch.

"Take a good look, you jackass. It's the closest you'll ever get to my natural color," she bellowed and then pushed me away.

Everyone held their beer high and laughed. I noticed Chopper's laugh most. Her head was thrown back and her mouth was wide open. She laughed so the world could hear. When her head came forward, I saw a tear. She jerked and shook her head quickly just at me. I nodded imperceptibly to signal agreement that I'd keep her secret, knowing my ass was grass if I didn't.

Tom was the skinny, superior, smug ass. We all liked him. It's just that we had this urge from time to time to punch his lights out. He was also Chopper's guy. It got him the pass he thought his intellect earned. No one had the heart to tell him the truth.

Fat Butt had short black hair, fair skin, was built like a line backer and had a yap in constant flap. As Bonnie to Chopper's Clyde, it saved her from getting fists shoved in it. She constantly bitched about her holiday ham hips. We joked about them.

"You glaze those hips with brown sugar, Fat Butt?" cracked Dave, unable to resist an occasional ungodly jibe.

Fat Butt threw a pillow on his face and sat on it. We all hid our laughs as Fat Butt bounced. Desperate for air, Dave waved his arms and kicked his feet.

"I have a nice ass," Fat Butt said, sedately.

"What a tiny tush it is," said Tom, barely able to keep a straight face until he laughed in a pillow.

"A cute little derrière," Chopper added quietly.

Fat Butt went to the kitchen for a beer. Behind her back was a chorus of bloated cheeks, circled arms, stifled laughs and Reverend Dave gasping for air.

Bill was the football jock rebel. He had a mind, mean left hook, a

Names I Can't Remember

love for the stage, and was an ape-man. Bill was a walking hairball. He shaved at seven, four, and ten but still looked like Bigfoot. His knuckles had hair. No one got in his face even if they could find it. He had a goofy humor and loved laughing, mostly from self-induced chemical imbalances. Bill became the traveling salesman from campus to campus with a briefcase drugstore. It bought him grades that secured a college student draft deferment.

Pompous Dave, not the Reverend, was a teddy bear and anal intellect. He knew a lot and had opinions even on what he didn't know. He swaggered like a leader that no one followed. We let him have his way because he did things we didn't have to. His ego was as big as his grin and heart.

Jake was the human computer and library. He was two years behind us in school but a light-year brain beyond anyone. He read at least a book a day, only took the tests at school, and got his one calculus test ninety-nine revised to a one hundred. His proof was presented at a mathematics symposium. Jake later roamed the world beating casinos silly at black jack. He was the only person who could count a six-deck shoe. Even this bored Jake. At the same time, he played no limit backgammon with the world's best.

I once asked him why he played both at the same time.

"Applying the number of each card to a fractal equation over a function of backgammon dice rolls determines the betting paradigm plus or minus," he blathered.

"O.K. Huh?"

"I beat the casinos using backgammon chips like an abacus, a Chinese adding machine. But now I can do it faster in my head," Jake said with pompous relish.

Pudgy Jake with glasses had a Santa Claus laugh. We all loved his smug ass, even when he had that superior twinkle in his eyes. He had a kick ass mind and raconteur personality that was gregariously entertaining. Yet his Christmas laugh hid a heart at a funeral. Jake couldn't do anything and seemed an emotional infant. Everything he put in a toaster oven on autopilot came out charcoal. No one could remember if Jake ever had a date.

In Reverend Dave's apartment, there were no tomorrows. Today's beer was cold. The music was mind-bending and the company was the approved elite. We had it all, we thought. Not one of us knew we were the fourth class passengers on 1968's tie-dyed Titanic and that pretentiousness and bull made a rotten life vest.

Bill and I proved it one coffee house Saturday. I acted and directed us in Albee's Zoo Story, a seemingly simple story about a bench, a dog and a depressing life.

What a great dramatic pause Bill had taken. He turned so slowly to me to emphasize the emotional turmoil I saw in Albee's text. His face looked tortured. Perfect! His eyes were full of the empty beyond the last star. Exquisite. He took my direction perfectly, I thought. Bill began to drool panic. He knew every word in the dictionary but none in the order Albee wrote. Bill was burning alive in the horror of stage hell. He was up; couldn't remember lines. Master thespian came to the rescue.

"What did you say?" I asked with sarcastic brilliance.

Bill twitched. His fear spread to me. Witty barbs escaped me. We crossed the stage with purpose. We rose to sit again quietly. We glowered with intensity, until the horror began. Actors in the spot-light of our own bull and ego actually thought we were writers.

"God sucks!" he scowled. Barrymore actor Bill was a Dick and Jane writer horror.

"Is that why dogs hump my leg?" was my snappy retort.

Albee wrote every dull and poetically horrible line but these two. The ugly lasted a life long ten minutes.

"When will a friendly wind *in the wings* blow holy words this for-getful day!?"

Chopper, Fat Butt, Tom, Reverend Dave, Jake and pompous Dave dangled a script in the air but didn't open it.

"Just one begs my soul," I pleaded to friends in the wings with the only script.

"Thou art one stupid director!"

Bill was a great actor. His Tom was brilliant to my sensitive but self-absorbed Gentleman Caller, said the school paper of our Glass

Names I Can't Remember

Menagerie. Writers we weren't. Our ego Hiroshima was him trans-
planting my heart without the anesthetic I declined.

Our brains hadn't disappeared. One astute wit in the audience
observed how they were dripping out of our ears. I thought impro-
vised banter might help us find the lines.

"Are we in Montana?" I sighed.

"Would you LIKE to be?" seethed Bill, waving a fist.

"You know what?"

"WhaaaaaTTT?" With that line, Bill broke two old theatre records.
His thirteen syllable what broke Brando's Stella record by two sylla-
bles. His clipped T spit distance was six feet, nine and three quarter
inches, a new world record. He got hit your insane scene partner in
the face bonus points.

We got the audience back for a while with the mime routine. The
rendition of "Dirty Old Egg Sucking Dog" seemed to go well. Teaching
Bill a time step didn't. My feet were sore for a week. We thought the
audience stayed due to our brilliant acting. Little did we know how
fascinating it could be to see dignity dismembered so efficiently.

It was a thunderous yet confused ovation of one-hand claps and
single finger snaps. With chests puffed and sweating bullets of relief,
we loudly claimed we'd gotten hold of the only copy of Albee's first
draft. We kept the BS going with tales of the scribe's secret rewrite
trips to Montana. Chopper, Fat Butt, Tom, Jake, Scotty, Minister Dave
and Pompous Dave were laughing their asses off in the shadows.

The memory of that night weeks ago warmed me. Alone outside
the coffee house door, I laughed at those self-righteous idiots I loved.
We confronted and defied authority at every chance. For graduation
rehearsal, we piled into Tom's van at sunrise. After getting drunk on
beer at the forest preserve, our pomp and circumstance was a bit
woozy and foul-mouthed.

On a cold Friday morning in February, these memories didn't fill a
growling belly. Gorging on desperation, fear and panic is a banquet
that starves the soul. Loneliness devoured my delicious memories
leaving bleached bone silence. I felt lucky. The sun warmed my body.
That empty room so full of smiling ghosts fired my spirit. Two hours

had passed. At least my soul had eaten.

Pacing, I thought of options that had all but run out. I had nowhere to go but had to leave the vacated parsonage. Living there secretively put Dave's job at risk. Before that was the party central apartment. The authorities let four troubled boys finish school living on their own. We shared expenses. We worked and partied hearty whether we wanted to or not once word was out that the four best rebels had a pad. Guarded by our own unmarked cop car, it stayed relatively calm. The worst tussle with the constabulary was the chick run-a-way that said she'd seek my guidance. The dragnet couldn't find her, so the boys in blue came to me. My call to her best friend found her and I told my private cop to buzz off. I drank more and worked less. With no job, my fellow rebels ousted me.

Home was no option. Dad had told me, man to man, it was time I go. Although I towered over him, I knew he was right and agreed. There's only so much coming home when I damn well pleased Mom's heart could handle before it cracked. The toughest of us all, she blubbered like a baby as I walked out with one bag and nowhere to go.

With my 1-A draft status, a job that met my standards was impossible. I wanted the comfort I was used too, not a cold water garret my pretentious drunk had earned. $1.65 an hour was the best I could find. I turned it down and mooched on Dave again. A $60 a week acting job in a kiddy theatre in a van company was beneath me. I'd rather starve on ego than earn a crust of humility. Daydream bitching was my job, making me a drunk nut.

Where are you now rebels loud, opinionated all?
You alpha, brusque, ideaed, pushy pimpled
Coffee house laughy, lonely, leaders tall.
How dare you leave me here alone.
Sizzle, snap and drizzle spat,
I'm your char-broiled steak dripping fat.

Are you getting answers from Merry Peter Paul,
Jimmy, Zep Led, Blues Moody and Dylan's call?

Names I Can't Remember

Simon so Garfunkled in Mellow Yellow
We're prom kings till Pepper got to the ball.
Crackle glimmer, spit shimmer, tease and moan,
Say you're sorry for my ham n'mayo home here alone.
Why not fuck the little old lady from Pasadena?
Or Woodstock to hell and back,
The day the music died in American Pie
'Cuz father knowing best was such a lie.
Pop n' zap, sparks smolder smoke so crawl you prick.
Take silent halls for Oreos in cream dipped thick.
Crosby Stills changed the world and Maggie May
Will feed me ever binged Ripple mistakes today.
All flowers gone in Alice's Restaurant
God damn attention's the only meal I fucking want.
Stare at my ember's glow, the flicker pale.
You'd crawl for celery and crackers stale.

Does the motherless child feel sometimes?
Tell me Dave so old and bloodied God wise.
You've mothered and fathered throughout the land.
Did rule makers ever dance to hopeless The Band?
Fizzle die crackle, snap and pop your belly yells?
Hot buttered, sour creamed potato for one soul sells.

Times are a changing, so said the door mouse in name.
Flappers never rolled joints, Miller never got laid
For a lousy string of pearls said Joni's circle game.
Tomorrow is no rainbow when sorrow is paid.
Yesterday, I drank my troubles seemed so far away.

Last warmth cools, the boxer, fighter by trade shivers
Here's dying fire truth in Brautigans' final gun mouth
Whispers,"In watermelon sugar the deeds were done and
Done again as my life is done in watermelon sugar,"
The last coal moans I'm dead.

I built the fire that night tenderly. A dented and blackened pot from the basement was my silver banquet service. A cracked jelly jar from the garbage was my leaded crystal goblet. Without any oil, I shook the pot on the fire vigorously, so not a kernel would burn. I covered it with a scrap of cardboard, so none would escape the pot and burn away in the fire. A tea bag steeped in the jelly jar full of fire-heated water.

The room clouded with my chilly breath filled with the aroma of fulfillment. The popcorn and hot tea would soon fill my stomach and warm my shivers like the fire never could. Rocking side to side in front of the fire, I was a huddled muck of anger, hunger and desperation wrapped in newspaper that stunk of decayed garbage. The corn danced to the fire's opulent rhythm of a Viennese Waltz I imagined. I slammed the pot down in the fire and began licking the stench paper like it was steak. I picked through every crease looking for any bit of meaning. The maggots were delicious. I opened my eyes and my belly seized. I was eating a bit of shriveled potato, rotted black and crusted with stinking mold. The music I heard was my gut-wrenching yowl of satisfaction and disgust. In one gulp, it was gone. I was a starving wolf on a frozen tundra worn down to skin, bones and fury with no scent of prey in the frozen air. I wanted more. I needed more. I couldn't take this crap. My feet pounded the floor as my fists beat the walls.

I broke. I crawled to the corner of the dark room and whimpered in a fetal position. My broken spirit and mind reeled. Sniffling, my eyes tightly shut, I was dancing in my banquet fantasy with Queen Satiated of Belch Burp.

She had slaughtered animal fat dripping down her cheeks. My tongue curled around my quivering cracked lips tasting the delectable dream. We swooned around an immense table graced in linen, overflowing in rich creamed desserts, succulent bloody beef and crispy skinned pig dripping in butter. The Queen swayed in delight and pulled her bodice lower. Her eyes were the dazzling rich brown of the gravy finished in sparkling butter. I whirled her near the steaming and creamy colored potatoes. Pulling her to me, I reached for the table.

"Naughty boy," she squealed, heaving her naked bosom.

Names I Can't Remember

"How delicious!" I moaned.

"Taste my bounty," said she, tossing her head back.

I scooped potatoes and slapped them in her valley of delight making her moan. Drizzling all with the steaming gravy, she heaved and sighed as I feasted wantonly.

"Dear God what a wondrous tongue, my boy!"

"You taste like contentment," I said, my face smeared in creamy white. My tongue smacked the gravy from her nipples.

"Try the beef at my nape," she cried. "Slower. Greed is foreplay only to the wealthy. Sample my sticky dessert," she whispered taking my head beneath her gown.

"I'll suck your delectable drippings dry.

"Licks not limericks, damn you, dear God."

The louder she screamed, the more viciously my rigid cock and slapping balls beat her cunt bloody while I rammed chunks of bloody beef down my gullet. The harder her hungry ass slammed back at me, the more cruelly my oozing prick ripped her asshole raw as I shoved creamy cake over my face and in my mouth. The more desperately she gagged for air, the faster I rammed my vile, exploding cock deep in her throat as I guzzled the wine flooding out of the corners of my mouth. I fucked her throat until I came although she'd passed out. Walking away, I licked my fingers dry of fat and cream, ignoring her beaten bloody mass laying there with come dripping from her lifeless jaw.

Popping kernels shattered my nauseating dream orgasm of cannibalistic disgust. Black, rotting potato puke drool was dribbling out of my whimpering mouth. I looked at what was once my feast the first night here two weeks ago. I saw disgusting, burnt, stale popcorn and tasteless tea. Trembling and in tears, I scoured the fire's ashes and devoured charred kernels. I guzzled, colorless and cold, dead bag tea. The hunger beat me down one last time. Begging for Reverend Dave to fill me with the God gas he spoke of did nothing. Starvation is a Goliath David's faith cannot slay. I chose to win or die.

In the morning, I walked the three blocks to the downtown section of Des Plaines. At Lee and Graceland was the small central Post Office. In the adjacent building was the Armed Services Recruitment Center.

It was Leap Day, Friday February 29, 1968.

A boy shivered his way down that street. A young lion swaggered in the center. At a lifeless, gray, metal desk sat a proud warrior with ribbons on his chest. The warrior said nothing. His confident cold look barely took note of the cocky young lion that had dared to approach his pride. When his eyes did meet mine, a cold fear struck me and I jerked to a stop. I saw a deep sorrow hidden behind a sly grin. It was his vacant stare that went through beyond and me to the somewhere that made Hell his home.

"Is this a good day to die?" he laughed uproariously, while offering me a seat.

A cold laugh made me shiver. Then came the moment of manly silence. His cock was bigger but he smelled my defiance. It was an instant filled with the destiny and instinct found in ancient caves. A boy stood before the hunter, stiff with pride and knocking knees, saying I'm ready. The hunter's eyes spoke a sadness that tried to push a boy away from fate. It was a wordless tale of fire and fear men alone know and makes mothers cry. A man's gotta' do what a man's gotta' do, our inspiring hard-on insanity.

I stared the warrior straight in the eye.

"I'm eighteen. If I sign now, when do I leave this screwed-up mess for a warm bed and hot food?"

"Tomorrow at O six hundred," he firmly whispered, setting the form before me.

I signed in a firm seamless flow. Out came other papers as he babbled, sure that my mechanical nods meant I'd heard every word. The sorry bastard had no idea how bad I'd kicked his ass. I'd just suckered him out of thousands of warm beds and hot meals. His wry smile said he didn't care. I was his cannon fodder quota for the day. He signed me for three years as a clerk, knowing ego would put a rifle in my hands.

He heard my belly growl. With two bucks, he bought my promise to be there at sunrise tomorrow. I went to the Mandas family diner for a blood rare burger, French fries dripping hot oil, and a headache cold milk shake. Sitting back satiated, I smiled. It was a great day belch and encore.

That night, I knocked on Reverend Dave's apartment window. The gang was inside as usual. The stereo blared over an argument about the meaning of Lucy in the Sky with Diamonds. I watched the argument without a word. Dave stood behind me. He alone saw the ticket and papers in my pocket. His sigh said he knew.

"Guys. Guys! I just...," I shouted, but was cut off as they all turned to stare at me.

"We need to name this, this damn place!" Dave shouted in anger that dropped jaws.

Shocked eyes asked why. Dave's lean begged me to change my mind. I turned away.

"We'll never, never have this day again. The God-damned coffee house should have a name, a name for all of us," Dave said, looking straight at me.

"I enlisted. I leave tomorrow," were the cool quiet words.

It was an earthquake of asses hitting the floor. No one spoke. They looked at each other and to me. A minister in tears looked at us all and put a record on the stereo.

> "I am just a poor boy, though my story's seldom told.
> I have squandered my resistance for a pocket full of
> mumbles such are promises..."

Pompous Dave tried to shove a ticket to Canada he'd been saving for himself in my pocket. His birthday was 365 in the lottery. I refused the lucky asshole with a smile.

No one knows why Jake the brain wasn't drafted. When this roly-poly star child in thick glasses walked into the draft board, he smiled like the devil and lectured them. He walked out grinning, with them shaking their heads. The Pentagon still studies his logic, sure it's a matrix for a propulsion system to get us to Alpha Centauri in the blink of an eye.

> "All lies and jest. Still a man hears what he wants to hear
> and disregards the rest, lie, lie, lie."

I never saw Chopper again after that night. She got the defiance beat out of her in Grant Park. The defeat pissed her off so much, she decided to see what all the anger was about. She bought a ticket on Asia Air and just took off.

Chopper became a Red Cross slut. With no papers and guts, she bullied her way up to every battlefield aide station. With an iron smile, she held hands with every bloody stump. She French-kissed every screaming face that wasn't there. She proposed to bastards screaming for Mamma, while medics argued if the guts in the dirt were his. Her foul-mouthed insults pissed off guys so bad that they lived long enough for her to finish their last letter, get the best blowjob ever and say I do. Chopper was there two years. One day she crawled into a foxhole at Khe Sahn and froze. Shipped home, she locked herself behind a door and cried for two years. They called her the acid queen.

> "When I left my home and my family,
> I was no more than a boy..."

Tom got drafted, although he had papers for grad school. The gang was sure he'd wind up an officer in counter intelligence kissing some general's ass at a linen covered table. Turns out he was a lowly private on latrine duty in some rear camp. One day while he was burning latrine honey pots with gasoline, the methane exploded. They scraped up what they could find of him and dumped it in a steel pot. The helmet was rested on a crudely drawn sign "died in the line of doodie."

Fat Butt became the most famous USO Donut Dolly. She handed out donuts and coffee at bases too small to get a show. She loved talking to guys about home. Her ass was famous and was pinched by all. She mooned every catcall. The artillery base she was on was creamed by friendly fire trying to beat back a human wave attack of enemy sappers: suicide bombs on their bodies. Fat Butt was mid-moon at the time. Somewhere in the jungle is a cross with her name on it, "Here Lays the Fattest Ass Ever. Thanks." They told her mom that her smiling cheeks comforted every soldier she saw.

> "Asking only workman's wages,
> I come looking for a job, but I get no offers…"

Scotty went to Grant Park. A gentle poet was swept up in a tsunami of nightsticks and snarling police dogs. His soul was drowned in the violent underground of the SDS.

When I met him years later, he was still kicking his opponents' ass at chess. It dumbfounded me. It was his private FBI agent. He stopped by each few months to pump Scotty for the whereabouts of political friends still on the most wanted list. Scotty sent him on his way, saying he hadn't spoken to them in years. I asked him once if that was a lie. He said checkmate with such charm it sent a chill up my spine. I never asked again.

> "Then I'm laying out my winter clothes
> and wishing I was home…"

Bill's luck ran out. A narc in hot pants busted him. She was kind enough to bust the charming jerk after they got out of the shower. He opted for the infantry instead of fifteen years. That didn't stop him. Deep in the triple canopy of the Ahe Shau Valley, he had a semsillia farm of the best Asian weed. Cured over opium coals, it's called killer Tai Stick. A half joint had you drooling for hours. Crazoid Bill would go out alone on patrol to water his crop. One day he stumbled on the lead units of an enemy battalion plowing under his valuable crop. Bill went King Kong on them and stumbled into the Medal of Honor. He was ripped at the time. Counting his cash later, he walked into a chopper tail blade. His legend lives. Three customers claiming they were just witnesses, said his headless corpse quietly got in the chopper counting money.

> "In the clearing stands a boxer
> And a fighter by his trade…"

A skipping scratching needle was all we heard. It was the hissing breath escaping young lives. When it ended, we were all so old, so very old. Terrified, each raised a hand like a child to get Father Dave's attention. One suggested a name for the coffeehouse. One by one, each suggested a name.

"Let's use them all," Dave sighed wisely.

In 1968, kids bartered dreams for beds and burgers and were never seen again. I miss those children, those cocky rebels in The Radical Ice-Cream Blue Rag Café and (ssshhh) Demolition Society. I wish I could have gone back to tell them how old killing, booze, and guilt made me. I couldn't. I still had to learn if we hadn't gambled our lives to beat the boredom with a joint of lonely, maybe we could have finished being young, tasting every morsel of life to come, for memories are feasts to the starving.

On a bus headed west, I was the one snoozing while others sweated. I'd forgotten the carousel cake with three candles in the Camel Trail bar. The mighty tree house built to see the dreams and dragons in the empty field of weeds out back decayed outside Des Moines. The cool kid in a Cub's uniform hugging a proud dad disappeared in the flat Nebraska wheat fields. The drunk, stoned on Southern Comfort, who pissed on Mom's paint by number Lassie, hopped a freight car in Missouri. I was in the third seat on the left smiling, while the smoky haze of shivered nights of stolen popcorn and dead tea faded in smiles mile after mile. In my head danced dreams of bloody beef, mashed potatoes swimming in steaming gravy, and a thick mattress covered by warm blankets.

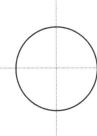

The Baha'í

MARCH 1968

"Break the load into small parts
so you are stronger than it is,
and carry it many familiar miles.
Faith is a journey, not a destination."

He was a quiet boy that kept to himself reading books of peace, and slaughtered an army alone with one word. His slender build was no threat. His pale, milky skin was unnoticed. His gentle demeanor sparked no conversations. In the first hours at the base, no one knew he was there. On a frigid angry day in Missouri, he was a warm breeze of serenity before a brutal storm only he knew was coming.

We were in a long, rectangular room with rows of metal bunk-beds divided by an aisle in the middle. The long sidewalls were mostly windows of six over six panes to sunrise a midnight space. They could jump-start a breeze that turned sticky, humid Missouri summer days into a tolerable sauna. They were days that made drenched-with-sweat clothes a second skin and fast, furious fucking the best way to cool off. On cold nights, the panes rattled the same rhythm as my teeth and moans.

On each bunk of squeaky springs were a rolled mattress, pillow, and a scratchy wool blanket. Kids with apple pie cheeks and mop heads shared fears and handshakes in arguments over upper or lower. Between bunks were tall, narrow lockers. They were that lifeless, baby poop, broccoli green. Freshly painted green footlockers were on the aisle side of each bunk. Overhead hung cone shaped lights spaced every few feet. The walls were studs and beams covered only by outside clapboards. The perfume was cheap cathouse: ammonia, testosterone and a spritz of confusion behind each ear.

The latrine was at one end. It had sinks on one wall and open commodes on the other, Army civil rights brilliance. It's hard to hate the guy on the john next to you if he has the only paper. The gray floor was spotless. The room inspired Santa to suicide.

In a quiet moment, I flopped onto the bunk next to where he was reading. As his slender fingers slowly turned pages, I looked around the lonely room and sighed.

"What's wrong?" he asked, putting a book down softly.

"The bed's warm. The food hot. It don't get it," I pondered, scratching my head.

"What?" he asked leaning in, to intently listen.

"I'm still hungry and shiver," I said, sadly.

"A three hots and cot enlistee? I bet a warehouse of W.W.II rations just emptied. Have you noticed, no stray dogs on this base?" he offered with a gentle poke.

He was from Chicago. We got lost in Chi-town stories of Uno's pan pizza, the Magnificent Mile, and Loop subway that rocked and rolled. I felt he was a remarkable man. His eyes, the mocha tan of steaming creamed coffee, were dreams that lasted days. His soothing voice was a peaceful soul, singing lullabies, milk and cookies with mom.

"My name is...,"

He raised his hand and grinned peacefully.

"What's wrong?" I asked in crinkled brow confusion.

"You gave me a great minute memory. Don't give me a lifetime of tears with a name I'll see on a monument. The memories of youth for grey-haired warriors should be hope grown in the field of not knowing the truth," he said with quiet firmness, while scratching his chin tilted high.

"Nice goatee and moustache there. Have a good scratch. You won't have it much longer," I kidded him, nervously changing the subject.

"It's my crucifixion," he said ominously.

His was the first of the names I can't remember. Years later, when I stared at the low black slab, I thanked him for that gift. If his name was there, I didn't know.

In the 60's Army, Basic Training was still assault and battery. It was mixed with Hiroshimic verbal and emotional abuse that, decades later, would get you a Not Guilty for killing Mom and Dad in the blame everything but your own evil era. The head bull guard in the prison was a short, barrel-chested, no neck, black, Drill Instructor in a Smokey the Bear hat. He had the nose of a champ that had defended the title too many times. His stubby hands looked like vices with hairy knuckles. He had a deep scar on his face and a chest full of survivor's ribbons. His cold, pinched-eyed stares rammed hearts into throats and knocked knees. He growled blood-curdling commands with the gravely grumble of a bull in heat. Silent, his scar and ribbons did the talking to every death row kid begging for a pardon.

The execution was at the barber shack where deafening razors cut the army style, bald. Shaggy-headed boys entered in tens and stood braced. Each thirty seconds, one of the ten chairs emptied. A stunned egghead staggered out and a jittering wavy-haired hero sat down. The cutters plowed over heads and faces like herders shearing diseased sheep to save wool. The floor looked like King Kong's hairball. Tips to charm or con for sideburns or peach fuzz cut got the Mr. Clean variation and no refund.

The Baha'i said nothing as his wavy locks hit the floor. The razor came to his chin. His gentle hand softly blocked the razor. The robot barber was stunned. Again, he raised his razor. The quiet boy's peaceful but firm stare stopped him. Heads turned. The buzz of razors died out. The clock ticked last tense seconds. It was high noon. With his back to the blazing sun, the Baha'i stood brushing off the last of the hair on his head. With his fingers, he gently combed his moustache and goatee while looking in the mirror.

The first thud of a heel hitting the ground stole every breath. The Baha'i stood straight and listened. Another boot heel slammed the ground. The Baha'i turned and faced Smokey, the drill instructor, peaceful to evil eye. A low mournful whistle was heard. Smokey smashed the boy's head with a razor.

The Baha'i didn't move.

Smokey bashed again. The Baha'i raised his chin. He showed his trickling blood and defiantly walked out.

A normal hour run before chow lasted three on the dustiest Missouri roads. Smokey made the boy carry the flag at the rear and eat the choking dust after emptying his canteen. Smokey didn't see when I dropped back to offer a drink. The boy refused.

"You got us in a pile of crap, you bastard," I yelled.

"Yes. I'm sorry," he spat out between gulps of air.

"Take a drink," I ordered him.

He brushed back my canteen with a weary hand.

"He'll see us. Take it!" I nervously demanded.

"I deserve it," he said motioning me back to the pack.

Running, I looked back. The crazy kid was smiling.

Smokey made us eat lunch standing at attention in the heat-stroke sun. He made the Baha'i do push-ups. Smokey drenched the boy with insults that would break a Mafia made man. Smokey kicked or punched the boy to hurt, not maim. He had the Baha'i strip, jog in place and scream the Star Spangled Banner. We ate dinner at attention in the heat and humidity again. The boy got his faced shoved in his food with every push-up, but wasn't allowed to eat. With every crushing kick, the boy smiled. At letter home time, Smokey made us scrub the Baha'i with floor brushes and lye. He then made the boy scrub the floor with his body. He let the exhausted kid have one drink from a flushing toilet.

The day ended with us all at attention next to our bunks. For the Baha'is' defiance, we paid the price of trying to sleep standing up. He was forced to do more push-ups and scream the count to keep us awake. After a few hours, Smokey gave a last insult, kick and punch to the Baha'i. When he smiled, Smokey left without a word. Later, drained boys fell into their bunks. His face calm, the Baha'i strongly did push-ups.

My bladder woke me at about 4 A.M. I tiptoed back from the latrine to my bunk at one end of the barracks. I saw one light still on at the other end. Unseen, I strained to listen and watched the strange sight of beater healing beaten.

The brutal D.I. was talking to the boy in a fatherly tone. Huddled together, the brute iced the boy's aches.

"Breath shallow, son. It hurts less," he said.

"Thanks," the boy sighed flinching from the ice.

"Gots to send yah to the shave tail Lieutenant, son," he said with a worried look.

"I know," said the boy looking in the man's sad eyes.

"Higher it goes is worser. Dey'll make me break you for dem scraggly hairs."

"What they mean to me is worth it," the boy said.

"I got a crease in ma chin here. Dem womens loves it. Ain't so sure I'd get the crap beat outta me for it," the bear of a man said chuckling and stroking his scar.

The Baha'i seemed fascinated with Smokey's scar.

"Son, soldiering ain't a democracy. If you vote who to kill in what kind way, damn wars would last forever. No fun 'tall," he chuckled.

"Behead every child so the next peasant won't fight," said the boy wincing and turning away.

"Boy, two things comes home, the brutal and body bags," the scarred man sighed.

"There's a difference?" asked the boy curiously.

"Killin's easy. Most likes it. Warriors walk off the field an' fight ta get his soul back at preachin."

He sponged the boy's aches and pains with cool water.

"They beat you. What was it like?" he asked, softly.

"How could you tell?" the D.I. asked warily.

"Not the scar. Your eyes. I could see you hated doing it," said the boy in a soft, firm tone of respect.

"That's why you smiled?" grinned the warrior.

"I could tell it pissed you off," smiled the lad.

"You ever tell anyone you had fun getting the crap beat out of you, I'll beat the crap out of you. It'll ruin my rep-a-ta-shun!" he grinned shaking the kid's hand.

"What was it like?" the boy asked again, cautiously.

"Ain't much to tell. It was different in my army. My D.I. still beat the life out of us, worse than me. He could beat a body, but couldn't go for the throat and humiliate the man. Can't beat a killer instinct in any man if it ain't in 'em," he said flatly.

"You fought with him didn't you?" he asked leaning in.

"Took that rat hole five times just 'fore Panmunjon. We'd go up with fewer guys and come down with more parts. The bastard wiped out two machine gun nests and waved us on for a glory charge. He'd carved a kid's eye. The kid screamed watching him eat it without flinching. He cut his balls off and shoved them in the chink's mouth."

The Baha'i cried.

"That bastard carved for five minutes. Kid was dead for four. The next step the prick took was on a mine. It was two miles to medics. I picked the screaming shit up and put one bloody mess in this pocket and another in that," said the D.I. in a dead tone.

"Saved his life," said the boy wiping his tears.

"Didn't know which mess was face and which was guts!"

"How'd you get the scar?" asked the boy trying to change the subject. The DI cut the boy with a steel stare.

"The bastard flailed. He got my bayonet and slashed. I tried to stop the gushing as he flopped to the ground. The faceless shit begged me to finish him. Get some balls for a change, he screamed. Could you face what I did, he yells. Kill me you chicken fuck, for God sake please, he yowled. I shook my head. I tried hating him for not teaching me this. I couldn't. You ain't killing the memory, just the mess that's left, he yelled. He grabbed my pistol and shoved it in what looked like a mouth. He was too weak. I put my shaking hand on his. He got this peaceful look and fainted," said the DI with a frozen face.

"You saved him from himself," said the boy of faith.

"At the medic station, they said we don't have enough morphine to let whatever that is die in peace. I healed him I said. They asked me why I carried him back. A mamma deserves pieces, not medals I said, emptying my pockets."

The Baha'i puked. The D.I. father sat there.

"Son, you have to be ready for that even if it cost me my rank and a stretch in Leavenworth. You gonna shave that hair off?" asked the D.I. in an ominous low tone.

"No," said the Baha'i wiping puke from his chin.

The warrior walked off. Slow heavy steps echoed like a moaning bell, tolling twelve while six lowered one. He turned. As the D.I. snapped his hand up to salute the kid, something hot and wet hit my cheek. They smiled. The boy fell exhausted into a bunk and instantly asleep, but smiling.

Smokey walked past without seeing me. I saw what hit me in the cheek and how he told the story with no emotion. His thumbnail pressed into the flesh of his finger had butchered it to the bone. It gushed tears his memory refused to cry.

"Is it that bad there? I need to know," I whispered.

A warrior walked off this battlefield in silence down a deafening trail of sorrow.

The next day, I sat on the john next to the Baha'i. It started with sharing toilet paper and daydream banter.

"Goatee will cost yah. Boy, are they gonna chew you a new asshole!" I argued, shoving a finger in his face.

He laughed uproariously. "I'm laughing with God. We've never heard faith defined quite that way. Mine's the hymn I sing from memory," he explained.

"Please speak plain. I went to school to pass tests not learn. I never took thinking," I said, laughing too.

After warm fire laughs, he spoke in a quiet reverent tone. "Baha'i. I'm a Baha'i."

"What's that?"

"I can't tell you."

"Guys are taking a lotta' crap for you. They deserve an explanation.

Refuse and you are in deep shit. You just told 200 guys waiting for execution you hid their pardons."

It got worse. The Lieutenant tried group pressure. After trashing our bunks and lockers at 4 A.M., the Baha'is' the worst, he made us stand at attention until the boy cleaned it all up. He ordered Smokey to run the boy until he dropped. Smokey ran him and tripped him each few steps. The boy refused to shave. Only I saw them smile.

Behind doors, the Captain yelled at the kid for six hours. I heard slamming furniture. He tossed the boy out and ordered Smokey to take him to the special live fire course. While Smokey fired rounds inches from the crawling boys face, the Captain screamed and kicked him. Bloody, the boy refused the Captain's order to shave.

The meeting with the major was quiet, and lasted minutes. After the kid left and Smokey had his orders, four other kids, big kids, from our barracks were seen going in. At two that morning, there was a blanket party beating no one stopped. At chow that morning, the Baha'i had a mush melon face. He hadn't shaved.

The Colonel had the battalion at attention. He presented a razor to the kid. He had the chaplain speak to him. The chaplain backed away, frustrated. Then the Colonel had the entire battalion march by the kid in single file and spit on him. The kid refused to shave. The Colonel ordered Smokey to take the boy to a private office. We heard the moans and thuds. I peeked. The kid was doing push-ups while Smokey kicked a pillow.

That night while the rest slept, I walked over to his bunk. He was shining his boots by flashlight.

"I used to look at the dome on the Baha'i temple just north of Chicago, wondering what it was," I said softly.

"Our beliefs are there, in many great books. They're there for you to read and believe or not," he explained.

"No answers first, huh?"

"There isn't any explanation. That's why they call it faith. I glory him with this hair. To cut it, defiles what I hold sacred."

He met the general. He came back to the barracks smiling. He was clean shaven. I rolled over on my bunk and faced away.

Names I Can't Remember

His gentle hand on my shoulder turned me towards him.

"Why?" I weakly asked.

"Faith won," he whispered.

"Your face is shaved."

"I believed his need for conformity in training, and he believed that my hair is my faith without explanation. I can grow it back after basic training is over."

"And you believed him?" I asked incredulously.

"I trust him, but I got the Army's word, in writing!" he laughed waving the paper.

"But you gave in," I said again.

"Have you ever seen a strong man carry a heavy load?"

"Yes," I responded looking right at him.

"And what happens to him?"

"Well... he struggles until it exhausts him," I said looking away.

"Right. If you struggle with the load one mighty time, you fall and never go on. If your faith is stronger than your back, break the load into small parts so you are stronger than it is, and carry it many familiar miles. Faith is a journey, not a destination," he sighed.

Basic was what it was supposed to be. We learned to arrange belongings in the same perfect order, eat puke food, exhaust our bodies, scream obedience, run, fall, crawl under live fire, march and sing as one while sleeping, rise in the dark, pee in public and all that other vital military stuff. Learning it took hours. Breaking spirits took weeks of individuality-crushing insults.

I slogged on happy in my gonna be a clerk cocoon. In the asshole trophy room sat a sergeant who'd sold used cars. He had my test scores, cocky kid profile, and a big smile on his face. "Gotcha," that smile said. I never knew what hit me.

They needed guys to be acting corporals in advanced training. Sign up, go to a two week leadership school and I'd get to wear a blue armband with two stripes on it. I would be in command, lead men from class to class and be able to give orders. "Give me that pen," I screamed inside. He wasn't done with me.

"Son," he said, "You are different from all the rest."

"I do believe."

"Boy, you are a leader of men, an Officer! Tell yah what I'm gonna do, friend for starters..."

I bent over, spread 'em, begged the Army to do it without Vaseline and bought a bright red Mustang with a transmission leaking sawdust. A quiet boy full of God got a General's promise in writing. I believed my schmuck's smile. When a slot opened up in Artillery Officer Candidate School, he'd shoot me right in it. To get that far from the battle job, I signed to start in the Infantry. That was the jackass option package I bought.

"The best officers are airborne, son. You get an extra hundred and ten smackers a month!"

"Airborne All the way, Sir!"

Right after advanced training, I'd be off to jump school. He figured I have an idiot so sign him up for idiot school. Wow, I thought. I'll jump out of a perfectly good airplane that has every intention to land. If I didn't splat, I'd get those cool silver wings.

I finished Basic Training in an idiot's bliss. I was a punk who signed up for three easy years pushing paper to get three hot meals a day and a warm bed. Now, I'd signed away the last of my youth to get a glory whore's gold bar, jump out of planes and lead boys to kill other boys. The ego of immortal youth forever digs its grave with stupid.

I never saw the Baha'i after Basic. I don't know if he grew the moustache and goatee back. I don't know if faith finally won. Maybe he lost that last battle. I don't know if he laughed at a jerk clerk now in the infantry whose draft lottery number was so high he would have never been drafted. I do know one thing. The Baha'i carried his load with a smile, one small stone at a time, down long dusty roads over many familiar miles on a journey going nowhere but to his soul.

> In spring came the Calliope
> Circus clatter clang and laugh.
> Dads hoist children shoulder high
> To watch clowns brightly pass.
> Lions roar from Main to Elm.

Names I Can't Remember

Elephants bellow, fingers plug ears.
Noise so loud the wind must whisper.
Yet, one by one, heads turn to the sky.

In the cool crisp blue on high
Soars a lone mighty eagle
Simply known as the Baha'i.

In his eyes was the warm breeze
On a crisp, cool night of fear.
His tender whispers touched our sorrow.
His every soft and soothing smile,
Each word of faith without any answer
Gave us rock-a-bye baby morrows.

He was the quiet man among noisy boys
Whose circus was gone and tears were real,
When shaggy boys became balded killers,
Screamed this warrior in whisper, 'no'
I'll give my body but never my soul,
And the river of peace began to flow.

Cotton Candy and kiss the girls.
Slam the hammer and ring the bell.
Blue balloons and popcorn gorge,
Giggle laugh yell as tigers paw,
The circus weekend is here and gone
From Main to Elm the wind whispers still.

In the cool crisp blue on high
Soars a lone mighty eagle
Simply known as, the Baha'i.

The Baha'i

Two's Company, Four's Impotence

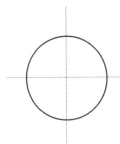

MAY 1968

"Whorehouses turn elated boys into lonely men. Mother Silkie was of mixed parentage, part poet, pimp, and poker player."

On cold gray days in the always lonely remember when winter of life, I think of the first crackling fire of my youth. She was the black and white woman in my tie-dyed love affair that rented passion by half-hours in a squalid room. I spent the last of my childhood for a vivid memory but got a faded crumpled photo under shattered glass.

The journey began in a spring sunset lit with the twinkling of firefly's pixie dances to the happy melodies of crickets. There are no wars when crickets sing. A breeze made my soul whisper and cooled a fiery day from hurry to stroll. The sky was a scarlet orange blaze streaked with the last of blue and gold. Mighty trees full of daytime color were black shadow cut outs swaying gently on a vibrant night canvas.

Lines of long, narrow, wooden barracks surrounded a vast, empty marching field. It would rest until sunrise. Then, boy legions would march, sing, and trample it with new scars; wide swaths of gouged and boot beaten grass. We sat on the steps at the end of the buildings. Thick rough planks and boards were slapped together and painted dull gray. They looked like temporary steps with no risers on a new house. It was a place to go when the barracks noise or smell was too much. In rare quiet times after class or chow, strangers shared cigarettes and lonely trying to make friends. It was Times Square on New Year's Eve in a boring and brain dead school for clerks.

Between exciting typing classes, the utterly exhilarating tests on filling out the ten page toilet paper form, and scribbling suicide notes on the assassinate a sergeant plans, we drank rivers of near beer; soda pop with an inflated ego. We had to drink a river just to get a buzz that wore off racing to piss every ten minutes.

I learned all the yelling, folding, marching, shining and killing basic training offered. Two weeks in leadership school got me the blue armband with corporal's stripes. I could yell louder, fold clothes more precisely, shine boots more mirror like, and take more degrading insults without tears. I never did learn how hospital corners on a bunk made so tight you could bounce a quarter off it made me a better killer.

Bull sessions on those steps were dull and always the same: Army sucks, chow sucks, let's get drunk, and I'm horny. With boys, those topics are epic tales of conquest.

I've forgotten what pimple farm punk said what. Was he the farm boy from Nebraska worried about rain and a lonely wife? Or was he the smart-ass from Bah-ston who pahked so many kaaahhhs in Hahvad yahd it made us sick? We all learned the unspoken rule. Every face was a memory to cherish. Every name was a monument horror to forget. Everyone was a rumpled green and bald graduate of the Gomer Pyle charm school. Our talk was as predictable as the fate of the toilet seat when a man goes to the john.

"This Army sucks," was his rapier opening.

"Chow sucked. What was the brown shit?" I grumbled.

"Last week's moldy green crap," he giggled.

"Sticks pictures on the wall real good," I cracked.

"Wanna' get drunk?" he asked.

"Nah. All that pissing is too much work," I groaned.

"Beat the crap outta' Sarge?" he said slapping my arm.

"And face the guy that kicked his ass?" I laughed.

"You horny?" he bellowed, puffing his chest.

"Ever notice how some couples in school suddenly stopped fighting?" I asked.

"Football jocks that used to beat on me, suddenly giggling at girls," he added.

"Greaser and surfer chicks stopped cat fighting."

"Just staring off in the distance, they twirled hair and scribbled new last names next to theirs. Maybe it was the pimple cream?" he wondered aloud.

Two idiots under the majesty of a Missouri sunset had no clue. Everyone had been laid but us. The more we talked, the stupider I got. I did the one thing no man should ever do in any locker room, tell the truth about being a "technical" virgin.

"I ran all the bases so many times. Just never slid into home," I finally admitted.

When I looked at his jaw dropped face, my puffed chest deflated like a kid seeing the F on his term paper. It taught me Men's Rule # 1. You can't win practice games. A million successes in cracking bra access codes, Fort Knox girdle hand dives, or I really love you best when I cum hand-jobs, gets you thrown out of the cave. No cave painting ever had Mastodons running from rubber tipped spears. Hearing that any boy hasn't is the same horror men show when learning stove and washing machine manuals don't exclude us from using them. Male B.S. is bold lies. Like when Ma sees us with our hand in the jar and our mouth dribbles cookie crumbs, she asks if we are eating a cookie, and we say no. It could work. Maybe mom's brain died.

My training buddy absolved me of the sin and called a cab to rush me to an emergency baptism. The driver entertained us with a southern drawl and laughter. We were typical Yankees that assumed talking slow made one stupid. He had fun toying with us, explaining the difference between oil and all.

"Awll y'all put in yer cahhh an' awll is evrah body."

"Right. Huh?"

"Evra body is awll. Awll y'all put in a cahhh."

The driver giggled into his radio mic about two Yankee whipper-snappers he was taking to the woodshed. He said he'd be quitting early after making his day on this trip. We men of the world asked the idiot question he always heard. Where can a guy get...? Before we finished, he asked us if we wanted broads. It shocked us that he knew. I guess he had seen the uniforms and dumb ass, young horny private signs on our foreheads. It only cost an extra twenty dollars, each, to get to the secret location. He drove in circles chatting us up with charm and driving up the meter. Never mind that the sign bathed in neon red, "Mother Silkie's Cash Bar and Xystusium Emporium — All GIs Welcome — If You Got It, We Hock It!" could be seen for miles from any highway.

Mother Silkie's had the charm of a traveling junkyard and trailer trash caravan that broke down across the street from your church. The juke joint lounge and bar looked like a pile of shipping crates roofed in tin and rotting side by side. Around it were a few dirty trailers with scraps of gaudy fabric hanging in the windows to block the daylight. Behind each scrap was a bare red bulb. Cab traffic from the base and the highway to the compound had worn the weeds into rutted mud long ago. The air crackled with the buzz of the flashing neon lure for Sodom and Gomorrah.

The doorman was a hairy it on parole for murdering three guys with a baseball bat. Rumor had it that after they beat him to a bloody pulp, he lost it and killed one with his bare hands, the other with intimidation, and the third dropped dead from fear. They say he got his parole because the board was too afraid to say no.

He ripped open our cab door and snarled, "Cash only. Clean girls. What you got, you didn't get here. Two drink minimum. Complete chicken dinner, twenty five cents."

He did very well on tips! We gave him five for drooling and ten to back him off. Silkie took pity on her only son and gave him room and board. His salary paid for ripped doors and customer's hospital bills.

As he said, "he looked at me side-wise squirrelly."

Rotting tool sheds in the suburbs were palaces compared to Silkie's. We walked through a flimsy hinge-less door that fell. The carpet looked and smelled like bettors had pissed in a pit bull ring on the bloody dead winner. Beer warped plywood on tall sawhorses was the bar. Plastic Woolworth lamps cast a faint red glow in the garage size room. The $4.95 lamps had melted to objet d' art lumps. There were two three legged couches the Salvation Army had rejected. They were the color of baby dodo. Dingy sheets were their stained covers. The place smelled like a truck of air freshener had just collided with an ammonia tanker.

We sat on two rickety bar stools and ordered.

"Two cold, very cold Budweisers, please. Real beer!" I laughed. My friend slapped my back in agreement.

"Warm Blatz or hot Blatz?" wheezed Mother Silkie.

Mother Silkie was of mixed parentage, part poet, pimp, and poker player. Her voice was a calliope caught in a tornado. Black as a moonless winter night, her teeth sparkled like diamonds on velvet. She lived on laughter and breathed a constant smile. A Camel cigarette never left her mouth. One replaced the other before it went out. Ashes fell in the valley between bosoms so full and round they put pillows to shame and created many wet dreams in lonely barracks. She flowed through space like a Ruebens balloon about to fly off under her fluffy high Afro. She was jiggling clouds of flesh covered in spray painted Capri pants and flimsy silk. Her fashion statement was to pile clashing colors in a heap and dive in. Chanel dies again when Silkie walks in but this brash bitch worked the room, mesmerized, and eased everyone. She knew that true style is revealing who you are and making work what no one else has the guts to try. Silkie was grandma serving her boys hot steamy muffins covered with warm icing. Show an empty wallet and she was a bull smashing out of the gelding shed with whomp-ass revenge in his eyes looking for the condemned idiot holding a bloody knife. Bought for ten cents and sold for ten bucks, she set down longneck flat beer bottles that barely made it through the blast at Yucca flats in 1947.

Names I Can't Remember

"Twenty bucks cash, PLUS tip," she sang through the cloud of Camel smoke.

So far, losing my virginity had cost sixty dollars to be well laid fully clothed without so much as a tingle.

"My boys, my boys, how isims y'all this fine day? Jes' look at dem lovely womens Iz got for yooz," she bellowed.

We said nothing. On the couch, sat Toothless Smile, Bathed Last Year, Flies Buzz Around Me, I Snores Like a Truck, and other debutantes at the ball.

"Some poet said, 'Kisses loves the heart but gold fucks the belly.' My boys, did you know the French crazies cut off heads and served them with bread-n-buddah? Dat is Silkie style! I love all my mens except the poor ones. Lordy, let's see that cash!"

"Silkie, where's my complete chicken dinner?" I yelled, full of sucker-punch-me bravado.

"Gives me a quarter," she said with a syrupy laugh.

Her spider net devoured me and wrapped me tight for a winter snack. With my two-foot cock ego, I slapped a quarter in her massive hand. She gave me a hard-boiled egg. She put my quarter in a giant bottle full of idiot change labeled "Silkie's retirement bottle, eighty-five." Mashing me with huge arms, she let me breathe when I showed her cash. A shadowy corner caught my eye. In a three-legged stuffed chair sat a quiet soldier that looked like a statue. All I could see was his silhouette.

"Who— what is that?" I asked gasping.

"Let that mans be," she sighed, walking away.

His distant eyes ringed in dark weary circles, cut through me, fixed on what only he saw. His cheeks were sunken. His body was rigid. His hands were claws on the chairs' arms. He was looking at the juke joint door fixed on his only way out. In a formal, dress green uniform, Airborne beret, and campaign braids, his chest was a salad of ribbons with valor V's. There was no fear, panic, or resignation in his cruel stare. The horrors he had survived and would remember forever had drained him of joy.

I kneeled and looked into his eyes. Slowly and tenderly, I put my hand on his knee. I don't know why. Maybe it was his look of the starving too weak to crawl to the banquet, the desperate to be touched but too dead to ask. He didn't acknowledge me.

"What happened there?" I asked softly.

He said nothing. His granite body didn't flinch. It was impossible to tell if he was even breathing. Mother Silkie's vice grip dug into my shoulder and jerked me back.

"Leave him alone," she said in a threatening tone.

"What happened to him?" I asked her.

Silence. The mother took care of her newborn. From a combat style pack ripped open on the wrong end, she tore the filter off a Kool, lit it, and put it to his lips. He dragged and exhaled. The sigh was the sound of the damned. She offered a sandwich she'd made. She set it next to him on the table by the other uneaten sandwiches. From a dusty ancient bottle saved just for him, she poured a tumbler full of Glenfarclas single malt scotch and fed him a sip. The ambrosia dribbled down the chin of a man with no soul to save at a last communion. Silkie filled it and placed it near all the empty tumblers. She looked at him. I saw his empty exhausted spirit cry in agony. His head turned lifelessly away.

Brass balled Silkie disappeared. A toothless bitch with a razor blade smile, nut busting dyke, earth mother, now Virgin Mary cared for her beaten Jesus. Her arms around this lost and helpless child let her be the mother she was before life chewed her up and spit her out. Whispered endearments made her the Gladys of old with a tiny house, garden, and swings out back. A scowl turned into the blushing cheeks of a new mother in a nursery of tenderness, forgiveness, and forgetting. Her baby's curling lips, begging tongue, and whimper was a different cry only mothers know. This was hunger. Her warrior was desperate for the peace and rest war ripped from his life. Brushing his wispy hair softly aside and stroking his cheek with a tender finger, she created a quiet cocoon where they alone could share this moment. She leaned a shoulder over to shield them from prying eyes. She got a fluffy shawl and small feather pillow. She primped it beside her heaving chest and covered her breast near his cheek. Her hand

Names I Can't Remember

reached under the cover, lowered her flimsy top, and turned his weary head. Ssshhing him, she drew his lips to her bosom. His lips opened and reached. For the milk she could no longer feed, she offered the suckling rest and beating heart lullaby he craved. Cupping her breast up and out to him, with his eyes closed, he quenched his hunger with her gentleness. Cradling his head, she breathed a mother's ultimate sigh of nurturing. Her eyes closed and her head fell forward in repose. Alone together, they were lost at the corner of I Need and Need Me. In a loud, smelly circus, they were in a silent cloud perfumed by talcum powder and serenity. Her head tilted down, her fingers softly stroking his cheek, Gladys sang.

"Bi...ohhh, bio baby bio. Bio bio baby bi..."

If it's easy to heal the weak, I watched what happened when the big man fell.

The moment was a feast of wonder. After seconds that seemed forever, I left.

Over a beer at the bar, I got over the last of the shock in me. The crude display I'd just been disgusted by became a tender memory. The worn out broad, so sure she had no mother left to give, fed the one so desperate to feel anything.

Sipping my beer, I heard the humming die out and a drawer open and close where Gladys put her shawl and memories away. Something hit my head so hard it nearly fell off. Silkie was back.

"You fucker's still wasting Silkie's time not spendin' nuttin'!" she snarled, her clenched fists and her balloon hips.

I tried to defend myself with a useless question.

"So, what is a Xystusium, Mother Silkie?" I asked.

"Cash! Get a bitch, get fucked, and get out! I heard that word and liked it right off. I figured if booze and bitches didn't work, I'd snag curious mens. Worked on you. A right snooty word I figger. It's a good bragging word. Nigger whore like Silkie has to show this fucked up world she has brains and pussy," said the slut Socrates.

"Covered portico or open court for athletic purposes," said the warrior in the corner.

"My oh my. I loves my mens. Thank you boy," she said filling his tumbler to the brim with scotch.

"Damn guy! I thought you was deaf an' dumb or something," I blurted out.

"Sssh. That's the first thing he said in two months he been wit me," she sighed.

"Shit, Silkie. He's a deserter. They'll throw him in jail," I argued.

"Son, this man done, done his killing. They have no use for him now. Told me so. So they leaves him with me. Look, you damned fool," she insisted glancing at his knee.

My hand on his knee again, he'd covered mine with his. It was the only time I think he saw me. His look was plea or warning. I didn't understand. He seemed to be trying to speak. Words refused to come out as his emotions retreated farther within. His cold hand fell and his head turned away. I felt a tight grip on my shoulder. It wasn't mother Madonna Gladys that had healed him earlier. Bitch Silkie had a hungry cash box.

With a snap of Silkie's fingers, her debutantes were all over us. One squeezed my balls while the other licked my ear. One smothered me with her tits while another rubbed my cock. Sticky sweat promises were made as these smiling buzzards fought each other for punk cash carcasses. As Passion riffled my pockets for cash, my cock got harder, began to twitch, and drip. All I thought of was the stench. I was surrounded by the stink of cigarette breath mixed with the odor of rotting teeth. I wanted to shove a spoiled sardine and rotten egg sandwich under my nose to mask the reeking armpits and pussies unwashed for days. My cock wanted to fuck them all. My heart ran home to Mom.

Silkie slapped her bitches back in line. The freebee tease was over. I finally took a breath that tasted sweat while she rubbed her palm, smiled, and glared at us to choose. Each of us sadly pointed at one of Mother Silkie's queens and headed to our prom in the seedy looking trailers in the compound. Once chosen and the money changed hands, these Cinderella's turned to scowling ugly sister cunts.

Yammering at each other about some monster cock that tore their pussy apart, they grabbed us by the wrist and dragged us behind them. We were naughty boys being taken for a spanking by angry mothers anxious to get back to the Soaps. Stumbling through the muddy yard, I watched bubble butts jiggle out of shorts stuck in ass cracks listening to their babble.

The trailers were flimsy walls that divided dinky bedrooms on either side of a hall a waif would be cramped in. As rooms, they were great closets. The mattress was wall to wall. A tacked up dingy sheet replaced the door that would have bumped into the bed. There was barely room to stand in the disgusting smell of sweaty sheets and body fluids. Clouds of lemon fresh and pine freshener left slime on skin and burned nostrils. Stink Foot and Rank Cunt plopped on the bed and yanked our pants down. Blabbering away, they washed our cocks and balls with a rag that looked like it was used for oil changes and grease jobs.

"Girl, this white bitch 'bout ruined my nails."

"Don't even tell me dat. I stopped goin' there."

We yanked our pants up. While our blushing cheeks returned to normal, our raging hard-ons went limp from nerves. Finally, we looked at each other in silent confusion asking the same question. Who was going to leave the room for this private first passion? We waited for either of them to get up and take one of us with them. The longer we waited, the more our knees knocked and asses clenched in embarrassment. My tender kisses by candlelight were drowned in a torrent fuck you girl guffaws. I couldn't look my friend in the eye. I wanted to run home for cookies and milk.

Our debutantes just yanked our pants back down while they splayed themselves naked on the same mattress. While one jacked and sucked, the other spoke. Our faces provided the red bulb glow.

"Try that hillbilly's shop. She knows how to do a sister's hair. Suck harder, baby. Da' boy seems a might twitchy. Scratch his nuts. Dey love dat, right boy?"

"Baby, I got me a fine hair place now. Come on, boy. Get it dancin'. I gots a busy day. The bitch there got it right. My head just tingles but don't burn."

"No burn," she said rubbing Vaseline on her pussy.

"Huh," garbled the one her mouth full of rubbery cock.

"How much you tip, baby?" she asked.

"I thought we already paid," my blush replied.

"Boy, I'll tell you when I'm talking to you. Get that white ass over my bizness and that rubber band will know what to do. Silly ass boy thought I was talking to him."

"Yah, Shirl. White boys—"

"Look the same!" they laughed waving our limp dicks.

They played with us without looking at us while we desperately avoided looking at each other. Their chatter became a dull din as I ran away in my head, screaming all the way. Where was the nervous tenderness? I wanted our hands to tremble as we touched and stroked each other until the windows steamed with desire. Rank Cunt was picking her nose while telling her friend about her blowjob sore jaw. I fought for a fantasy to stiffen my ego and stop my knocking knees. I wanted her to fumble with my zipper while I fought with the clasp on her bra. She reached for a nail clipper to clip a hangnail. The hard-on I almost had went limp again. I wanted our tongues to swirl and swoon my virgin tango. She popped a zit on her cunt. My stomach rumbled with disgust and I fought the urge to puke. I wanted her to say she loved me. She was laughing in my face. I sniffled like a bully beaten little boy. The more my soul begged for breathy sighs and tasting each other's sticky sweet fingers, the louder she laughed.

Listening to everything about laundry soap to Richard Roundtree's fine black ass, boys humped with fully limped egos. When needed, they'd firm us up with a quick yank or suck, shove us back in, and continue their coffee klatch without missing a breath.

At some point, our asses flinched and they shoved us off. These pros had sperm radar between their legs. It could sniff out a testicle twitch in a snowstorm. Before we blinked, they wiped clean with a grimy towel lying on the floor and turned us out. The same burning cigarettes we set in the ashtray when we entered, we smoked on the way out. I guess I came. I wasn't a virgin. I wasn't a man. I was a cock with an empty wallet, broken heart, and a lonely, desperation to be Silkie's 'baby.'

It was a quiet ride back to the base. Whorehouses turn elated boys into lonely men. The cab was full of sadness. Whatever love was, it wasn't that. It was a man's lesson in humiliation when mother and tears no longer heal.

We sat on those barracks steps again. We smoked, laughed, and patted each other on the back. We turned a blind date with a six-foot geek wearing coke bottle glasses and watermelon pimples on her face into Romeo and Juliet.

"Was that really your first time?" he asked.

"Yes," was my slow, sheepish admission. Silence.

Then his laughter erupted and obliterated me.

"Shut the hell up out there!" came the bellowed chorus from the men he woke.

He danced a giggly and finger pointing dance. I defended with tales of conquests at home. He couldn't hear me. It was the fifty other boys in boxer shorts that flooded out of the barracks to join the humiliation dance. Failure and shame by mob is our right of passage. Guys from other barracks awoke and joined the fun.

"Ya'lls first time," giggled the hillbilly.

"Yes. Just ask the other thirty guys that asked me that," I hissed.

"No practice, boner boy?" said one poking my ribs.

"Yah, but I ran out of willing heifers, farmer!" I yelled in defense.

Guzzling Army 'near beer,' a tribal party happened. A radio blared. In a mesh garbage can, a fire crackled, and cast shadows of boys prancing in the crisp cool moonlight. Ancient caves and teepees emptied while the women slept to leave us howling at the moon, sharing bloody beef, and reliving the hunt with puffed chests that hid the failures. Cracking voices rang out tales of hefty cocks so rigid she surely loved it. The night wore on and the fire fell to glowing embers until a strange thing happened. One typist boy at the Devil's dead man ball slapped me on the back and smiled, then another, and still another. Loneliness brings out sympathy in boys. The crowd thinned to a few that watched a dying fire in silence. Jokes turned to distant dreams and yearnings.

"My Mustang's tricked out cherry. Me and Kate at Lookout Hill, top down, the 8-track, and just talk. Most times we didn't do anything," said the sheepish Jersey boy.

"First time I got inside that trap girdle, I didn't wipe my finger off. You shoulda' seen guys smelling that finger I showed off," I proudly laughed, waving a finger.

"The one you felt up before you even knew her name?" asked the Kansas farmer.

"That's her. At first I thought she was easy, but she wasn't," I smiled, shaking my head.

"What was she then?" stammered the Boise cowboy.

"Well, fooling around to her was just... fun! You should have seen her smile. In the whole year we dated, we never went out on one date, not one," I emphatically added.

"Dated but didn't date?" asked the sandy haired one with glasses. He was a trusting kid that believed anyone so we were always putting him on with wild stories.

As the tribal fire sizzle spat, wannabe warriors in boxer shorts listened to legends.

"We always parked and fooled around. Man, the stories we invented; games we never bowled, movies never seen, and pizzas never eaten. On the rides home, she put her bra back on and my boner went down. We'd practice our story. God, we laughed."

"Groovy. Did she ever get you—"

"ALL the time... once I got the guts to pull her hand down there," I snickered, giggling like a girl.

Cave boys howled in flickering fire shadows.

"Slowly, I stroked the back of her head and— "

Their she's gonna gulp guffaws cut me off.

"While she stroked and squeezed—"

More yowls. Miles off, a wolf got curious.

"He pushed!" yowled one.

"Her head moved... on its own! She kissed it," I whispered, softly.

Stunned silence.

They loved my great make out spot; the doctors parking lot at the hospital. It was private, dark, never patrolled, and doctors were inside for days. Only once were Steel Girdle and I caught. Well-steamed windows didn't bust us. I had my foot on the brake. While we squeezed in gooey delight, my foot pumped away. A gray haired guard eventually knocked on the window thinking a doctor had left his lights on.

I got applause with the tale of how we did it in her house. While her brother and sister watched TV, we were in her room. A Bible belt kid gulped his beer, begged for popcorn, and took notes. He scribbled lots when I said she stopped wearing the hand trap girdle after I asked. She loved showing off and changed in front of me to model clothes. The guys leaned in to hear how I said, don't dress, and we wound up in bed, naked.

"Lower naked-ocity? God!" sighed the kid from Boston.

"I was hard as a rock. Then she whispered in my ear."

"She wanted it. She wanted it!" yelled a few.

"You should lock the door," she said.

They gasped for breath and laughed at the picture of me waddling to the door with my pants at my ankles. Back in bed, we fumbled and stroked. Had either of us known how to execute what we both seemed to want, we might have. The moist and gooey fumbling went on. They got very quiet hearing about her pushing my head down.

"There it was, the promised land inches from my nose. My face crinkled from the confusing yet intoxicating perfume. Then it hit me, what do I do with it?"

Heads leaned into a deafening silence of stupidity.

"I kissed it... like kissing her mouth," was my whisper.

"Ahhhhhh," was the tribe's confused sigh of agreement.

Shadows and shivering boys danced in the dark. Taunts of lost virginity were forgotten. The tribal fire cooled to the echoes of the fading youth laughter. In boring typing class the next day, every worldly man, bold liar, and boyish virgin smiled, except one.

I was afraid of yesterday. Like a slick from the womb baby, I suckled a first desperate breath that's every warrior's last gasp for mom. I'd lost what I'd never had to a body part who didn't care I was in the dingy trailer. The trial fire and stories of last night meant nothing. In clerk class in the morning, I held back tears typo after typo. All I could remember was Madonna Gladys, Child, and a hand on my knee.

In the shadows of smiles are satin sheets,
Dreamy music tingling the skin so joyously.
Candle dances flicker desire everywhere
Giving her yearning learning silken heart
Into my open arms so strong yet trembling.

The wonder of all those years in skin so soft,
Her eyes afire she flows deep into my arms.
The touch, the touch, just her touch so warm.
Her scent fills me so, draws my moist lips low.
Jewels of passion slide on heaving breasts

Hold me dearest, please never let me go.
First night is our forever my heart says so.
Teach this strong one how passion grows.
Rest; let me rest in our arms and sighs.
She rises, I fall, two alone in one new love.

Each new touch a wondrous shiver
With laughter we bravely roam
Kisses dancing with smiling sighs
And words of all our dreams yet to come
Be with me, I in we,
Our rainbows will fly in cloudy skies.

Tender touches yearning eve to morn
I is thee, we are me, in laughter love's born.
Lets us live our virgin's night now and always.
In my arms she rests to love again aglow
We looked so long to love and be needed so.

In the long, lonely winter of my life, I remember her.

Names I Can't Remember

Mom should never see her son lose his virginity.

The 19-year-old punk given the responsibility
for 50 other punks' lives.

Names I Can't Remember

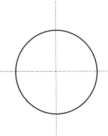

Oleanna

September 1968

"God would let me forget the names but force me to grow old with memories."

We were boys chasing snowflakes with our tongues and men whose courage was a magic bean in a field of sorrow nurtured by mothers' tears. Gazing at vast, green marching fields in the red Georgia clay, we wandered outside the barracks. Young lions with new manes but no scars made alliances with steely glances and piled duffel bags for shade. Yelling, pissing, marching, shining, folding, and avoiding play bullets in unison made us invincible killers hungry to blow off men's faces. Behind wary eyes were coward mamma's boys that found their war at an ego circus.

Home was Infantry Officer Candidate School. Banners extolled the mantra "Follow Me" outside the warrior palace of brick and plywood. Floors were sparkling tile, not splintered wood that creaked. John stalls had doors! We had rooms instead of an open barracks of snores. Each slept four or less if you had big balls or were intimidating. Meat was steak not shit on a shingle from a can. While training, we were temporary sergeants. The tastiest bait on the hook were the salutes from subordinate enlisted men.

Our part of the base was a vast marching field of jade green grass a half-mile square. Wide swaths of dead grass beaten down by boots streaked the green sea framed by a road. On three sides of the field were barracks. The fourth was the forest for war games. Each side was a battalion field of three training companies with two hundred boys each. Companies had a portion of the field with lumber obstacles for training. Each company had a barracks of three floors with a blacktop courtyard in front.

Each 6 months, a thousand new 2nd Lieutenants were cranked out. This is minus the 50% that failed to measure up or just quit in emotional and physical exhaustion. Winners went to Vietnam. No one asked what dragon was devouring all those princes to the Kingdom of Stupid.

We were here to learn how to lead in combat. It meant learning traditions that made slaughter a hell I'd keep a brother from by locking him up but live again if I could. It started with the boyish screams Follow Me in a hail of gunfire and ended with the glimmer in old soldiers' eyes before the tears. The mantra, the men come first, helped turn bloodbaths into victories. By smoky fires of glory in ancient caves of honor, boys hear mystic tales of lead by example. The brave never surrender. We dig a grave, hop in, and fill in the dirt smiling. The same gladiator fairytales that filled us with pride would be the lead in the paper and headstone title months later. Some stood boldly in the mid-day sun with wind in their face. Clouds of cigarette smoke and laughter billowed. Two hundred men of nineteen told war stories of surviving brutal 3 A.M. inspections. We were the next aggressive calves in the hamburger line.

Uniforms were the dark green of new fabric. They were rumpled not pressed or starched to death. Helmets were the ugly bumpy green of standard issue. They had no decals or gleaming paint. Our boots were shinned but also standard issue. They weren't the classy jump boots with stitched heels and toes or the glare of a mirror spit shine.

The first eight weeks, we would be these ugly Basics. If we lasted and measured up, the next eight would be as Intermediates. That meant uniforms faded and stiffer from starch, helmets painted glossy black, spit shined jump boots and black scarves. They were the mythical medals for punks fulfilling their destiny as men to compete, excel and lead. In truth, they were the scars for enduring pain, constant humiliation, and our spirits screaming to give up. Half would make it all the way to Senior Psycho. That meant the crushing abuse would end with a gold bar for Stupid and the balls to gamble boy's lives on our decisions.

If an Army marches on full stomachs, it wins because waiting makes you homicidal. The jock showed off the cheerleader's panties. The scrounger auctioned smuggled Budweiser. The intellect had his Proust upside down. The poet read the whimsical drug fantasy "Watermelon Sugar." I asked if Brautigan's "ideath" was "I – death" or "IDEA – th." He scribbled furiously. The nose picker tasted a prize. The dork cleaned thick glasses. The solitary kid, hid. The pimple popper let the juicy one bleed. The freckled farmer wrote to Betty Jo worried about mythical Jodi we'd sung about while marching. Jodi, unfit for any Army, was a horny devil, and traveled the country seducing wives and girlfriends. The Army loved aggression from sexual tension. They never heard the squeaky bedsprings at night. They made the enemy Jodi's Asian cousins.

Sticking my helmet under my ass, I stared at that sea of green field. It was soothing and mysterious. The sun bouncing off something caught my eye. It was the jump school wings on my chest. I quietly hummed the Airborne "All the Way" marching tune. It was a nothing tune, really. Add words for any task, problem, sorrow, and count to four then back down made it the one size fits all inspiration. I stroked the wings. Boys are proud of the crazy things they do. I'll never forget the same expression of terror on all those young faces. We were going to jump out of a perfectly good airplane that had every intention of landing.

The wings were my only pride. I earned them for guts to be nuts. I took exhausting abuse for four weeks to do what few had the courage to try. I earned my wings early. The usual sequence is Basic, Advanced Training, Major Skill School, and then jump school or other optional killing courses. A typical Army screw up had me in jump school and home on pre-combat leave until someone saw I was set for Infantry OCS. None of this mattered until a real officer got pissed. I had what he didn't.

I remembered the hillbilly with heart in jump school. He was the best good old boy Billy bubba with the most heart and least ability. He worked twice as hard to fail twice as fast. He never complained. At each obstacle, after every character assassination, and every boot in the ass, he got up and tried again. One day, he flopped in his bunk and we talked.

"I jest kain't figger it, you damn Yankee," he smiled.

"What's that, you cousin fucker reb?" I answered with a shot to his arm and grinning a goofy smile.

"I don't get it. I can take out a possum eye with a rusty rifle. All this is a dang foundin' me like a cornered coon with whup ass on his mind," he said, shaking his head.

"Maybe it's time you quit before they wash you out."

"Never. Don't aim to start now. I'm right 'preciated for you not a jokin' like the rest. Man who walks away from a righteous fight's still a coward," he smirked.

"Hmmm. Do you have any idea what's wrong?" I prodded.

"Nary a musin'. They teach me an it jus' don't sink in. I try to do it all and I jus' get hurt worse. Maybe I oughta' listened to that draft doc, you figger?"

"What draft doctor?" I asked, leaning in.

"Damn Yankee tells me I'm deaf in one ear and blind in the other eye. I says I knows. Never stopped me plowin' bottom land in a storm with a three legged mule."

After I laughed my ass off and slapped the daylight out of him, he was off to sick call. The war meat grinder needed hamburger so bad he got one of those hey you, how many hands I got hearing and eye tests. I never saw him again. The gang signed a letter I promised to send. We got a scrawled response from his family in Pig Jaw. He died pulling that three-legged mule out of a flooding sinkhole. We bought a Silver Star at the PX and sent it to his Maw. I told her the Army sent it to the barracks by mistake. The fake citation read his unit gave her son the Silver Star with V for courage and kindness above and beyond the call of duty. We got a last letter from his mother. She must have practiced that chicken scrawl thank you for weeks. Along with the neatly folded scrap of paper, was one of Pig Jaw's finest wild flowers.

My roving eye spotted someone across the road at the edge of the vast marching field. A boy, maybe a bit older, was staring out over the field. He was looking at something he knew was there but couldn't see. He stood out from the people walking because of his darting eyes hidden by dark glasses. His lean frame moved in a calculated fashion. His head was in constant motion to see if anyone was looking at him. He seemed worried about being caught. He tried so hard to not be noticed. I noticed. As I walked over, I spotted the Air Canada return ticket in his back pocket. I saw a few words on the crumpled letter in his hand, "Dear brother, I was awestruck," was all I could see. A worn out stateside paper told me he was on the run, desperate for a taste of home and relief from the loneliness.

I looked at the horizon over the field that fascinated him but saw nothing. Looking at him, those intense eyes so moist and focused, I knew he could see it.

"Is something wrong over there?" I asked him softly.

Silence. Turning to me was his only recognition. The anger and sadness in his eyes startled me. They were sunken, sleepless, and lost in the anger about to explode or crumble in tears. A blue warrior had to feel what inspired his gray brother so. He begged for an answer with those eyes. I had nothing to give but the comfort of standing at his side. His chin sank to his chest and he turned to stare again. His shoulder touched mine the instant he sighed and rested. I stood with him in silence, seeing nothing. Like a stoic chief, he read his brother's words, stood proud, tall, and pointed to the horizon.

It was a dusty puff of red Georgia clay in the distance. Faint crimson in color, this small cloud so close to the ground seemed to be the signal of the first cannon fired far off before the roar reached my ear. Two boys watched in curious wonder. The puff grew, rolled, billowed and rose to the sky as some mystical herd thundered closer. Faint crimson turned deep scarlet the closer it came. We stiffened and stood taller.

Faint at first, it was the deep, rumbling moan of a distant tribal drum welcoming the ominous clouds of a Serengeti monsoon. One massive voice was approaching. It widened eyes and dropped our jaws in that peaceful awe just before fear daggers the heart. Closer, the rumbling became a melody. It was a warrior chorus of angel song that shivered the spines of boys with manly four-part harmony:

"oh - lee - anna,
Oh - lee, Oh - lee, anna.
OH! -Lee Oh-Lee, OH! - Lee Oh-Lee
OHHH - LEE, OHHH - LEE - ANNAHH!"

Sky blue shining helmets rippled like a proud mighty wave. I needed one.

Virgin white scarves adorned the senior warrior gods with honor. I craved one.

"oh - lee - anna,
Oh - lee, Oh - lee, anna.
OH! -Lee Oh-Lee, OH! - Lee Oh-Lee
OHHH - LEE, OHHH - LEE - ANNAHH!"

Jump boots pounded the earth as one thunderous crash of might. Heels and toes dazzled like diamonds that earned the right to be worshiped. My soul groveled for them.

"oh - lee - anna,
Oh - lee, Oh - lee, anna.
OH! -Lee Oh-Lee, OH! - Lee Oh-Lee
OHHH - LEE, OHHH - LEE - ANNAHH!"

As the class of seniors thundered close enough to touch, the sound filled me with envy. Oleanna, the word sung over and over in angelic harmony, was a constant melody of bravery, the tempo surprised by sudden ego solos. It wasn't a toy of boys lilting by, it was a single man machine crushing punks with bravery and tempting every dreamer to join the parade. It's a sound that stiffened flags and spines to face the thunder of defeat.

I saw the stiff, creased uniforms. They weren't flapping in the breeze like mine. They were faded to pale green by experience that had proven itself. They weren't the gangly, giggly virgin green of what I wore. They were rock hard from being starched to death with self-confidence. My fatigues were a Jello erection. Their pockets were so glued shut they looked like drawings. Hidden buttons left ringed impressions from blazing irons and steam. They remained stiff in the dripping sweat Georgia swelter. Changes were made to break starch twice, thrice a day. Gods must look like Gods.

I couldn't see their eyes. They were hidden under shiny sky blue helmets with the OCS emblem on the front. Their square clenched jaws protruded from under the tipped low rims. Their helmets weren't the dull, uninspiring, and pimply green thing I wore.

The boots were a wave of diamonds roaring by. The leather was a sparkling mirror reflecting a universe of bravery. Stitched toes and heels were exploding novas. They were chariots for invincible legions not the half-assed polished goof boots I wore.

The ex-patriot brother was gone. Together, we had watched conceit march by, crush humility, and bury youth. He wanted no part of it. I wanted to devour it. He waved. I wished him well in a lonely cold water flat in Canada where every knock on the door or coded letter condemned him to fear's death row. I wanted to be a killer. Glory buried my fear. It would rot with my tears hidden from those close until exploding in the quiet gray years alone or in wordless glances with one who was there. It's where names I can't remember are shrouded by hell's rainbow of regret.

There was nothing extraordinary about the entire six months of OCS. Like combat, those months were eternities of boredom interrupted by insane heartbeats of emotional and physical exhaustion. Souls for hell scorch in purgatory first. I learned to inspire and lead but not about life or death. I survived on glory and bravery but starved, refusing to eat the truth. Classes had me ready to fight for glory. Soldiers kill to survive. Leaders survive not killing. Others might die based on what I did. Not one class taught me what I needed most — how to carry a gold bar made of lives.

God would let me forget the names but force me to grow old with memories.

I remember the trainee's wife that made extra money getting uniforms to and from the laundry stiff and starched. Her married daughter seldom asks about dad who lives alone in a dump shack deep in the northwest woods.

I remember the joker who spit lighter fluid fire to shock us. His soul and face always smiled. His name is never seen on the sliver where the low black slab begins.

I remember big brother teacher. He taught me how to soften new jump boots until they were comfortable second skins. I hear he stares at the locked ward door and out the window a lot, drooling between convulsions of memory.

I remember the gung-ho bastard that loved every abusive minute of OCS. Glory ran in his veins and hooked him. I saw him on his way to war. His eyes were as sunken and dead as his soul. He jumped out of a chopper anxious to kill again and ran the wrong way. His head exploded in the tail rotor. It's said he kept firing for a minute.

I remember the wolf pack. It was my triumphant return to Rome via Waterloo. I was student company commander for a critical exercise. I was terrified but knew my bluster and brashness would get me through. All that sleeping I did in class didn't give me a clue as to how. A smart-ass needs no talent. Survival starts with belief not fact. A smartass only needs balls.

I took command calling the company to attention. Having just torn my pants ass to knee rushing out of the barracks did not inspire. Giggles and snickers echoed as I began the ten-mile, heavy pack march to the exercise site in sweltering heat. Calling cadence and commands for two hundred kids stretched over a hundred yards shook me. Luckily, the end of my company wound up where the front had gone. Eight miles out, the real officers decided the barracks were dirty and we must return to clean them. The exhausted men complained but obeyed. Busy work done, we headed out. The officers hovered at my side trying to terrorize and break me that I would now fail at this mission. Student platoon leaders told me how exhausted the men were. They needed water, rest and time to care for blisters. The officers pushed me. I pushed the men harder. I found the men's agony in my exhaustion. The officers yelled more. Despite their anger, I ordered a rest. After all, who was in command? Panic won. At a bridge near the mission site, the wolf pack attacked. I was told the enemy might ambush us. We must cross at a double time march. My exhaustion was breaking me. As the company ran, four real officers surrounded me smelling blood. They tore at my flanks of conceit.

"Your men are going to get killed, Captain!"

"You can't make it. Give up command!"

"You know you want to, loser. Save yourself!"

"Do you surrender command, Captain asshole!?"

I ran in a panicked sweat, looking at my men and tired with each deafening insult. At my weakest, I drooled a "yes." I couldn't take the pain. I wanted to give up. I didn't give a damn about the men. The wolf pack devoured me and tore my flesh with insults. I survived flailing my arms to grasp a last breath of anger.

"You sorry sack of shit! You are a commander."

"Those lives depend on you, you pussy!"

"I'll save them, mamma's boy. Do you surrender command, captain shithead?"

"No!" I yelled, my emotional bones picked clean.

I learned that command is one second fear, one week anger, and one eternity of guilt. I'd hated myself for the coward's yes I took back. At the exercise site, I passed command on. The new student leader boy's eyes begged my dead man's soul for a way out of the grave that buries every mother's son with his words or actions. I spoke with a father's silent sorrow that didn't heal his agony. He would have to face his own wolf pack. The leftover idiots survived the rest of OCS.

We earned our powder blue helmets, white scarves, stiff uniforms, dazzling boots, and got into the hamburger line smiling.

It ended with our Lieutenants' gold bar. Our first truth was how senior sergeants retire in opulence. After the ceremony, the real company first sergeant stood outside. As each butter bar Lieutenant came out, this thirty-year man from D-Day and Inchon snapped a crisp salute and held out his palm. We returned the salute, added a "carry-on First Sergeant," and slapped a new silver dollar in his hand. Each six months, tradition put a smile on Top's face, silver in his pocket, and a fifty-foot sloop in his future.

There is one person I remember in detail and with fiendish glee. He was Lieutenant what's-his-name. What a succulent affair of teasing and rebellion it was. He was my training officer. The gold bar he wore didn't satisfy him. I had something he didn't have. It made me stand out from all the rest. Different is Army sin that shivers God in the factory where all cogs are crushed to mold one killing machine. It was a joy pissing him off, flaunting it in his face each day. That I was entitled to do so made it more delicious. The object of his fury and desire was a small set of wings on my chest. The wings were for graduates of parachute school. We all sang Airborne, All the Way! I was the only prick trainee in a thousand who was actually Airborne. Not even this training officer had gone to jump school. In the your cock is as long as the number of medals you wear contest, I was pissing on what's-his-name's pride.

One day early in training, I pinned on the wings I was proud of. During the pre-dawn inspection by flashlight, the glint of metal on my chest caught his eye and he was on me like a fly on a fresh kill. The how dare you idiot screaming ensued. Later came my epiphany of brilliance; medals need shining! Then, they glitter and glow by sun or moon. I shined the ridges off that bastard and enjoyed every knuckle-busting hour. Classmates envied those wings with grins and slaps on my back stiff with notice and pride. A fanatic's drool at the corner of Lieutenant what's-his-name mouth was best.

Oleanna was the warrior gods owning the soul I proudly surrendered. Its dark side is the sadness in the old lion's eyes too feeble to hunt and the yawns when the glories are told to the young lions in the Pride who have not yet killed.

"Go home, old lion. Sing these boring, snoring laments of boots and scarves to cubs who give a damn. Your rituals are for headstones not headlines. I won't sell my pride for your memories. What do you want to buy, toothless one?"

"A life lost in hate I wish to save you from."

"You old fool. Why do the old lie and nobly claim to teach when the truth is all they want is forgiveness and escape from regret?"

"I can't feel. Say I'm not horrible. Say, I know now how important the glory, I see why you spent your last snowflake and green grass giggle for a bag of magic beans to grow weeds of sorrow tomorrows. Are my scars of survival worth the feeling I gave away? Tell me, please. Why do I want to be a God, to hunt, and kill once more?"

Oh-lee-ANNA
Oh-lee, oh-lee-ANNA
Oh-lee, oh-lee, oh-lee, oh-lee
OH-lee, oh-lee-anna!

It's the sound I remember.

Not one stood out.
But the mass that mattered,
Crashing waves of bravery,
Steel tall, erect, square jawed
Warrior winds of Agincourt
God's swords pounding Normandy
Blood to break the fort
A cold lunch of death and Sauvignon
A supper untouched of dead soul sorrow
Forward follow me tomorrow
Virgin white Crusader's banner
About the neck
The mourning silk to dress the dead

The symbol of the sorrow suffered
And right to die so proudly bloody free
Screaming we are the warriors
You want to be

God's dance in rhythm all the same
Singing angels song in glory
Of balls to lead in blood and dies
We are the square jawed chosen ones
To wield the sword of lies.

Grim Reaper leather dazzled
Bare knuckle to black diamond mirror
Coal dark angels glint and dance
In rhythm to the dead we lead
This string of black pearls undulate
On a milky bare soft tender neck
Come love me now, lay down to die
At crest of wanton heaving breast

So many dreams
In a life of schemes
And drunken sadness sung.
Fill lonely with anger, leap and soar,
Or suicide scribble love being lost.
Wandering to the ice-berg candy store
Pay gimme gotta get I in frozen frost.

Oh-lee-anna, Oh-lee-anna let me be thee
Warrior God, Schlub, Billy Bubba, all pimply me.

I heard warrior's words
Singing angel song.
Come do the devil's dance

Of defiant youth indifference
Bet gray life for bold blazing blue.
Hey stupid, your boys live or die
Depending on shithead you.

Vast rolling green on red Georgia clay
Angel God warrior soul soaring song afar
Schlameel, Kaleel, Mario spic Dick and I
Can shithead, baby ass face me be what they are?
Stiff marching, faded starched green
Heel an' toe in blazing mirror black
Bravery rammed up your ass an' feathers preen.

Bass, baritone, tenor and alto melody
Follow Me in noble four part harmony.
Remember when I think its time you go
Looking up firm father said.
Where, what or will I do — you'll know.
Make mother's cry sons gots no bed.
Be three hots and cot worth betting dead?

Oh-lee-anna, Oh-lee-anna let me be thee
Warrior God, Schlub, Billy Bubba, all pimply me.

Two Wounded Sparrows

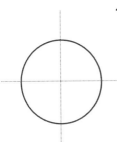

APRIL 1969

"Our first kiss came as all delicious first ones do. It's remembered for a lifetime and comes in a quiet moment, gently and by surprise."

Her broken heart and romantics' eyes saw delicate bone china in a paper plate world. Linda had jet-black hair and smooth ivory skin. Her black Irish hazel eyes were framed by pencil thin, velvet black eyebrows and thick, sensual lashes. The sparkle in those far away eyes came from tears always there but never set free. A petite, curvy woman, she moved with the charming southern grace of a lazy river in June.

She was twenty-five years old, a recent divorcée, and a civilian secretary. I was the nineteen-year-old virgin Lieutenant noticing this Mrs. Robinson. She didn't look like temptation but dragged me to that dark side without much struggle. In 1969, divorcée was the term for all single women even if there were large bruises under high collars and long sleeves. In this humid Georgia spring, Linda wore the highest collars and longest sleeves. Until sundown, I was the sober executive officer of a parachutist training unit. I fell in love one hangover at a time.

We shared a someone, anyone hold me feeling that hid behind wide-eyed gazes and hearty laughs. As she tenderly arranged her desk menagerie of porcelain, I could hear her heart that loved too early too often. She'd rather have a wastebasket full of broken hearts more than soggy tissue. As she watched me sign papers and gaze at billowy clouds out my window, she could hear my heart that loved too late behind a cracked mask of pride. We were two wounded sparrows with broken wings of loneliness.

I pushed paper every day so slow that cold oatmeal was an erotic fantasy. For an Airborne Infantry 2nd Lieutenant that gorged warrior Wheaties for six months I would have preferred the jokes at an accountants convention. For fun, I got drunk on base at night and rode my motorcycle to the local dry town hot spot. The Arby's 2 A.M. late show was mopping and ketchup refilling.

I watched her often while I signed papers a sergeant filled out and shoved in front of me. For all I know, I shipped fur coats to Asia, ice to Alaska, and stolen jeeps to the sergeant's home. The joy of my job was falling in love and offering gentle smiles mixed with kind words to a beauty about to crack.

Our offices were the headquarters. It was an ugly duck rectangle disguised as a swan. Thick layers of dazzling white on plain clapboards held it together more than nails. The trim was unit honor blue and gold. The one storey, hundred foot shack looked tired from holding up so much paint. Out front, the colonels' manicured lawn was plush green from constant watering, while non-command grass elsewhere looked like dead corned-beef hash in the Georgia sun. The lawn was edged in whitewashed rocks. Three flags celebrated the glory of country and Airborne All the Way!

Inside was military spic-and-span. Stick to your ass vinyl furniture was ugly gray steel that survived the blast at Yucca Flats. Walls were mock wood paneling covered with ornate citations for bravery, widget management, pictures of presidents, and former classes. The floor was thick, gleaming, and dull gray asbestos tiles in a checkerboard pattern. You could eat off it if you liked a half-inch coat of wax with your powdered eggs.

My desk was in the open lobby area. I was the S-1 Administration Officer and Executive Officer of the training unit. I could see the first office on the narrow hallway leading to the other end of the building. Linda, the colonel's secretary, sat in there.

Further down the hall, were the offices of the Staff Sergeant that really ran things. He was the guy who knew what the hell was going on. I never saw him except to sign some cryptic form that only he understood. His door was always closed. Behind it, I heard the constant clatter of an old adding machine and giggles. He had to be totaling all the stuff he'd sent, under my signature, to his secret warehouse in suburbia. The last office was for the battalion Sergeant Major. As far as I could tell, his only duty was to yell "attention" when the colonel entered his private door near his office at the back.

After the personnel, bravery, honor and efficiency forms, there was nothing to do. If I wasn't daydreaming leading a charge up San Juan Hill or committing eighty proof suicide, I was watching and knowing Linda from afar.

We both wanted others to like us more than we did. I'd watch her surrounded by soldiers all needing a problem solved now. She'd beat each problem into submission. She'd shush each man out and close her door. Through the crack, I saw her dance, smile and celebrate in victory. Then she looked around that empty room, crashed in her chair, and began to cry as she petted one of the delicate figurines on her desk. I knew that solitude of the mighty, afraid to show how much they need to be needed. We talked with sneaky peeks and sudden looks away when the other looked up. We shared a teenage need to reach out and the fear the other would pull their hand away.

I wanted to ask, "Do you go to crowded parties and wander empty heartless rooms alone?" When I asked her to fix my toilet paper order form, did she whisper, "Do you eat one-dish meals in margarine bowls like I have at home?" Did she catch me eyes shut, inhaling her lovely lilac scent? Was I that stupid to never see her hand waving more my way? Why didn't we ever share a gutsy laugh over our expertise at Christmas dinner for one? She was busy crumpling in her chair when her he beat me calls to mom rang unanswered. I was occupied sneaking a drink from the bottle in my drawer. We'd quickly pass each other pausing for an instant hoping a desperation hug would leap out of us. We handed each other papers but backed off when the time came. So many times, we poured two cups of coffee and drank both alone.

The first moment we ever shared in the office was a nervous laugh at the bulletin board. Each of us denied being the author of the joke memo to the Army brass in DC. It said we had the sharpest pencils, cleanest whores, and ten times the needed one hundred-dollar widgets that cost two bucks a pop off base. Our relaxed smiles and reaching eyes were a great kiss until we noticed our sighs, beads of sweat, and nervously parted. Walking by Linda's office, a perfumed Kleenex whooshed out of a brightly colored box. I glanced and saw her dab and gently pat tears at the corner of her eyes. Confused, I still didn't understand why women can't stand mussed make-up. I guess agony has to look good.

"Hi," was all I could manage.

"Hi," she whispered trying to turn her gloom into a smile. In that agonizing forever pause that quickly filled with apologetic twitches, I watched her. Her small hands with those long and slender fingers fluffed the fringed collar of her bright summer dress. With smooth and graceful moves, she checked each sleeve and evened out nonexistent wrinkles in a puffy skirt. It gave her the time to straighten her back. It's that erect posture of dignity and pride all Southern women have, even when watching their husband's lover dress or the Yankees break down the door to Tara.

She found her composure. It didn't hide the fragile cracks in her Southern pride; the delicately laced hankie crumpled and damp always in her hand.

"How'd yah get that bruise?" I asked in a whisper.

"Why, what do y'all mean, Lieutenant?" she asked, coyly fluttering her lashes and turning away.

"Ma never believed me when I didn't know too," I stammered as she bristled, raising her chin in defiance.

"No one... nothing beats— bruises— a Southern woman ripens," she sniffled into the tissue.

"I'm sorry. I'm always too fucking curious."

"Lieutenant, I am appalled at your language," she said primping up a frilly collar.

Bruises from him or not, her chin just got higher.

"I'm always sticking my nose in other people's stuff. You suppose that's why I never get asked to hang out a second time?" I said, with rare honesty and a tense giggle.

Her answer wasn't a nervous smile but one that told me I almost made her laugh.

"Thanks," she said, like a bluebird greeting the sun.

"For what?" I asked, curiously.

"For a smile I truly felt. Do you have any idea how hard it is for a Southern woman to smile constantly when she'd just as soon chew someone's eyes out?"

We laughed. At last, a friendly moment with our guard down. Her stiffness relaxed and I slouched in a chair at her desk. With a graceful hand and gentle touch, her slender fingers flowed over the delicate porcelain figures on her desk. Her eyes seemed to be misting and her drawling Southern voice drifted as if in a dream.

"Did y'all learn anything in OCS?"

"I make a tight bunk and can out spit-shine the best," I said, sarcastically, while puffing my chest.

She laughed demurely, hiding the joy behind her hand. She was a woman of the Old South where ladies learn it is impolite to laugh bawdily. A lady is soft and quiet

"Do y'all know why Southern women titter behind fans?" she asked, impishly humored by her own joke.

"Why?"

"So Daddy dasn't hear and, God forbid, change his will," she said with glee. "Isn't it sad?" she said, cradling a figurine in her hand.

"What?"

"That a little girl's bedtime stories never have the same happy

Names I Can't Remember

endings when she's a woman."

"Huh?"

"Lieutenant—"

"Doug, please!"

Responsibility was pissing me off, but my rank being a joke made me angrier. I couldn't wait to command a unit so my gold bar would get me what I deserved.

"I'd like to be me instead of a cocksucker Colonel's errand boy. I went from num-nuts to Lieutenant in six months. So far, all glory means is being the officer in charge of blame," I snickered.

"Foul mouth and all? A tad crispy but full of Southern fried charm. Doug, then, it is. Feel free to call me Linda."

"Tell me, Linda. You like making funny cracks don't you? I've never thought Southern women were like that."

"Then, you haven't met many. I suspect y'all haven't really met any true Southern women, just Scarlets," she offered, with an evil glint in her eyes.

"Scarlets?"

"Our term for supposed women of the South in trashy books. Scarlets are cartoons not rich, long, dark, and delicious book chapters as Southern women truly are. As we say after too many mint juleps, a true Southern woman is front door Scarlet and backdoor harlot," she sang, with clipped precision and pride.

"Is that so?" I asked, with a grin.

"You bet your sweet ass," she bellowed, slapping her thigh as if she had jugged the last of the white lightening over her crooked arm. "Thank you," she said, in a whisper.

"For what?" I asked.

"Y'all see, we have something in common. I like being me instead of an expectation. Thank y'all kindly, Douglas. 'I've always depended upon the kindness of strangers,'" she finished with Blanche's girlish giggle and cotton-candy fragility.

Her flirtation surprised me. It was the only time I remember the boy called Douglas feeling like a man.

We laughed and smiled the early evening away as she told

me her tale of a broken heart and what's-his-name. Linda told me Southern dramas are never the sins of Rhett or Robert E. The South decided that all tales of their troubled daughters had to start with dull Yankee names like Sam, George or Leon. I listened with my chin in my hands like a boy mesmerized by mamma's bedtime tale. She reminded me there were always the Billy Bubbas and Willie Joe's. Women of breeding and property never marry those sharecropper, 'shine running, and coal dusted men. Those names were saved for the distant cousins. They married other thirteen-year-old cousins and bred the crazy aunts Southern families proudly display on holidays or at family reunions. The crazy ones laughed bawdily with loud passion not titters behind flitting fans that sounded like someone stuffed a cork in their ass.

I listened to her sordid tale. It started as they all do with we met at, built to a roaring blaze with blame, and ended with the tears of a wounded, guiltless storyteller. At times, I nodded and stroked her arm softly to reassure her because that's what I thought I should do. I had no idea if it was right. She was twenty-five, vulnerable, and there. I was nineteen, horny, and feeling lucky. I waited in sympathetic lust.

She talked about the happy but few, early days. Her fragile smile disappeared as she held back tears. Her deep hazel eyes, so warmly soothing and passionately moist, mesmerized and tempted me. I sensed her fear when she told how he beat her but had my eyes on her tits. Her lithe arms, like the swooning necks of swans, conducted the story's music. Beaten, he left her alone and was gone for a drunk of days. Her head fell gently on my shoulder while she spoke of the lonely nights. Her words came like stifled whispers through the crisp hankie held to her lips. I wanted to stroke those milky thighs.

Drained of her grace, dignity, and pride, my wounded sparrow fell into my arms. Her moist, hold me eyes looked up to me. I saw who cares I'm twenty five and you're nineteen hunger. My fiery gaze was no blazing romance. I was desperately remembering opening bra clasp techniques. I felt her short and quick breaths push her breasts into me. Her hand gently rested on my racing heart. Our breath warmed the need between us like the stormy wind over the sandy dunes on a fire sky summer evening. Her lips begged me. My oozing cock had to wait. I had to stop my hands from trembling.

"Ahh - ten - HUHHH!!!" the Sergeant bellowed as the old man entered the office.

Rolling down the hall like a bull elephant, dripping and swollen between his legs and sniffing estrus, he passed our offices. He didn't see my trembling hand sharpening pencils in her office and she nervously stacking papers in mine. Our almost romance ended. It felt like we had nearly been caught by her father and my boss at the same time. We shared a guilty glance of desperate desire.

Over the weeks, one of us would occasionally catch the other glancing their way. Like ex-lovers who must work together, we nervously avoided each other's eyes and paths. We were so terrified by broken hearts, we starved rather than feed the hungry lust filling us.

To avoid Linda, I took long lunch walks in the woods near the office. It was a dense and peaceful place. The sounds of the birds, insects and rustling leaves was like the tender touch of a soft lullaby that let dreams warm you to sleep while smiling.

Once, a campfire scent caught my attention and I walked towards it. It was rough going through the tangled bush a mile or more from any base building or trail. I stumbled into a clearing hacked out of the dense foliage. There was a small fire of twigs and a mound of tender tree bows formed as a mattress.

I turned to leave and jumped in terror. He was there. He had the distant empty soul look of a killer. His sunken steady glance pierced my heart. His rock steady fingers caressed the razor edge of his knife while his gaze drooled over my eyes and throat. He had gorged on death and either decided he liked the taste or jungle was the only home he had now.

Catching my breath, I noticed boots I'd never seen. Thick canvas sides were worn thin. Black leather had been rubbed raw by many miles and battles. The deep brown stains of very old blood, I noticed most. Were they bloody memories he refused to wash away and must hold close to know he wasn't crazy? Had I invaded his sanctuary from being called baby killer? His tattered jungle uniform hung from slumped shoulders. On his head was a headband from a scrap of torn green T-shirt. A bushy beard covered his I'll eat your face glare. He stunk from utter surrender and a mountain of self-hate. Slung at his side was a beat up rifle that a clenched fist hung onto like a life preserver. Looking at him, I knew why no one had the guts to take it from him when he got home.

"Come on. Was it that bad? Couldn't handle it huh?" I said, brashly, with a cocky smile.

He said nothing. All that was missing from those dead eyes was the pennies. His lean, battle muscled frame ambled to me. His grimy hand reached for my chin. Turning it from side to side, he looked at the creamy colored skin so young and tender. Was he looking for the boy he used to be? I saw the crude tattoo on his forearm. It read Class of '66. He was a year younger than I but had the far off look of Omaha Beach nightmares.

As I tried to ask again, he fired near my feet. Every time I tried, he fired until I turned to leave. Doofus me didn't know he was offering me the chance to leave with an answer or my life but not both. The shots said I had to get my answer the way he did.

Having a last thought, I stopped. I heard a round click into the chamber. I put my pack of cigarettes on the ground. I also left him the half-pint of booze I kept for walking highs. I think I saw a nod of thanks, the only sign of life. I turned and walked a few steps. Turning back to wave, there was nothing but a smoldering fire.

Linda and I had our moment when she escaped to a cheap motel. To my erection, it was a dim French Café with candles, wine and poetry. In truth, the candle was a fake light bulb, the wine was a half-empty jug of sour piss, and the poetry had the emotion of a premature ejaculation.

Her ex had called. His reconciliation was giving her only one black eye. She called me. I was nearing my blaming others nightly blackout from a single malt scotch ego fantasy with a twist of suicidal self-loathing in a two buck rot gut reality. In tears, she asked me to come over, now that she was safe in some No-tell Motel.

Home was a rented trailer off base with the military trailer trash.

Rows of slender white boxes were side by side with half-repaired cars and trucks out front. It was like living in a dollhouse version of motel chic. The feel was like a cage for humans when the pets took over. The fridge kept the beer cold, the john and the shower worked. To a young punk, it was perfect.

I grabbed a book and hurriedly wrapped it in floral tissue. I was blasted enough to not care if she noticed the paper was only six inches wide and had perforations between the sheets. It was a book by the Popsicle poet of the day. In McKuen's sugary *Listen to the Warm*, we found a Southern passion that sweltering eve. Most of the night, we talked. It's a shame men don't know what foreplay listening is.

Seeing delicate her in that Lysol perfumed motel room was a surprise. She'd escaped the brute, grabbing Southern grace as she ran. On a rickety table was some girly froo-froo guys don't see unless they're on the TV or the toilet. It was a small stuffed animal, Woodstock from Peanuts. I picked it up although she asked me not too. It covered a rather large hole in the table she'd tried to hide.

With that teasing smile, her quivering voice said, "Style is but the grace and trickery that hides wrinkles, or the reality that daddy cut you out of the will." She turned away to push up the dark glasses hiding her black eye.

I loved how she looked even in casual clothes. In her plain slacks and floral blouse, she still flowed in graceful arcs through space rather than just filling it. Her nails were done in a cool baby blue. Her jet-black hair was combed smooth to a bun at the back with a shimmering yellow ribbon. It let her long porcelain face stand out like fine bone china. Her Scarlet's rebellion was bright red lipstick that put the spotlight on round and voluptuous lips that were forever teasing and pouting. For me, the highlight was the lacy collars on any blouse she wore. Never loud or raucous, they were always the slight and polite touch of gentility she required in her life, even when she was the one telling the dirtiest of jokes.

"In watermelon sugar the deeds were done and done again as my life is done in watermelon sugar," I whispered. McKuen was so sappy; I quoted my favorite, Brautigan.

Two Wounded Sparrows

"Doug, it's beautiful. Whatever does it mean?" she cooed, leaning in a bit closer.

"Not the slightest idea. I dig it because it sounds groovy," I said, like a goofball so proud of his stupidity.

"Yes, I think that's lovely. You must love words," she asked, scooting over on the cheap bed. I was the idiot in the room that didn't notice she was smoothing a space for me and had her lips ever so slightly parted and moist from her slithering tongue.

"I saw a play. Weird. It seemed so... warm up there... safe? Like I could hide behind the lights. It's funny."

"What, silly," she said, with a tempting throaty sigh I still hadn't caught on to.

"Nothing."

She sat me next to her and stroked my hand. I was relaxing not forcing charm.

"It was more than that wasn't it?"

"For a junior high talent show, I was a sad, Emmett Kelly clown and sang *Whenever I Feel Afraid*. Got the worst stage fright. I sounded like a cat being gutted."

I hadn't noticed she was holding my fingers to her cheek as I stammered on trying to breathe.

"Safe it ain't. I did some cool stuff in school and the community theatre. Bored and drunk, I wandered in the Springer Opera House here. All that red velvet, golden gargoyles up high, plush seats, and blinding lights. It was all..." I gagged.

My fingers weren't the only things tingling as I mumbled on.

"The dust in the air danced like fairies. It was a... I dunno. It felt like I was inside *Leave It to Beaver*. Four people eating the same hot meal together. I felt so at home there."

A little moan escaped her lips. I gasped. Being seduced scared the crap out of me.

"I bluffed my way into Funny Forum as Milos Glorious. Drunk was the only way I survived the singing with a voice that thinks a C-note is a hundred bucks."

When she looked into my eyes, she nervously jerked back and

turned away. Softly, I touched her shoulder

"I can't. I'm twenty... more than one and you're—"

"An officer?" I think she wanted to laugh.

"Don't most girls fudge their age by ten—?"

"Five... maybe a tad more," she said nearly smiling.

Turning her I said, "Makes us the same age. Far out!"

When we stopped laughing, we saw our lips just inches apart and turned away. Her chest heaved as she closed two buttons she'd absentmindedly opened. I was wringing my hands trying to dry the cold sweat. We looked at each other with the same I'm sorry on our lips.

Her eyelids meekly sank. Her Scarlet chest heaved with desire. My knees knocked from Mother Silkie debutante anguish until I noticed my bulging crotch. The passion and fear beating the crap out of us lost to our young love tenderness. Our first kiss came as all delicious first ones do. It's remembered for a lifetime and comes in a quiet moment, gently and by surprise...

>Gardenias and Mint Juleps met in fantasies
>Eyes locking over lost dreams
>Resurrected in cheap motels
>along with erections and raised nipples
>We cried over somethings and laughed over nothings
>and forgot where we put the memories
>Black hair draped across bare chests and
>fingernails scraped bare backs
>Sucking breaths and sucking mouths
>belong to lovers and children
>We were both tonight
>We were neither tomorrow
>Keep your eyes closed i demanded of myself
>I might remember the hooch
>Keep your eyes closed she screamed in her mind
>You might remember the thorns
>But for tonight my love, whoever you are, wherever you
>   are

Two Wounded Sparrows

we are here, you are here, I am here...
And the memories can be flushed down with the spent
   rubber
once again, the sparrow dies.

© 2004 Mariah Hochhauser

"The sun's down. I'm tired of being Scarlet. Don't hurt me," her husky voice whispered as she trembled nearly crying from lust and fear. Her shaking lips parted.

"I can't. Just ask Mother Silkie," I said, with a goofy sigh.

Her eyes slid closed and she shivered. Her lips drifted across mine like a puffy cloud in a bright blue sky. The lingering moment was warm, moist and so feather light. So slowly, we began to move, touching and tasting each soft sigh. I tried to calm my nerves mumbling idiocy.

"You're familiar with Brautigan, Hemingway?" I babbled, as she nibbled my lip.

"Hmmm. Tasty, your lip I mean. Brautigan? Hem-ah-who?"

"Drunk Yankees that ate guns. Great typists. Lousy shots," I whispered, gasping.

"After Mitchell and Faulkner..."her hand drifted lower. "Southerners tend to be a might distracted," she said squeezing. "The South shall rise again," she cooed.

Humming Yankee Doodle, our giggles exploded and we fell apart like kids. The sun was dying embers of today's dreams, soothing orange and red so intense it streaked the sky with tomorrow's hope. Maybe it was the evening glow flowing through the window and filling the room with the shimmering light of desire. Maybe it was the laughter that let us finally trust one another and be less alone.

I stroked her jet-black hair. She leaned her cheek into my hand and kissed it. She kissed the tips of my fingers one by one. I stroked her milky cheek and her porcelain smooth forehead in gentle circles. She leaned her head into my chest. Our arms reached for each other and we drew the warmth nearer. We begged for tenderness with whisper sighs. It was an embrace of the drowning, desperate, clinging to a life

Names I Can't Remember

raft of loneliness and sharing one last heartbeat.

She leaned back and turned on the radio.

The look in her eyes was a quiet, intense gaze of an erotic wanting, a willingness to take and give. Slowly, she removed the ribbon from her hair and let her jet-black mane fall free. To music whispers, she swayed from side to side, her gaze fixed on my eyes. A button opened, then another and a frilly high collared blouse floated to the floor. The music drifted here to there and back again and the slacks fell in a heap. Her head fell back and circled round and round, her hips pulsed slowly. Wisps of silk and lace were last, and naked she stood, her chin high and proud, her chest heaving with desire, her hungry gaze demanded, "Want me."

The touching began each to the self for the other in a tribal dance. She moved like a liquid flame to our fire music of hunger. Her hands slid over her body holding her breasts high. Her tempting hips undulated. She opened her thighs while stroking and tempting. Licking her fingers, she held out her hand to me only to take it back. Her head falling back, she pinched rigid nipples, and sighed.

I missed the best of her sweaty tango. I was the num-nuts hopping about trying to kick out of starched stiff uniform pants. She was kind enough to not laugh when I hunched over after the zipper nicked my rigid salute to her temptation. My erotic Chaplain moment ended when I stubbed my toe. I fell into a chair not sure which hurt worse; my cock, toe, or ego.

The music groaning, she flowed to me. I bumble fumbled trying to remember what went where in lessons I'd never had. Her hands on my shoulders, legs outside mine, eyes locked on mine, she lowered herself and held me. Her sshh calmed me. In her eyes, was tenderness that got everything where it needed to be at the right time. Her head fell to my shoulder. Her trembling hand reached for the lamp. A dark room full of passion and loneliness flooded with her tears and our don't leave me moans.

In the quiet of the last deep dark before morning, I left her sleeping. The punk drunk in me was terrified not knowing what to do next. I had no idea that the best thank you kiss over breakfast, not a cowards' apology left on sleeping lips. Needing a drink was always my excuse for running from the joy before it ran away from me.

I left a note, "Linda, A while ago, I met a wise woman. She told me affection is a fifty-dollar bill. Love is a hundred extra. She was wrong. She never met you."

For the last of my childhood days in Georgia, we were grownups again, silent and too embarrassed to talk or try again such a carefree night of passion. Her broken heart had not yet healed. I had overseas orders coming soon, salutes to throw and booze to guzzle, while worrying about gold bars that seemed to get heavier day by day.

My armored knight tried to mount my white steed and charge to my damsel's side once more, but I fell in battle. Drunk one night, I decided to walk to her house ten miles away through the trees and bramble in a straight line, as the crow flies. It seemed noble. All I did was get drunker along the way, sprain my ankle and stumble into my office at the barracks halfway there. I slept off the hangover on that couch. The next day, I rode home on my motorcycle while my ankle throbbed. I never saw her again.

On red Georgia clay I bellowed a brave marching song. Hundreds of boys in the company following my cadence call, beat the earth dead with the pride of their pounding boots and raised billowy clouds of dusty honor. Marching to the bloody boxing matches pitting each unit's best against the other, my chest swelled from this junk of power I was hooked on. Overhead, I saw a solitary sparrow too far behind to catch the flock. A wounded wing could not beat back the wind no matter how hard its heart tried. I didn't see it fall. I was too hooked on glory to notice another wounded sparrow reading a note and crying, one more wounded sparrow unable to keep up caught my eye.

> Will you love me in the morning when I'm gone?
> Or am I the stranger that filled lonely till dawn?
> Ahly ahly unson free, there's no more boy left in me.
> One potato, two potato, three potato more,
> Five potato, six potato, seven body bags more.
> My mother told me to pick you.

Names I Can't Remember

Show me yours and I'll show you mine.
Raise your guts and leg one arm, don't whine.
We love sucked we me thee in summer sunshine
You touch me at every sunrise one more time.
I remember every shiver so very long ago,
Every laugh, every giggle, every tear you cried so.
Did you find a hero to heal the heart bled for me?
I remember every frightened tremble you shared,
Each soft scared kiss, wanton caress given so free.
When snowbird friends lovers leave with every chill,
The wounded sparrow sings in memory still.
Her jet black lion's mane hair,
Sparkling, seductive hazel eyes,
Embarrassed blushing cheeks,
Crisp crinoline swish, lacy neck
Lady like proper buttoned high,
Trembling soft creamy thighs,
Hitch in her git-a-long giggle,
Tushy shimmer shake and smile,
Mint Julep proper front porch Scarlet
Rebellious hippie wanton sundown harlot
Dance the misty Varsuvianna one more while.
Ah the cheap fruity wine of long lost smiles
Is the dusty bottle vintage I sip in gray days now.
One summer soldier that hopes she remembers
The sandbox days of one last, lazy summer
When love was what yah gave in smiles
Not what yah got in cash and carry sighs.
Let me lay my head softly one last time
In your lap, stroke my hair and lick away the lies.
I give you a summer soldier's smile
Now and old warrior's silver streaked glee
The wounded sparrow still soars mighty
In the fuck me suck me in we thee free.

Top: In front of bar – King, Queen and the bar where I became a drunk; Center right: Mother/son – before the blast at Yucca Flats; Center left: Baseball uniform – Remembered this all my life. Thanks Dad (even though Ma probably bought it); Bottom: House – Castle with the dreams and dragons in the field of weeds out back.

Names I Can't Remember

The Last Bloody Warrior With a Mile Long Prick Is a Guilt Wielding Mother, One Pissed Off Chick.

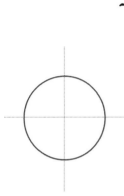

OCTOBER 1969

"A charming tornado, the words diplomacy, judgment, or taste are Greek to her. She's rusty blade honest. In her family, you were loud, tough and fed or dead."

I don't know the color of my mother's eyes nor do I ever remember her looking into mine and saying "I love you." This chunky Depression dame has a bawdy laugh and a husky voice dream to be a saloon singer. She beats life instead of living it with time payment passion that fails to forget or forgive. Her hugs and compliments were four walls and a full fridge.

She left a Minnesota farm for the stage. A bum killed her dream wooing and knocking her up. Her sequined dress for opening night was tenderly packed away for a little while. My diapers were applause in a smoky bar of her broken heart. A gumball machine music charm replaced the man with the eye patch she imagined at table one. Cherished Rosie Clooney records were sold to pay for an apartment.

The cement worker was a drunk. Money she'd saved for a voice coach bought the truck the jackass was too drunk to drive to the next job he'd be fired from. After slinging hash and cleaning up his vomit, she cried and sang torch tunes listening to the radio late at night.

When the wacko beat her, she ran home. Grandma said she'd made her bed, lie in it. Money from her band bought two bus tickets to Chicago. The foreman said he didn't hire single broads. She asked how many men or pregnant married women quit his crappy job? She said a desperate bitch with a hungry kid and no husband wouldn't. Her bluntness and flirtations got the job. He never got the date. Oiling a machine, she fought to remember tunes she once knew by heart.

Too many lonely nights lead to my sister. Voice lesson money covered my sister's adoption costs. Even this ballsy broad knew greasy spoon waitress tips from her pinched black and blue ass could only keep her and one kid from starving. She figured my sister deserved a good home. Two jobs paid for the cab rides I demanded and the special tuna casserole four times a week. Little girls with cupcake and candle smiles pissed her off. Walking paid for my little man suit and her fifty buck Studebaker. She forgot where her sparkle gown was hidden. Spotlight dreams drowned in scotch and sore feet.

When I smashed my head, she ran, carrying me bleeding, miles to the hospital. Two minutes later or a eighth of an inch to the left, I would have died. Her money for a piano player and one-night showcase paid the doctor bill. By only eating at work, she paid for a brand new Philco TV. Uncle Miltie with cheap scotch was the only dream left in the haze of her unfiltered Chesterfields. Her smoky lounge was now a bed so I didn't have to sleep in a drawer.

Names I Can't Remember

Her bawdy smile increased her tips. The owner at the Camel Trail didn't need a bat to roust drunks. He had a single mom in love with scotch. Looking at her, they timidly left their cash and balls. Her cherished crystal tip goblet for her lounge act was full of dead dreams. I got a carousel cake. She never rehearsed again.

A caring girl died but a dame baptized with resentment survived. Any paycheck better than every dream was the religion she fire and brimstone preached to all. No one could stand her for more than minutes or her family for more than days. We got tired of her regrets rammed down our lives.

Strangely, the early suffering years were good, filling the lonely with each other. I was too young to know how much mystery meat she served to buy me everything I smiled or whined for. She bought it all for me to hide the anger that I kept her out of a dingy rehearsal room with stoned horn players. My coos and drools punched her with guilt for dumping me with strangers every day. Boilermaker beers and shots served on the third job trucker bar paid for my bow tie, new pants, and shirt, picture with Santa. When I busted my glasses again with an I don't know how Ma grin, her going ballistic was better than no attention. My Mamma please begging sent her on suffer dates with horny drunks just to borrow his dinner tip for glasses. We smiled in many Mom and little man pictures near Lake Michigan. Hers hid a self-loathing because the little prick looks like the sperm donor that beat her. My buggy wheel racer surprises never pleased. She taught me what-the-hell you jerk was a pat on the back. I ate insults to keep from starving on her compliments. Surviving for two sucks when one is a babied punk getting clipped toenails by the one with pennies in her apron and a black-and-blue ass. Why didn't she tell me? It would have been nice sharing anything. We spoke defiance, scotch, and conflict. Anger and resentment were I love you.

I hate her. I need her. I respect her. I don't love her, could be a lie. She wouldn't let me. At the Little Big Horn, we alone would have slaughtered Sioux and killed each other with devious manipulation. A chat is a bloody victory shoving our right down the other's wrong. I'm the child born of horny, not hope, life long friend she's never had, and enemy never beaten. I am her tears still searching for a faded sequined gown. She's better at life. I starve it dream to dream. She gorges on it a buck at a time. It's a shame we can't set aside differing dreams and settle for respect. Survival is our French kiss incest.

She is the second youngest of the twelve of thirteen who survived. I'm the oldest of four, the urban rat that gnawed at her guilt. Maybe she hates me for all the crap she ate from ten older siblings. Maybe I resist because I didn't get all the milk I demanded. Maybe she hates the responsibility I was not the applause she craved. Maybe I hate her working that made loneliness my best friend. Maybe we need each other too much. We are the best of enemies. One lonely moment at a time in a house at the corner of hope and despair, I became the ELDEST son, oldest ENEMY.

She learned life on a farm in Minnesota from matriarch Louise. She raised twelve during The Depression alone, after Grandpa dropped dead. In the only picture of him and his mules, he's the one in the Sunday suit. I guess he got tired of looking at a mule's ass all day. Grandma made muffins for grandkids, withered children with mild glances, and broke a hip yanking out a sapling at seventy-two.

She's the toughest broad I know. Her name is Joy.

Her will could pull a plow. Ma is five foot nothing at 140 to 200 depending on what diet failed her. No one dares tell her she is short or that her hard hair beehive is a weapon, not a style. It's her right energy and take charge way that wears out a wrong world. At Waterloo, her mouth would have kicked ass. She owns the piano at parties. She was a living hell stand-in for my aunt when her daughter married. My cousin barely survived all the guilt pampering meant for my sister. Joy sings a hearty tune, tells a bawdy joke, stuffs you with food, drinks you under the table, has a heart and sex drive that could entertain an army. It's her withering will and utter lack of sensitivity that makes the world tolerate rather than enjoy her company. Everyone craves her as a weapon or problem solver but does their best to survive her in five minute blasts. She would insult herself worse telling a nigger joke to a black customer and not know what shocked everyone. To Joy, the only insult is silence. A charming tornado, the words diplomacy, judgment, or taste are Greek to her. She's rusty blade honest. In her family, you were loud, tough and fed or dead. Alone, she raised me to survive and dominate despite any odds. Insults and grudges are our family heirlooms. If I weren't just like her, I'd be gay.

We managed some touching moments. Age 8, I had gone to wee wee and found that he had left the toilet seat up the first night he stayed over to swap spit with Joy. In the morning, Joy found me snapping Tony the Tiger between the eyes with the balloon I'd found laying on the floor by the john. Stammering, she did her best to explain. I understood Miss Kitty and Marshall Dillon really liking each other. It was the part about the vegetable patch with the pink and blue pumpkins that threw me."

"You tryin' to talk 'bout babies? Tommy Svenson tol' us all about it. It all happens at the movies. First..."

"No! I've, seen movies. What did Tommy tell you?"

"Well, the night before you make a baby, a guy takes a girl to the Dairy Queen for a banana royal triple split with hot fudge and nuts. Then they walk to the movies."

"And that's how Tommy says you make a baby?"

"First the bleachers."

"You mean balcony?"

"Braces."

"I thought you said bleachers?"

"Bleachers, braces, balcony then baby. Golly, you said you knew this stuff? The girl waits under the football bleachers. The boy hides his sweaty hands, shuffles his feet, and says aaahhh for a long time. The girl blushes until she says the magic word uh-oh. Then the boy puts his mouth on the girl's 'cuz you got to lock braces to start the baby. The boy and girl yell so the baby knows it's time. Then, the movies. Got it so far, Ma?"

"No."

"Ma-a-a. That's where they get the double butter for the popcorn, and JuJu-Bees."

"God forbid forgetting the JuJu-Bees."

"Black JuJu-Bees! The girl picks the popcorn and JuJu-Bees out of her braces until the boy sneaks his arm around her. Later, he has to get the blood back in his arm. You can't make a baby with a sleeping arm. Now, they make the baby with googy."

"Googy?"

"The boy's face gets all googy, he does a titty twister, and she slaps him hard in the face."

"That's it?"

"The girl goes to her aunt's for six months 'till her folks argue about a baby name. The popcorn wizard leaves a baby in the hamper. It stays with her aunt and the girl goes home. Tommy's brother said that's how you make a baby. Ma? What's titty twister?"

"Never you mind."

"When will I get my braces?"

"Never! Not for a long time."

"No sweat, Ma. I hate popcorn. I love JuJu-Bees."

"Why me? What did I do to deserve this, God?"

"God? That's about cheating on a spelling test."

Ben was a shoe salesman for O'Conner & Goldberg's chain of eighteen Best Quality and Clean Family Stores in all Chicago-land. I thought the slogan meant that was where you bought a rich family with no dirt on them. Joy served him the meatloaf special and he never left. He smiled when she said she wasn't married. They joked about popcorn for one at a Cary Grant feature. When he heard about me, he poked at last Monday's mystery meat under this Wednesday's gravy. She gave him a double slice of peach pie and suggested a new Cary Grant picture. He smiled.They got married. After being around so many single moms, a man was just someone who didn't bitch about the toilet seat being up.

When they left me with the bitch for their honeymoon, I learned hate. The witch took in cast-off kids. I was the only one that would go home but no one told me. It taught me how to say I love you with revenge eyes. I showed deep affection for the honeymoon desertion six years later getting drunk, wrecking the den, and pissing on her favorite paint-by-numbers collie. Even with someone to blame for leaving the toilet seat up, I hated Cary Grant pictures.

Names I Can't Remember

Joy had one good friend. Lila was a roly-poly mamma mia from down the block. I guess they made it work since they were opposites. Lila liked being a wife and mother. Joy didn't mind it as long as the paycheck cleared, the fridge was full, the bar was stocked, and she could afford the same stuff Lila had. Shopping was their clash of wills, a ballsy female Oscar versus Felix.

"Where's your list, Lila?"

"Right here, Joy," she said pointing to the crumpled wad of coupons in her fist.

"I mean a list, aisle by aisle, item by item. How do you expect to save any time?"

"You take the fun out of this. Shopping is buy what you want not what you need."

Lila leaned and lolled along with her cart. She didn't walk. She waddled side to side in a gentle rhythm. Her four kid, pasta, wine, bread, and wide load hips swayed and knocked things off shelves.

"I just finished off aisles 6 and 8," Joy would say scribbling entries off her list.

"What happened to aisle 7, Joy?" she asked tasting cookies from the bag that committed suicide on her gnashing teeth. "There's a new cracker tasting in aisle four."

"Too salty. Don't bother."

"I love salty!"

"Well your hips don't. Try the grapes over there."

"Slow down! Your Scotch and water ass ain't winning any prizes. Shopping is out of the house. You get that?" Lila said, to keep Joy from running out of the store.

"Fast bitch! You bringing coffee cake later?"

"Don't I always, slow fat ass?"

They always managed to finish shopping without killing each other. Their differences seemed to be the glue that bound them. To Lila, jokes and insults were I love you. To Joy, they were you're the only friend I have.

It was my last 4 weeks at the suburban house on Peter Road. They were my last chance to laugh to hide emotion, truth, and fear. I left the house whenever I could.

Our house was a place to sleep and raid the fridge before going out. My folks hobbies were TV and cocktails. A deep conversation was pass the salt and pepper. When it came to work, customers, or how we had out-foxed someone, we were endless orators of ego. Our family moments were four TVs on the same channel in separate rooms. We were strangers that shared a mailbox and bathroom.

Often, one parents' seat was empty at meals. They weren't evil, but worked conflicting schedules to pay for the palace of silence. Dad managed two shoe stores now. Mom worked as a waitress at The Hapsburg Inn, a family restaurant where haute cuisine was gravy with the mashed potatoes and fried chicken for four. Both worked late evening hours. Our family meals were usually warmed over or eaten in shifts.

The best pre-war days were Sunday morning breakfasts. Even if Mom or Dad had to work, we had those. The meals were hearty and loud. French toast, eggs, bacon and or sausage would pass from the kitchen through the slit in the wall to the dining room. We all bellowed choices to short order cook mom that already had them cooked and all the pans washed.

At our house, being loud or screwing up was how you got the most attention or any attention. She and Dad shared the same depression survivor theories of parental nurturing. They said I love you with paid bills and food. A pat on the back was the paycheck from the job you found on your own. A hug was a color TV. How do you feel was instructions for cooking dinner on the oven door. Family outings were mad dashes to the john during the commercials when fresh cocktails were poured. A compliment was getting yelled at for my last deliberate screw-up. I'd graduated from the Cool Hand Luke school of family values, "Lord, love me, hate me, jes' lemme know it!"

"How do you want your steak, Doug?" Ma would yell from the kitchen while sliding it done on a plate.

"Just show the cow a picture of a match and throw him on the plate, Ma," I said .

"Well done! I want that son of a bitch dead just this side of a new sole for my shoe. How can you eat that bloody mess?" Dad would yell, shaking his head.

"Gives the cow a chance to fight back. Right, Ma?"

"This one had a mean right hook when I beat the crap outta him. So, keep your guard up. I swear I heard a moo when I threw yours on the broiler, Doug."

The meals were the same chatter of shoes sold and chicken dinners served. I thought marriage was more about competition and clinking ice than companionship. Ma was seldom in her seat to eat until the rest of us were pushing back from the table. This, too, was a lesson from her mother. The cook gets to eat when all are served and the pots and pans are already washed. She'd wolf down her food and then make the drinks.

Dessert banter was light at first. They blabbered about nice customers, stupid ones, and how they always knew best what customers needed on their feet and in their bellies. After ten years as an only child, I now had two pre-teen brothers. They hung out with it all until the urge to head to so and so's house hit. It was time to split when Ma sat down to a clear table with the bottle of scotch in her hand.

"So, you lined up a job for when you come home?" she said, with a steely gaze.

"Why? I'll just waste the money on cheap booze, bad cards and boring women!"

"You'll work at my store, till you get settled," Dad would whisper trying to put space between us. He was sipping his cocktail while we were pouring our second.

"Seeing anyone?" she punched lightly.

"I'm going to war!" I jabbed, dancing away.

"Well, you know us two, born horny and gonna die that way. Just curious if you're getting laid," she slammed into me like a fierce uppercut, followed by a heart laugh.

"I prefer love over convenience," I whispered, masking a vicious jab. She offered a good one smile with a vicious wink, slammed her glass down, and poured drinks.

"No job, bumming around here, or sponging off those jerky friends at the church again?" was her one-two punch.

"Na, I'll just starve in the theatre so I can watch you go nuts and drool screaming where did I go wrong?"

Dad and the boys had left. This was the Dick and Jane story time we never had and the affection neither knew how to show. Attack was the emotion we enjoyed sharing. Getting drunk let us both win without feeling regret for beating the crap out of the other. There was no discussion of me going to war. We would have had to say how we felt telling the truth.

Dad had his new no one drives my car but me wheels. In the space left over was Mom's current bucket of used bolts. It was a faded green Oldsmobile 442. Its asset to any punk kid was that ugly as it was from age, it had bucket seats, sporty lines, and a hot rod engine.

My buddy Bill and I decided we needed a last night ripping the town a new asshole. This was hard to do since Des Plaines had no ass. The sleepy Chicago suburb's claim to fame was that Ray Kroch's first McDonalds was here. It was a place for fifteen-cent burgers and actually watching them change the numbers on the sign.

Bill and I knew which beer stores would sell to us without I.D. We drove, drank, and hit all the hot spots. After that fifteen minutes passed, we drank more. We stopped by Abraham, the gnarled tree at Dead Man's Curve, to take a much-needed piss. We argued if "ku-ku-ka-choo" was a walrus fart. At his house, there was no formal goodbye as we were too drunk to think of that and I still had ten days leave time left.

Bill hung onto the car door in front of his house. He sucked on the quart of beer and passed it inside to me.

"Here, take a jerk, you drink" he yelled, shaking the bottle and peeing on his foot.

"Ahhhhh, I could piss a river of drink, I could. Give me the bottle, kind sir hairball."

Weaving, Bill looked at his empty hands like a terrified child. "We been robbed. Police! Some rob has crooked our bottle," he yelled, falling and laughing.

I giggled while passing the bottle back. "I gotta piss a take." I wobbled out of the car and peed in the street. Getting in, I took the bottle back from the laughing bear of a boy with a bushy beard. "Did you know someone stole your toilet?" I sputtered.

"So you pissed on my carpet, you jerk wad fool" he giggled, passing the bottle and belching.

"What is happening?" I yowled at the cool night.

Bill got quiet. He had that same look of panic that night we both went blank during our Zoo Story stage debacle. "You, you could stay here with me. We could deal dope in Canada or just hit the road. That's war man," he said, with a sad look in his eyes.

"And miss my war?" I yelled squealing the tires.

Moments later, Abraham had a new wound. Mom's sporty car with bucket seats looked like it lost a street fight with a garbage truck. I was drunk enough to roll with it and not get a scratch. I split before the cops. Her sports car rattled and smoked like a moving storm cloud getting bigger and darker.

At home, I managed to get the car in the garage quietly. Sneaking in, I went to the den bar. Sipping Chivas, reality hit. I wrecked the car of the only dame with balls. When the sun rose, mighty warriors who had never beaten each other would clash again. I was ready, Airborne All the Way, and a Lieutenant in the mighty infantry on his way to a glorious goddamn war!

The clock ticked. Spurs jangled. Sagebrush and dust devils swirled on empty streets. Terrified citizens peeked from behind curtains at the rock versus the hard place. This dusty cow town wasn't big enough for Matt and Miss Kitty. It was high noon.

Like a chicken seeing the supper axe, I ran. I'd rather face buckets of blood and guts than a pissed off mother. I silently mashed clothes into my duffel bag, shoved in Chivas and Seagram's 7, called a cab, drunk stumbled and tip-toed out at 2 A.M.

Waiting for the 7 A.M flight to San Francisco, I began sobering up sleeping in a chair at O'Hare. It all made sense. I had about a week left on my leave. I'd bunk at the bachelor officer quarters, see Frisco, eat bloody beef, and stay blasted.

The base was a bore. I got tired of TV. I was alone. The bloody filet mignon was tasteless. I needed a bust out move to have some fun before my war started.

I found it in the Haight Ashbury underground paper in the Crash Pad section. They were free places to sleep from an hour to forever depending on when the Twinkies and dope ran out. Why not spend the last hours at home with fellow hippie freaks? The reality was they lived sex, drugs, and rock and roll that wannabe me had only dreamed about living.

I was the best rebel a white bread suburb had. I was sent home for sideburns and no-no Blue Jeans. I'd run away to Malibu once and gained a rep. I'd buzzed the school on my Honda motorbike. I finished school in a party central apartment with four other rebels. I was as artsy, fartsy, surfer dude in powder blue Levi's and bleeding Madras shirt, hippie freak as you could be in a cocoon of hypocrites. Sssshhh. We had two Negroes at our school so they had someone to date! We were perfect Wonder Bread liberals too stupid to see our KKK hypocritical pride that we let our showcase lawn jockey house niggers have a sex life.

The LSD freak's roach motel crash pad was in the slum part of Haight Ashbury. Even the rats had moved to the burbs. His body slept on the floor. His brain was in New York. His attention span was on the road in a flowered bus. His age was hidden beneath pillows of hair on his head and chin. He thought his name was Malcolm. His rainbow colored, smelly clothes could have walked away from his skinny frame without him. He said soap is for straight people and parents. He was fascinated with my buzz cut and uniform. The flop was piled with garbage, almost empty pizza boxes, and bags of half-eaten Oreos. He peered into the hole in the floor to the apartment below, waving and smiling.

"Hi Mrs. Mendlebaum," he yelled, at the dazed broad in a pink moo-moo, scratching the scabs off her needle marks.

"You eat you junkie freak?" she barked, smiling.

"I took double speed and morning mescaline. I'm cool till lunch or maybe next Wednesday. This is my new roomy, star child," he showed her, pointing to me.

"No. I'm Doug, not star child. " I said, poking him.

"Ooops, body rush. He's no I'm Doug, not star child. Meet Mrs. Mendelbaum, the lady in the hole in my floor."

"My name's Doug, not star child, you stupid fuck," I added, while jabbing his arm.

"Far out, 'nuther rush. Correction Mrs. Mendelbaum, this is my new roomy, Doug not star child, you stupid fuck.' I think he's a Romulan."

"Get some Cracker Jack, you fucker. What's left of your brain is the prize inside," said the feisty wench, wrapping a rubber tube on her upper arm and pulling it tight.

"Far out Mrs. Mendelbaum. Remember, dirty needles..."

His voice drifted off in search of his brain. While he shook and wiggled, I sat Malcolm down and wiped drool from his smile.

"Don't ever cover that hole. It's a window to the time space continuum. Bowls of soup come up like messages from the gods. Groovy. Totally weird man."

"She feeds you so you won't starve, you crazy idiot!"

"The god's a woman? Does Mrs. Mendelbaum know? Far out hair, man. Have you met my roomy Doug not star child, you stupid fuck?"

"No man. I'm... forget it. Yah. I met him."

"Hey, Doug not star child, you stupid fuck, meet Forget It. He's crashing here too. He has hair just like yours, man. Far fucking out. The invasion from Geekoron."

"The army took my hair and gave me these clothes."

"Army? The invasion has started. Mrs. Mendelbaum!"

"No. I joined our army, Malcolm."

"We have an army, man? With a Malcolm? Bummer."

"For the war. I'm going there."

"Hey Mrs. Mendelbaum, the tribe's at war on Geekoron. Tell me, Forget It, and tell Doug not star child, you stupid fuck too, what's happening there?"

Malcolm's eyes rolled back and he took off for Jupiter. Soup arrived daily from Geekoron on a stick through a hole in the floor. I escaped Mom's revenge and watched his brain fry laughing and getting drunk. Rolling a joint on his sheepskin degree, he was happy. He'd found the only practical use for a Liberal Arts Masters.

Half-ripped and all drunk, I sat on a window ledge and counted stars over the bay. A rumble in the sky interrupted my giggle-fest. It wasn't rain my tongue was set to anxiously taste. Unseen black helicopters sneaked through the velvet black. I could see the fanciful lights where they landed. I was sure it was the Geekoron invasion looking for Malcolm. I laughed. So many times the rumble came, I had to know. Stumbling through the city on and off buses or in and out of cabs, I somehow made it there.

I saw them clinging to the tall wire fence that kept the people away from the truth on the small pad at the base. One of her hands was clenched on the fence like she was trying to hold herself up or hold back the anger. In her other hand, was a damp lace hankie. Standing tall, stiff and silent, his arm was around her. It wasn't clear who was holding who up. I could see the flecks of gray in their hair and K-Mart in their clothes.

One after the other, kid soldiers carried long slender bags out of each chopper without speaking and set them on the runway. When the chopper was emptied, the soldiers got in and it took off to get another load. In the dim glow of landing lights, these macabre lines of dominoes waited for the final ride home.

"What happened?" I whispered to them.

They took a deep breath and turned. The agony in those eyes took the place of words. Slowly, they walked to me. With a quivering chin, the father's hate filled eyes bore into me. The mother stroked my soft cheek and then froze. Raising her chin, she looked at my gold bar with those agony eyes. I saw all she had left was anger, no matter who was there. All she saw was my gold symbol of authority that put her son in a bag on the Tarmac. She spit in my face and walked off. I had my answer. It was in the chopper that I watched thunder through the night sky until it was quiet again.

In Des Plaines, a father in a garage was screaming bloody murder. In the kitchen, a mother who didn't give a damn was guzzling scotch and crying her eyes out.

Names I Can't Remember

We began in the spring time days.
Tuna noodle casserole so damn special,
When hard ain't so bad shared together,
Colorful carousel cakes in the Camel Trail bar,
Cabs she can't afford and a fifty buck Studebaker car.
Summer's playful prancing glory never spoke
Of desperate winters passed that shivered shook souls.
Bloody eyes, beatings, lies, little girls given and lost
Beat back horror with smiles, never give in to the frost.
Dagger hearts with guilt, win with tears at any cost.

Last living gladiator, she looks on from up high,
While warriors young, drunk and fucked so stumble,
Yelling, screaming of the glory on this day to die.
Adorned in peacock feathers, peach fuzz mighty prance,
Age frenzies youth to bleed blood, the unwhispered lie.

I am invincible, come fill my cup again and once more
Silly dilly dance and prance, bring me the ugly whore.
Smear my slashed face with scarlet hot and so sweet,
I am the fearless mighty never fought don't fuck with me,
Blind to a trail of false fearless dead ever behind thee.

I was once the boy beaten down, taught to win,
A new warrior standing ready in the blazing sun.
Helmets gleaming, swords honed so razor thin,
Steel gazes, chests puffed for the battle to be won.
The bloodiest battle not taught, a horror such a sin,

The last bloody warrior with the mile long prick,
Is a guilt wielding mother, one pissed off chick.

The Hillbilly, Nigger, and Spic

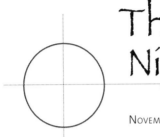

November 1969

"I brought paupers' treasures to life's manger. Their blazing fires of survival to warm me through the cruel year and cold tears to come blessed me. They were the gold in my bankrupt soul."

Awn-lee thang that'll drop quicker than hillbillies, niggers, er spics is 2nd. Lieutenants, Ya'll" said the first. "Stay the fuck away from us, Hefe," said the next.

"Shove the bar up your ass so your head has company. The brothers need something to laugh at," said the third.

These grinning faces were the squad leaders taught to follow my every order; Hillbilly, Nigger, and Spic. I must have slept through the how squad leaders show their respect for their new brave and bold commander class in OCS.

Tawny Spic spat a wad of cigar juice on my gleaming boot. Skinny Hillbilly kicked some dirt on the sticky mess. Monster Nigger mixed it all together with the heal of his worn to raw leather boot. They flashed me fingers and laughed. Later, I learned their humiliation was a survival lesson. Shining black boots are a target.

"Where's your Lieutenant? I'm the new platoon leader," I asked hesitantly. One scratched his nuts.

They all looked at the body bag waiting for the morgue chopper. Nigger with the bands of machine gun ammunition defiantly crossed on his bare chest, measured me. With command intensity, I drew up to demand respect after their insubordination.

"Is that how you greet your commanding officer?" I stuttered, weakly. Another popped his gum.

"Ya'll pissed?" said Hillbilly.

"What ju gunna do, Hefe?" grinned Spic.

"Send us to the fucking war?" yowled Nigger.

Hillbilly, Nigger, and Spic spat in my face.

Macbeth's lost soul witches had buried another offended butter bar. They rhythmically shook hands and cockily walked away. On a Honda scooter, a war orphan, now teenage Asian pimp had just pulled up with his merchandise. The girl looked like his little sister. She was. At the stack of ammo crates, my squad leaders took up their game of cut-throat spades. Hillbilly took an iced Budweiser a coke kid had stolen from the rear without paying the going price of two bucks. Kicking the yammering merchant, he popped the top, guzzled, and slapped down the Jack of Clubs looking me in the eye.

"Ya'll think Lieutenant wants to Court Martial my ig-or-ant hillbilly ass?" he smirked.

"Send us to a cell with a soft bed and hot food? Madre mia!" said Spic pulling the pin on a grenade and handing it to me. He trumped the Jack with the spade King.

With one hand, Nigger viciously slapped the Ace of Spades on the trick. With the other, he pushed the teenage hookers' head deeper on his cock, thrusing his hips meanly up..

I was the sweat monsoon trying to re-pin the frag with a Jello hand. I saw the dead Lieutenant had shined boots like me. I kicked mud on my boots and finally breathed.

The Hillbilly, Nigger, and Spic

After my ego and weary ass sank, I surveyed my kingdom. On the horizon, a mile off, was the South China Sea bay. A few thousand yards to my left, were two hills three hundred feet high covered by jungle. This small valley was a checkerboard of rice paddy plots. Each was thirty feet square and filled with shallow water held in by foot high and wide dikes. Two lanes split the plots surrounding the village fifty yards away, the blacktopped Highway 1. I was a few miles south of the old capitol Hue in the northern most province of the country divided by war. On my side of the highway, was the other dozen or so thatched roofed and tin huts that made up the village. To my right, was the small, stone, and mud orphanage/church run by Asian nuns. To me, it had the intimate charm and patina of a peasant congregation. I chuckled. God didn't give a damn for this priest-less outpost where every hut still had altars burning incense to the only poor man's gods that mattered; rice, rain, and rest. I was sitting on the crumbling stoop of the small, mud straw, and cement rice house. The tiny building was my platoon's headquarters that once stored village rice. Inside the building with half a war ravaged roof, was one open room with a stage-like rise at one end. A few windows with no glass lined the crumbling walls pockmarked by bullet holes. Sitting there and watching my boy men play cards, guzzle, yell, and snore; I strained to hear Oleanna. There were no angelic and melodic echoes of glory and honor here. The air was filled with the stench of beer, in your face acid rock, and defiance. Listening to the fart contest that smelled like rotting souls at the intersection of blood and guts, I stopped craving glory and started to devour fear.

My welcome committee was made up of the three senior Short Timers. These are men going back to The World in less than ninety days. Their helmets or floppy bush hats were covered with X's or numbers counting down from ninety. Short, meant you had killed and survived the blood letting for the first nine months of a twelve-month tour and were getting close to going home.

It didn't take much to tell new arrivals from Short Timers. New guys were scared to death and Short guys were scared angry. New Meat were terrified of dying every second. Short Timers were terrified of dying the second before they got on the chopper home. New meat were the guys in dark green uniforms who huddled en mass. We hid behind curious questions, whispers, and I don't know glances to one another. The guys with balls wore the ultra light green, washed to death uniforms, and hid in loud guffaws, card game wars, or belches. The one blood contract: no one talked about fear or dying.

We new meat nervously looked everywhere for any threat. We fidgeted, stayed away from locals, wore heavy protective helmets, constantly wrote Mom or Babe, and had shined boots. Short Timers swaggered with shoot me mother fucker defiance. Chests were bare. Headbands full of peace symbols were helmets. Ragged T-shirts blared crude challenges; "Yea though I walk through the Valley of the Shadow of Death, I am the meanest bad ass mother fucker in the valley." Shorts laughed and slapped cards that cracked with the pop of rifle fire. New Meat were silent, having yet to learn that loud defiance is the only wish for the helpless in a fear typhoon.

Hillbilly, Nigger and Spic came to me alone with lessons for their lives, not mine. New meat must stay far away from all Short Timers. We did stupid things that got them killed. We clanked from carrying loud crap that signaled the Dinks. We didn't smell like jungle. Our shaving lotion, soap, and the milk we drank made us perfumed targets. We walked near trails into the booby traps instead of safely in the thickest jungle. We didn't know the jungle cackles an out-of-tune symphony. Death was the sudden sound that stood out. Us new guys were like nervous teenagers at the front door. We'd forget to pull the trigger, run, or we would just freeze. In war, kills are how you measure the length of your life and cock. Fear keeps you from killing yourself with stupid. Evil irreverence was the Nam warrior's rifle. News from The World said how hated was our glory war and we. It made fear your Mom. Hillbilly, Nigger, and Spic taught me to ram my tongue down her throat and fuck the shit out of her with a rigid hard-on of defiance.

Living little boys here were wrinkled teachers. My squad leaders taught me how they survived so my orders wouldn't get any of us killed. Alone, soldiers die. Together, they live. My training was how to fight. In the bush, the lessons were how to live. Home taught tactics, loyalty, orders, and the noble bravery of Follow Me. Here, the final test was wear dead enemy ears so the next surrenders before the battle.

I left the crumbling stoop of the rice house and went inside. The card games, beer guzzling and grab ass was confusing. I had been trained to lead men who were listening, not ignoring me. Buried in my confusion were the yet to be learned lessons that command is taken, not given, and respect is earned, not demanded. Inside were lumpy piles of rucksacks strewn about the barren room amidst snoozing men. The hillbilly radio operator was on the raised stage area reserved for the squad leaders and I.

This boy was a Rembrandt of confusion. His hairless pale face was checkered with acne. Yet, this punk who probably never unhooked a bra, was conducting a High Mass of survival. The pope of pimples baptized and caressed that radio like the Christ Child. He precisely wrapped the handset in plastic to save it from the monsoon rain crucifixion. Tenderly, he folded the antenna in half and tied it down so it would not catch on underbrush, brake, or be a tall noisy signal to a distant enemy to fire here. He cleaned every crevice on this lifeline to rescue or firepower. He twitched when I wandered too close.

"I said stay the fuck away from me!" he said, waving an angry finger in my face.

"But you're my radio-man. How do I call for artillery or ask the old man for help?"

"Asshole! When Dink shit is falling from the sky like Georgia summer gnats at a watermelon convention, y'all think I know how to yell into the radio, 'We're getting our ass kicked. Send lottsa' bombs now!' as good as your sorry Yankee ass?"

"There's a little more to it than that, private."

"Personnel asshole fragmentation devices please, Sir!"

"You forgot the map coordinates."

"In front of the hillbilly 'bout to rip a dumb shit Lieutenant a new asshole and shove his face up it!"

"That ought to do it."

Our laughs broke the tension. I saw him trying to hide his smile. I hung my legs over the edge of the stage and lit a butt. He sat next to me and I handed him my pack as a peace offering.

"Staying away saves us. A radio is a target. Dinks know the guy next to the RTO is the Lieutenant. They shoot at him. Kill the head of the snake and the rest can't fight. OK?"

"Thanks."

"For what? Those slant eye fucks are crap shots. It's my ass! Pricks aiming at you or the radio hit me. Smart ones figure out the truth, shooting a radio screws us all, not just you. Any prick can call for artillery. We pre-plot shit hit the fan fire the night before and call it all at once, not one by one. We lose as many radios as Lieutenants now."

"The truth?"

"It only takes a day or two to get a new Lieutenant but a week to get a new radio".

My RTO had a long neck and a large Adam's Apple. He spoke in a squeaky high voice and walked with a goofy kind of galumph, loose and lanky like a bloodhound. His teaching wasn't noble. It was selfish desperation rammed down his throat by other living Short Timers whose trust he'd earned. Still, he twitched because of the radio that made him a target. He complained to himself in whispers. Bitching is the only thing that relieves the constant pressure of knowing some idiot out there has a bullet with address occupant engraved on it.

He spoke of the bottomland back home he hoped to farm with kids and Betty Lee. I saw his worried, sad eyes always looking down. Absentmindedly, he stroked that radio like the son he spoke of. It brought mail, pizza, bullets, body bags, and choppers home to hugs or hearses. He carried that burden papoosed on his heart like a baby tenderly wrapped in his arms. He refused to admit he'd scratched Billy Joe Jr. on its frame. It was the son he feared never having, his death sentence. It made him the brave man every boy aspires to be and the one he didn't know he already was.

I stayed away. He smiled at me from then on.

I left the rice house to him. It was sacrilege to invade his communion of hugging his radio and writing Betty Lee. I wandered through the tangled mass of card playing and belching pimpled warriors outside, beyond our compound with no barbed wire.

Near a dirt path at the edge of the village, a creaky and bent spine old man with the weathered skin of gnarled tree bark was filing the edge of a hand scythe. His hands trembled with age but I could see the tenderness and precision in his strokes practiced over so many seasons from starvation to abundance. He looked up with a smiling, toothless grin. In his eyes was the twinkle of pride misted by sorrow as his gaze drifted to my rifle. Mumbling words that meant nothing, his actions made clear what he wanted. The old man didn't need the pigeon-language English part Asian that locals and soldiers used to communicate. His heart spoke a wisdom I could clearly hear. Those trembling arthritic hands guided mine with the file over the edge of the scythe. He adjusted my motions to a smooth and precise flow while smiling to encourage me. I saw in wise old eyes, a fathers sorrow. For a moment, I was the grandchild the war buried near the edge of his village. Looking at his rotting teeth blackened by the Beetle-nut treat chewed by the locals, I wanted to see truth in that smile. There wasn't any. Was he the old man-father passing on his wisdom or a cold killer having me sharpen what he'd plunge in my back? With no front line or enemy in uniform, suspicion was our only common language.

"What's wrong here?" I begged, in a whisper.

My words confused him. His face crinkled. He did a strange thing. His trembling hand reached and touched my heart. He looked deeper into my eyes as he touched my pounding chest. He knew. His calm wise nod told me where to look. His frail arm paned the horizon of so many water filled plots and then to the misty sky. He walked away without a word. I knew. Leave me to my rice and rain. His silence yelled, guns and words feed no one.

When I looked down, I saw the lesson he'd left me. I had interrupted this hunched old man sharpening a scythe and shitting at the same time. Piles of shit surrounded me. I had walked into the land used as the village toilet. No time, effort, or land was useless here. Even the exhausted land was enriched while it rested. A wise old man snuck another lesson unspoken into my rude intrusion. I was the only useless shit here. I killed for ideas not food.

I wandered back near the rice house and watched a poker game.

Spics' grin was wide and inviting. His mouth was fully open showing white and perfect teeth. It was a friendly smile punctuated by a mouth full of mangled cigar stub. He spat tobacco juice regularly with the bravado of Ali standing over the beaten, bloody bull, Liston. He was a short, barrel-chest, husky man of nineteen that loved to wear his shirt open to reveal that olive toned hairy chest.

Sergeant Spic was cocky and full of nasty charm. It was the last of the boy inside fighting to run from the killing man he'd become. It put a twinkle in his eye that dared, catch me if you can, what devilish prank have I just committed. The days I plopped on a mud-filled helmet or rose from a nap to fall from laces tied together, he was cockily posed grinning my way like a wicked leprechaun claiming innocence but giggling with glee.

He wore his steel pot back and to one side. He was the happily married, no cracks about ma, kid from Central Casting in war movies. He was everyone's buddy, father yet champion in battle when he growled to calm his men by making them more afraid of him than dying. The strap for his helmet swung freely as he swaggered.

Slapping a trump on the ace, he slipped me a lesson no one saw. While the rest groaned and guzzled beer, he yanked the sleeves off my bootlaces and tucked the frayed ends tightly under the crossed strands. His deadly stare made sure I knew that any noise gets you killed. With a public fuck you finger for the crowd, a private wink for me, and tobacco spit, he waved me away having added days and battles to my life. I wasn't sure if I should kiss him on the mouth or kick his ass. A wink back was fine for now.

Nigger survived his own hell in the role of the intimidator. His job was to make everyone fear him from afar before he did a damn thing. His teeth were as white as clouds. His skin was as black as a velvet sky never warmed by any star or moon. He was tall, with a brick shithouse build and scowl that made anyone imagine their casket lid closing. When his white fangs glared against that oily black cloud of skin, I felt the frigid shiver breath from his dead heart.

The diamond jewelry of his haute couture hate look was the heavy machine gun slung under his arm and the bands of ammunition crossed on his bare chest, no matter what the weather. He polished each brass casing to a dazzling shine that could be seen hundreds of yards away, day or night. In a quiet moment, someone tapped my shoulder and pointed toward this messenger of death. Before each night's march to an ambush site, noisy boys fell silent to watch the gladiator Pope of Vengeance present his deadly challenge. This boy didn't swagger; he sauntered in rhythmic and defiant indifference to anything or anyone. Beneath the massacre sunset, he walked alone a hundred yards beyond the edge of the village. His steady and fearless bass voice bellowed to the faceless enemy hidden in the jungle beyond. The ominous echo of his voice pleased him.

"Here I come motherfucker!" he screamed with the dazzling brass on his slick black chest and white target painted on his back.

This faceless someone whispered in my ear and made it simple, "The more fear I give and killing I do, the sooner I go back to the world!" He told me the tale of the Mongol hoards. Warrior Kingdoms surrendered without a fight hearing messengers describe the path of bloody, severed children's heads as the Mongol's left. He never spoke to me or anyone again.

My unit had its two usual and heavy M-60 machine guns assigned to two man teams. Nigger carried alone a third he'd acquired, plus double the heavy ammo. Everyone seemed to know our Alpha warrior could be counted on to attack in a fury of selflessness. It was his job and he did it without anger. He saw his job simply; make every other warrior who sees him choose this good day to die.

No one crossed his path or stood in his way. Death was the poetry of his swagger. We knowingly accepted his public and loud sermons of hellfire and brimstone. His truths were spoken in the serene clarity of a kid who hid the Bible in his pocket, filled with crumpled pages of verse, and letters never sent home.

"Why?" I asked that first moment I stumbled into his private time.

Quickly, he hid the Bible and crumpled pages. He growled at me. It was that everyone gets one question then stay the fuck away look that made me shiver.

"He who is fear, has none. I AM the Cadillac nigger. Every cock-sucker, motherfucker, swingin' dick in MY bush is nuttin' but a nickel-an-dime Pontiac nigger."

"What the hell is a Pontiac?" I asked, loudly.

Silence. His gut carving scowl encouraged a friend's timid answer.

"Poor Old Nigger Thinks It's A Cadillac."

From then on, our eyes greeted the other in silent respect. I avoided his space. Never did I cross his path or speak without being scowled at. He honored my gold bar by never ripping my face off. To Hillbilly, Nigger and Spic, I brought paupers' treasures to life's manger. Their blazing fires of survival to warm me through the cruel year and cold tears to come blessed me. They were the gold in my bankrupt soul.

> Look at their baby butt faces
> These back seat Romeo's
> And touchdown maker's chests puffed
> With the succulent, sweet scent
> Of home plate on their fingers
> Glee in their boastful eyes
> The boy's names have vanished
> In warrior scarlet memory mist
> Were they Bubba Willy, Digger, and Rick,
> Now Hillbilly, Nigger and Spic?
>
> What happened to their names?
> Did I ever know the names
> These warriors at my side?
> Command, kill, protect and hide my fear
> Boys whose lives crushed my butter bar soul.
> Are the names lost in blood on my trembling hands?
> How I hate them for that burden
> In their what do we do now looks
>
> I want to tell so much more

Of the Hillbilly, Nigger and Spic.
I want you to know they loved Ma
Their favorite possum, chitlins, monocot
Loralee, Shateekah and Angela back home
Their dreams in poetic rusty cars
And water color music that soothes then rocks

Did I ever know their stories
How brave in battle they were
To make you proud of them
And I that lead
I want to tell you they danced with glee
Chocolate cake finally here from home
Cocky grins and swagger stories tall
From well fucked an sucked
Battle breaks in Bangcock all
I want to tell you to be proud
When they heroically saved, did they ever
Or ravaged the enemy by, or was that never
He stood alone in the face of, did I dream
Risked their lives by, or was it nightmare scream
And oh YES the time they...
I want to tell you they lived
How they sang and danced
At orders home deliverance
How we talked and cried
Of home, or have I lied
Did he tell me of the gas station
He dreamed to open
Baby buggy wheel racer that won
Kids to bounce on his knee
Dentist he dreamed to be
Finally losing his virginity
I want to tell you 'bout the Montana ranch
Cattle, kids and calico print kitchen curtains

Names I Can't Remember

Rockies to Red Dog far and wide
Or had they died
We had a contract scarlet signed
On silence and survival C-rations dined
Stay the fuck away they sang
Only you drop quicker
I see the feelings so damn well
Wanting they and you to know
Where are the names
Why can't I tell you
What is the trick
For Hillbilly, Nigger and Spic
I can't.
I don't remember.

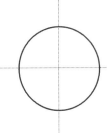

Saddle Up!

November, 1969

"Winning is for politicians and historians. Walking off the battlefield is the only victory a warrior prays for."

I shoot the first mother fucker that salutes!" he scowled, pointing his pistol at us.

A Colonel raised his hand.

Blam! The dirt between the Colonel's legs exploded.

"Or cocksuckers who ask questions before I finish."

The Colonel lowered his hand.

"Breathe, you son-of-a-bitch!" the teacher, ordered.

The Colonel breathed.

Alone in my rice house, I remembered that In-Country School days ago. It taught me to crave survival while OCS and Oleanna rammed honor and a glorious death down my throat. Neither taught me what the hell to do. How do I lead hilbillies, niggers, spics, and brass nuts killers with itchy trigger fingers ramming defiance up my ass? Sucking my thumb seemed good.

In-Country School had no walls, books, or tests. The diploma was a kiss from Mom or a body bag. New arrivals to the 101st Airborne Division sat outside on rough bleachers. Splinters in my ass kept me awake. Beyond the open-air classroom were hundreds of plywood and tin hootch barracks. Piled sandbags on the outer walls were rocket attack protection in this safe area behind the lines. Officers and enlisted men took classes together taught by psychotic assholes with 45 caliber chalk. Teachers were angry and unschooled men with the only credential that mattered. They were alive.

"I keep brave men that made it this far alive that you'll try to kill with stupid. Forget the crap you learned back in the world. Books let glory win the wars because no one has the nuts to say how much young boy's blood the victory cost. You did not expect me to shoot at you. To survive, remember the only rule in combat, there is none. How many of you warriors have pissed your pants?"

Honest hands trembled rising. One was the Colonel's.

I never saw Teacher's face. He was everything Oleanna I detested. His uniform was ragged. His canvass sided jungle boots were dirty raw leather. He wore no powder blue helmet or virgin white scarf to inspire. He intimidated with a ragged headband of torn T-shirt and muscles earned from humping hundred pound rucksacks, ammo, and dead men. His oily un-bathed skin stunk. While I cringed, the cocky bastard stood proud and tall as if daring hidden snipers to kill him now. His ice-cube funeral eyes screamed, "don't fuck with me." I felt like he was crushing my balls in one hand with the saber of rebellion in the other. I hated his guts but devoured his survivor Bible.

"The enemy wears no uniforms. Deadly looks friendly," was his in a North Pole whisper. His deadly gaze drew our eyes to the kids and old people being dragged away. Guards held the homemade bombs and blades locals had hidden behind smiles.

"Ditch those stateside new green duds for faded. Dinks spot that fresh green in this worn out jungle," he said, scratching his balls. His other hand pointed to the body bag detail near the chopper pad just yards away. Loaders in tattered and faded green tossed dead meat in factory fresh green into body bags.

"Don't shower! Stink like the jungle to live, you dick wads!" he screamed, sniffing out perfumed morgue material.

Sniffing the air, students and the carcasses reeked of shaving lotion and soap perfume Dinks smelled miles off.

"Never salute! Officers hate being pointed out and Dinks are punks with rotten aim," he snickered. He pointed at a pile of bloody mush with his arm in a rigid salute.

"Tear off rank markings that are bulls eyes!"

I was staring at the three dead Lieutenants wearing gold bars being zippered in.

"Never drink local bottled beer with a crimped on cap," he shrieked. He took out a bottle of the so-called Tiger Piss, pried off the top, and poured it on a rock. We listened to the crunchy sound of the ground glass in the liquid under his heel.

"Check, always check, the teenage whores' mouth and cunt for razor blades!"

Teacher tore his shirt. He had fresh and deep scars. Then he showed us the cunt's shriveled tongue he glued to his rifle butt like a notch in his six-gun. "Revenge is the only excuse for fuck-ups."

"Densest jungle is safest. Nothing is what it looks like," he taught, walking us on the practice course. The smartass spotted the mock booby trap on the path and walked around it. Bang! The laughers ran the other way. Blam!

"You idiots are dead from doing the easy and obvious!"

The punk who checked his crotch before his buddies got Teacher's left hook.

"To you, the jungle sounds like screams at a wake. It's a symphony of life. Death is a new silence or the one sharp and out of place sound," he said, walking into a bunker. No one noticed the rustling go silent or the sudden whoosh of air; my first rocket attack. He laughed as the tidal wave of assholes and elbows panicked in.

"Shoot where the hit and run enemy runs to, not fired from," he growled, pointing and waving his scarred arms.

We were on his live fire course not a safe one back in the world. Safe ones had barbed wire to crawl under taut and set high. The machine guns had bars under the barrel preventing low firing. Teachers had tangled wire that tore your flesh and some short-time cocksucker standing over you firing shit-your-pants distance from your nuts. Teacher gave the cockiest of us a magazine and bullied the punk to fire at him. After the jerk let rip a full magazine over Teacher's head and ran for cover, Teacher's single shot exploded in the mud next to my trembling hand.

"Love your rifle more than every buddy, any, and the best pussy you wish you had. A clean one saves you both, more than love yah letters to mamma or Betty Lou," he said grabbing a rifle one of us had just cleaned. He slammed and jammed it and his in the dirt and mud. His fired. I guess the mud was too afraid to clog his.

"Winning is for politicians and historians. Let them have the medals and body bags. Walking off the battlefield is the only victory a warrior prays for," was our Moses' eleventh commandment for parties not wakes at home.

The graduation ceremony for In Country School was a final reminder there was no Irving Berlin in our rock an' roll reality. Half the class got honey-pot duty. Fifty-five gallon drum halves filled with piss and shit were dragged out of the endless lines of out-houses. Gas was poured in and burned until the pots were empty. The other graduates filled a mountain of body bags at the morgue chopper pad. It was Teacher's simplest lesson without a lecture. Privates to colonel's burned the worst and buried the best. The sadness of every In Country class was the graduates burning shit always finished first.

The acrid black smoke billowed in the sky like the Grim Reapers' shroud choking the sun's hope to death. I watched chopper after chopper rise and disappear into the velvet stench. Long after the last honey pot was cleaned, the choppers kept thundering by carrying a body bag army to the last battle between dad's quiet, mom's tears and a room to clean but never to change.

I watched the Huey UH 1-Ds rise. Their squat snouts and bulging windows made them look like evil dragonflies. Their blades sounded like a mighty black stallion pounding the earth. Door gunners hung cockily out of the open side bays with their guns ready to blaze. I wanted to be one of those outnumbered horse soldiers headed into the deadly night to rescue some Custer punk butter bar. As a lone chopper thundered towards me, its Satan stare and hundred man fire power turned any raw beef courage I had into creamed chicken shit. I heard Hells' symphony of slaughter, cavalry of salvation, coward's courage, and rescue for the next breath dead.

Satan's chariots were also angels of hot food, mail, orders home, ammo, firepower, reinforcements, and one hell of a ride. To grunt foot soldiers, choppers were what OCS powder blue helmets, gleaming white virgin scarves, and spit-shined boots were supposed to be. If Oleanna was boy bullshit, choppers were the truths of men. I watched one rise steady and even as Teacher appeared from a shadow. I exhaled a fearful sigh. His hand touched my shoulder.

"What the fuck is going wrong here?" I whimpered.

"You'll learn, son. When they scream into the sky and rattle like a bucket of bolts about to explode, that's when they're off to save your ass. When they limp through the sky moaning low, they're full of body bags."

When I turned to thank Teacher and beg for more answers, he was gone. The last chopper screamed into the dark with urgency.

I jumped on a truck headed for the front lines the next day. It was making a quick stop at the body bag depot. I shared the ride with other New Meat. I was too crushed to see or talk to them. All I saw was the fresh carcass with a gaping hole in his chest and a smile on his face. I cried wondering what forgotten survival rule was hidden behind his only smile I ever saw. A serene but angry killer was dead. Teacher was going home at last.

I was dropped off on the hill top artillery firebase of my company commander's HQ. He was a cigar chomping, skinny, little jerk, 1st Lieutenant with a hooknose. For a couple of nights he ordered me to tag along with a platoon and get the flow of things on the night ambushes he ordered us to set. I copied his swagger. In my mind, I was his John Wayne that looked like Gomer Pyle.

The firebase was the end of my youth. Wannabe Viking me had hot slop food, real toilet paper, jerry rigged hot showers, radios that

Names I Can't Remember

played music, not desperate calls for artillery, and bunkers with dry beds made of ammo crates. The damp bunkers were full of rat traps that caught toes while the rats laughed and gorged on cheese. I shivered until my turn for guard duty. I had to stay on top of the bunker outside. John Waynes warned me not to move around.

Minutes into my 2-hour shift, my boredom and ego got to me. I strutted atop the bunker of sandbags covered with tar. Chest puffed and humming Oleanna, I gazed at the defensive wire ready to slaughter the enemy. The dense fog made the bunker tar slicker. I kept strutting. Thud! My invincible ass fell to the muddy ground below. All I heard was laughing boys, guffawing rats, and my ego deflating. It's hard to inspire with a muddy ass.

The second night, my CO sent me on a night patrol as an observer. I decided to leave my poncho liner at the firebase. After a rifle, it was the favored equipment. Feather light, it kept you warm even when soaked by a monsoon. I wanted to sleep warm and dry when we got back in the morning. I'd show these hardened vets leadership, courage, and smarts. I proved what an idiot I was. That night in a driving rain, I shivered in the mud. Cupping a lit but mushy butt in my hand was my only warmth. The guys laughing and smoking under their warm poncho liners drowned the machine gun Samba of my chattering teeth. The next morning, they dried poncho liners draped over their shoulders in the morning sun. At home, they snoozed as I found mine gone. They laughed as I bought it back from a coke kid for twenty bucks and a red face.

Coke kids were wise-ass hustlers getting rich. They sold everything including beer, cigarettes, pop, and sisters. Every rural village had a gas generator to run an ice machine for the cubes to cool beer and pop stolen from the rear and sold to us in the bush. Kids with plastic bags full of chilled cans popped out of the densest jungle. Cash was their childhood while papa and mamma-san eked out a starvation life in rice and pain paddies bombed out of existence by red, white, and blue freedom.

After three days of screw-ups, my old man assigned me.

At my rice house HQ now, all I had to fill the lonely was panic.

Nothing made sense. At In Country School, I had chicken shit idiots like me around for warmth. Now, I had a soul frozen by fear and killers who didn't give a damn. My platoon was having fun. Boymen were playing raucous animated card games. Snoring filled the air. Coke kids screamed out sales pitches. Guys were writing letters. One boy was reading. It looked like a tie-dyed revolt at the animal house fraternity of Pimple Pussy Pie before the chicks split, the beer and weed ran out.

Off to the side, was my platoon sergeant with a face crevassed by more this day lonely than I'd yet lived. Most of the sergeants here were three stripes; trained in ninety days shake n' bakes. At least OCS cannon fodder Lieutenants got twice that training time. The extra months meant we learned just enough to grow our ego to a dangerous size. I got lucky. My platoon Sergeant was a four-stripe career man. Maybe this was his second twelve-month tour here, he fought in Korea, or was a W.W. II dinosaur. A fourth stripe meant he knew what was really going on and would keep me alive if I didn't piss him off with new Lieutenant orders or attitude. His stripes and past inspired. His looks didn't. GI Joe or John Wayne he wasn't. His jelly belly, cheeks, and ass looked like Ralph Kramden had been drafted. Even with his waddle, he intimidated with a don't fuck with me glare. Everyone had that look but me.

With his strong sad gaze fixed on me, Sarge walked over. Teacher said if I was lucky and got a career sergeant, let him run things until my brain and ego diarrhea ended. It made sense. I stood firm and ready to put Sarge in his place with what I'd learned. Decisive and strong words would let him know it was MY platoon now. I would let him have a free hand for a few days. He stopped nose to nose. His glare chewed me up, spit me out and kicked my ass from hopeless to helpless. Drool was my decisive command decision. In his yawn, was a belly laugh too bored to explode. He walked away.

"I want you to know one thing," I finally stammered.

He stopped in his tracks but didn't face me. I wanted to brace him at attention with my bravery. I wanted my powder blue helmet of glory and virgin white scarf of leadership to pucker his asshole.

I wanted my gold bar and wings suffered for to smack his ass in place. I searched for cold clear tones to tell him about the traditions I squandered my youth on. My spirit would calm, inspire, and ignite a blaze within to follow me fearlessly into hell. When I was finished, I'd excuse him to do my bidding.

"Ah, run stuff till I get my head out of my ass," I bumbled staring at my feet.

He grinned. I saw in his wise eyes my diminutive father I could have thrown across the room saying, "You've made your mother cry too much, time for you to leave." I saw in Sarge the same truth that made me leave silently. It was the strength of a warrior who'd seen too many good days to die and survived them all.

I stuck out my hand.

"Yes..." he said with long pause, "Sir," he whispered taking my hand. My shake was firm but sweaty.

The sun creeping lower caught every eye. Sarge's glare got colder and harder. I saw this Dad ready to beat the crap out of me. Sarge saw men dying in his frightened son's eyes. My pudgy, nondescript Staff Sergeant stood unnoticed in the middle of that noisy circus of boys. Bare chest kids were slapping cards down like drunks swatting a cheap hooker's ass. They screamed arguments over muscle Mustangs and Mary's killer tits. Tops popped to drown the fear guzzle by guzzle. Sarge's ominous scowl was the gray rain drowning the rainbow of his laughing children. In his eyes, I saw a father crying anguish for his sons he must feed to the violent night. He turned to stare at me.

I saw agony and pity, so cold and raw it buckled my knees. With a quivering lip and worried look, I wordlessly asked him as I'd asked so many strangers before, "What went wrong here?" His answer was his weary gaze. It forced on me all the lonely of command that he carried for me. As the eyes of all those boys bore into us, I slumped as each life laid its future on my gold bar shoulders. Sarge's moan passed me the hole in his heart gouged by all those empty, open and waiting graves. I must now lead Tinker Toy boys turned killers.

Sarge's chin sunk and he closed his eyes. I didn't understand his strange look of hopeless relief in passing command to me. My jaw slowly dropped as his Grim Reaper arm pointed my eyes towards what was about to happen.

"SADDLE UP!" was Sarge's hell dog growl.

Refusing to look at one another, they lowered their zippers. Limp cocks pissed away the fear in noisy splashes that killed you on a quiet ambush. My trembling hand fed me from my booze canteen. While my acolytes pissed the communion helmet full of angry wine, my aged whiskey tasted like fear on the rocks with an acid twist. As they shook their cocks dry, I escaped my fear seeing Mom making her new Lieutenant his last French Toast.

A pack of Kools was opened, combat style, at the bottom. The pack was passed sacredly man-to-man like communion wafers. I bit my lip as they smoked a last calm moment. Non-smokers sucked hardest. In the choking cloud, I fought to remember Mom flipping my charred, bloody beef on the grill swearing the cow just mooed.

The scrawniest kid anointed himself Pope Assassin I with a head-band scrawled with Biggest Bad Ass Motherfucker in the Jungle. My gut seized. My mind raced back to the Coffee House rebel leaders as we danced around a sunrise fire before graduation. I saw my warrior priest assassins defiantly adorn themselves with peace signs, torn shirts covered with fuck you blessings of might and fear. Gasping panic, my pounding heart screamed out to the old tree Abraham to calm me. I had to dry heave but couldn't.

Faces that had not needed to shave since last week were black-ened with mud. My sweaty skin goose bumped, went frigid, and shivered when each took out what might be his last letter home. Inside, I was in that suburban classroom where I strutted tall and proud before classmates while waving my test with go to hell to the asshole teacher scrawled on it. Each warrior sealed my fate forcing his maybe last letter in my quivering hand.

A punk with stateside orders for tomorrow rebelliously tied a thick metal disk between his eyes. I couldn't keep looking at him. I was somewhere on an old airport road racing my screwed up go-cart that ran faster when you let up on the gas pedal. I stared at the kid drawing a bulls-eye on the metal disk. My go-cart sputtered dead out of gas as my heart drained of hope.

My shoulders lowered watching the kid who wore coke bottle glasses and refused to kill insects. In magazines that held twenty rounds each, this battle hard killer loaded each with only seventeen rounds because his pants filled with shit when twenty jammed his rifle. My eyes welled with I can hide here and be loved as a tearful, standing audience applauded my triumph as *The Glass Menagerie*, Gentleman Caller.

A New Meat fumbled test loading his magazines. I began to mumble Oleanna as that kid saw warriors tape theirs together in twos. The bullet ends faced in opposite directions. As the kid bumbled, a warrior released an empty one, flipped it, and rammed in the other with lightening speed. Combat has one truth: the dead load, the living fire. My Oleanna angel song was now fingernails on a chalkboard for the army of hearses slowly passing.

Mamma's boy loosened frag pins. I had to pee but watched him straighten the bent pins that must be pulled out before it could explode. Straight pins could fall out at the wrong time but pulled out faster. When being overrun, he who pulled and threw fastest lived. I tried to piss away my fear. I saw me back in the world by the streetlight outside her house. Writing horrible love sonnets to the girl with braces that let me feel her up once, my burning cock pissed nothing.

A two-left foot Doofus tied a knife to the back of his hand. The tip extended just beyond his fingertips. Everyone heard me gagging on the tune to Oleanna. My trembling body and chattering teeth was all I felt or heard. His eyes shut like the black night that would blind us all, Doofus slashed the air to practice killing who's there but can't be seen. He smiled. I stopped singing. I'd forgotten the Oleanna glory. All I remembered was the Dean sending me home for too long sideburns and jeans in school.

Iowa baby face honed his bayonet to a razor's edge. I couldn't feel my clenched fist. I watched this kid that had fainted at the sight of the Malaria shot needle slice his finger raw to test the edge of the bayonet and then suck his own gushing blood happily. What was left of me had just crawled home starving after running away to California. When Iowa kid sliced his finger a second time and deeper the third, I was gorging Mom's cookies hot from the oven. When the killer in front of me smeared his blood on his face like war paint, I puked, and fell to my knees.

Hillbilly point man slid a twig in his rifle barrel to feel enemy in front of him he couldn't see. It helped him survive moonless and starless nights so black, you couldn't see your outstretched hand. He learned it from men that bumped into death before they could see and kill it. I sniffled. Hillbilly tied a squealing rat to a bush, blind-folded himself, and swirled to disorient himself for point man practice. He sniffed and sensed his way. When his rifle stick bent on the rat, he fired and his freehand holding a knife beheaded the rat mist. His bloody face smiled. Gasping for air, I turned away. I fought to remember anything not so disgusting. I saw the last of the rebel in me that cut school for the first time roaring by the campus on my Honda 160. While the smiling hick kid tasted the rat blood on his face, shit filled my pants.

Spic reading baby names moments ago viciously snapped the wire of his garrote around a ration box. I couldn't look away. The cans spewed jellied guts but refused to die. In frenzy, he pulled tighter. Despite the handles, the garrote's twisting wire between his fingers slashed his flesh. Escaping, my mind drifted to the boat and grimaced while cousin Bruce ripped the hook from the mouth of the old scarred fish gasping his desperate last breath. I saw Spic's eyes pinched thin with vicious indifference. His hands gushed angry blood from the wire that cut his flesh deep. Cousin Bruce made me hold the dead fish high. Spic was licking his blood.

With his last boy's breath, Nigger slid into an envelope scented violet paper graced with tender poetry he hid from the others. Spent, I dreamed of the burbs and the three trees in front of the three bedroom, twenty three five bi-level. With his next killer's breath, Nigger draped the necklace of sandal scraps from fifty-one kills around his neck. I sighed at the same sized trees planted together that grew tall, medium, and short like we brothers three. A strap sup-porting the heavy machine gun Nigger carried alone cut his bare

Names I Can't Remember

chest. He checked the massive ammo belt fed to the gun over his shoulder and wrist. All stood far away from the poet of death with the killer stare. I was pushing my baby brothers through the snow on a sled wearing that goofy earflap hat..

Reverently putting on his yarmulke and prayer shawl, the medic whispered. I was jumping in the back seat of Dad's racy Ford with fins for our Sunday ride to the ice-cream shop. "Shemay isroel adanoi alohnu, adanoi achad..." was the medic's prayer that the dead, wounded, and battle wouldn't leave time for later. Praying, he checked his medical pouch. I was giggling in the tree house complete with roof, ladder, and balcony Tommy and I built on stilts because there was no tree. The medic put opened Morphine needle-ettes between his lips for the speed needed to let the screaming boys trying to shove their own guts back in with a gushing blood mangled stump die with goofy smiles not crying momma tears. Around his neck, he draped a dozen shirt scrap extra bandages after measuring them on his own belly. Moaning the last of his prayer in tears, he rammed bullets in his magazines. I was nervously telling Tommy about loneliness and thirty aspirins I'd swallowed.

Sarge walked to me and gave me a chance to be spit on at home. He poured the helmet full of my men's piss over me so I'd stink like my jungle survivors. I was remembering my naked brother Dave spraying me through his crib's rails. Sarge said this stench masked the perfumed soap, shaving lotion, and smelly bug juice that marked me dead man. Not one New Meat ever refused this ritual baptism. Sarge finished demolishing my ego. He faded my fresh green uniform with mud. All I saw was Mom suckling Dave when I stumbled in. Sarge ripped off my rank and unit patches. While Mom yelled, I stammered after accidentally sitting on baby brother Brad. The career man taped my noisy, dangling dog tags, and tucked away my floppy loud bootlaces. My feet fumbled every-which-way as Mom's water broke in the kitchen. Sarge threw away the crackly paper candy he saw me hide that Dinks smelled, heard, and blasted at. I was aimlessly picking weeds in front of my new house to make my own private yard. Sarge beat my boots raw with a rock to kill the shoot here shine.

I was standing tall by Dad in the Cubs uniform he bought me. Sarge rammed the last vicious ritual of life down my throat with a bloody lip uppercut reserved for officers. I was in Mom's arms as she ran to the hospital covering the gushing hole in my head from cracking my skull on playground cement. I said nothing putting my jaw back on my face. I understood them now. Taste your own blood now, not in battle. In combat, an officer has no right to fear.

The sun was dead. Boys closed caskets. Warrior eyes darted left and right. The spaced, single file line passed me by. One began to whistle Custer's *Gary Owen*; an Irish piper's *Black Knight* moan on the heather shrouded in highland mist. One then another savage whistle joined in. I stood tall in my little man suit while Mom snapped a Kodak. Headed out into the bloody jungle night, each killer slapped a letter in my hand and spit in my face. I licked mushy icing from the cake carousel at my third birthday in the Camel Trail bar where Mom hustled tips from maybe Dads. Sarge held his rifle high with his thumb on the safety for all to see. The sky cracked and thundered a symphony of thumbs clicking safeties off. Kids come thee killers to this lock and load cry of Beethoven's da' da' da' dum dirge lullaby.

Oleanna was dead.

"Sir? Get your fucking thumb out of your mouth!"

I was the womb slick baby suckling at Silkies.

"Thumb? Not my scotch?"

"Bullets now, booze in the morning, Lieutenant. Say something, Sir. Act brave for them, dammit!"

"Holy shit. What the fuck have I gotten myself into?"

Mamma daddy I did it whee,
Tied my shoe one two three.
Can I go out and kill today?
Aren't you very proud of me?
Two, four, six, eight,
Who do we decapitate?
Hit 'em hi and hit 'em low.
Extra guts, where do they go?

First base to third nearly home slidin'
Smell that finger guys, I ain't liein'.
Did she suck it, did she gag?
Is my cock in the body bag?
2 good 2 B 4 got 10,
Most likely to succeed,
Captain of the varsity,
Best butchering silently.

Sweet cologne shrinks pimples.
Can't makes babies the first time.
Yeast in cider will get you high.
Slashed ear collectors never die.
One potato, two potato, three potato four,
Tree house, mini-bike, back seat score,
Dick and Jane sitting in a tree
K, I, S, S my killing spree

Eeenie, meanie, minie moe,
Catch a nigger by the toe.
Is this his face I don't know.
If he hollers let him go.
Eeenie, meanie, minie moe.

Where oh where does the last childhood roam?
On walking dead boy's faces spit on at home.

Checked jacket: Killer Graduates 6th grade.
Dark jacket: Virgin Jr. High Graduate

Names I Can't Remember

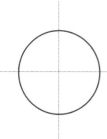

Virgins

December 10, 1969

"We shared the quiet of war;
where boys bury a hell of names
so men can survive a life of
memories. The price is sadness
and turning away from wives.
Love never heals war."

W e were the two that had not yet killed; virgins in a cat house with teenage hack n' slash killers and horny nymphomaniacs. I was twenty my first day in command and swaggering on the rice house porch. I looked like Custer telling my men we could kill Sioux with bullshit. Inside, I was sucking my thumb. The other virgin was a Corporal who quietly read Dickens and Plato. I saw a lost poet among assassins passing out guts and legs to screaming stumps.

The Corporal was out there in the bright and hot morning sun rising over the football field sized yard in front of the Rice House. My men fought for space to fill their canteens and shave at the small, mud, and straw well a few yards to the left by the hedgerow. The noise was getting louder from the trucks, buses, and black French cabs on Highway One. Yammering locals with sacks over their shoulders stood on each bumper and running board of every overloaded vehicle moaning its way to Da Nang in the South or Hue in the North. While villagers scurried across the road to rice paddy plots on either side, Sarge was tossing mail to the crowd surrounding him screaming "here" in the muddy yard. They laughed and ignored me except for the razor sharp glares that told New Meat me stay away.

Inside it was dark, cool, and quiet. I sat on my HQ stage area and plotted night defense fire alone. The isolation made my heart race, my breathing rapid, and shallow. Boys with Dink ears hanging from their peace sign necklaces were sleeping like babies. I wanted to give back my gold bar. My indifferent assassins that had body bagged friends, put marks on their helmet covers to count days and bragged how few they had left. Their noisy bellows puckered my three hundred and sixty five day asshole. Last night, my guys had held enemy guts in the air and were now chasing teenage hookers and writing mom. As commander, I could watch the party not join. All the meat grinder defiance I saw was turning the respect I'd hoped for into hamburger. My reward for being called Sir was the lonely of having their living or dying depend on what I decided. I was the deaf father with his back to his sons yelling I can't swim.

Four hairless chest killers slapped cards on an ammo crate and yelled at each other. My heart was at home, my eyes on the forty aspirin lined up on my desk. I saw the sad Corporal wandering the noisy circus desperate to find anyone with a book in his hand without the word Ka-pow on a four-color page. I saw the papa-san and mamma-san, teeth blackened by the local Beetle Nut treat, giggling at the private tasting their sour gift. I was remembering mom, dad, and my brothers, ten and twelve years younger, piling into the Chevy for a ride without me: the leftover kid from the old days. The Corporal had set up a chessboard and meekly signaled for a player. After fuck yous and fingers, he played alone and lost. My killer gang in OD green swarmed each other playing tackle football with a stuffed sandbag and taunted one another with touchdown roars. I remembered being in my room at home gagging on sorrow, the pills I'd swallowed,

Names I Can't Remember

and tears of isolation. The Corporal tried to make friends offering up some cookies he'd gotten from home. My assassins covered in crude tattoo peace signs devoured the cookies and left the Corporal eating crumbs alone. I watched my men boys compare killer tits girlfriend pictures. My soul was running out the back door to tell Tommy next door what I'd done while inside, mom, dad, and my brothers watched Bonanza. Here at the Rice House, was my swarming family of young lions with blood soaked faces from tearing into a fresh kill carcass and a Corporal leaning against a tree and sobbing. I cried a dry tear soaked in lonely. Hell was feeling like Eden with all this company.

I was learning command reality and hating their guts. I was blaming them for the get called sir sucker contract I signed freely. I was afraid to know or like them too much. Booze helped me figure out I didn't have to feel guilty if I got a stranger killed. It was all their fault. How dare they take my Frisbee free for all years from me. I wanted to carve their eyes out for keeping me from getting stoned with the Coffee House white bread rebels. Shivering nights, rancid popcorn, and sour tea didn't seem so bad now. I despised them for dumping their lives on my soul and not letting me have the glory Oleanna promised. I wanted to rip their bowels out and they died for never giving me the salutes I'd suffered for. I reviled them for relying on me and puking insolence in my face. I had to hate them because I couldn't run away and was worn out from hating myself.

Officers in larger units had each other to share intense command frustration with. I had no one to explain why I hated the responsibility that was strangling me. As the only officer in an isolated bush platoon, I had to choke down this fury alone. There was no mom's lap or Silkie to suckle. Booze was the only friend that hugged me.

It was my first day in actual command. What was I in command of? My heart pounded like a mother's agony cries while a sad soldier with a telegram knocked on her door. I had thirty-five boys proud of shaving with razors they had secretly taken the blades out of. What was the elevated commander's end of the Rice House for? I was wrinkled with confusion and panic. This was what I led but what do I do to command? Had I slept through that class too?

Career man Sarge wandered over. Again, he had quietly observed everything. When he spoke, it was gently and to the point, not the self-satisfying melodies I sang to please my ears. He stood and looked out with me. I felt safe near him. I turned trying to form a question. Silence. A nervous cough was all I could manage.

"You hate them don't you, Lieutenant?" he said, flatly

"How did you know?" I asked, incredulously.

"Lieutenant, hate's all any soldier has to hide fear. Go speak to them," he said like a priest's blessing before the firing squad aiming at me. "Be you, not the puke you learned in OCS. Anything but, I'm firm but fair," he said pushing, then pulling me back.

"No firm but fair speech, Sarge. Do they want to know what kind of man I am?"

"Go! They know," he said, holding me. "You're a dead BSer or live shooter. There's no maybe with bullets."

"I see. Actions, not words," I said, stepping off.

"Say whatever comes to you... but none of that, the men come first crap. When the shit hits the fan, every swinging dick here checks his own ass first."

"You got it, Sarge, no lies."

"What are you waiting for?" he said, grabbing my arm.

"Maybe I should take notes?" Still, he didn't let go.

"Don't flinch," he said, jerking back my collar. "These men are scared shitless. Although they know you are too, they need to believe you're not, so no swagger. They know when the BS bull has no balls. "

"Right. Show 'em my balls and guts. Why, Sarge?"

"Tell 'em you'll get your head outta' your ass as soon as possible," he said, not letting me go.

"Why do you call them men? Not one's over nineteen."

"Boys show up here, son. It takes a man to stay."

"May I go NOW?" I said, fighting his mother hen grip.

At that instant, a soldier wandered by within earshot of our conversation. Sarge stiffened, knowing he had the sergeant image to protect and booted me on my way.

"God damn officers with fucked up questions. I'll retire when the army replaces shit head officers with sharper pencils and cleaner whores," he barked.

No one looking, Sarge winked, "go get 'em, son."

I walked to a tree stump where the virgin Corporal was having a hard time writing his letter. I watched him start and stop until he noticed me. He looked up with a distant look in his eye. He was a fair-skinned kid with freckles and glasses. The round wire frames were as fragile as his personality. It seemed he hoped the boys would take orders from the stripes he wore, not him. He kept to himself and read a lot, a quiet kid with strength of character within, not a foul mouth muscle personality without.

I planted my feet firmly and looked deep in his eyes with a steady and meaningful look. I waited for Sarge's advice to come out. The Corporal looked up at me shielding his eyes from the sun. Silence. Sarge didn't tell me about the why in terrified young eyes asking me for an answer. It was the instant I let life hurt me. In front of me was a kid scared he was going to die. His eyes were begging me to please get him home to momma. I let him see that his Infantry god warrior on a white winged stallion down from mount Oleanna was an arrogant jerk with knocking knees who sold his soul for glory he hadn't the bravery to pay for.

"You ain't gonna kiss me are you, Lieutenant?"

"Hi."

"Huh?"

"I'm just as scared as you are," I said without flinching. I saw Sarge smiling and scratching his chin.

The Corporal and I grinned. A tense moment melted. He tilted back the tip of his helmet with a breath and his shoulders slumped down as the fear drained. Seeing this, my ass unclenched and I didn't shit panic. Somehow, his fear made me more confident

"I'm trying to write Ma what it's like here. It's my first day. I don't know what to say. Every time I lie, how OK it is, I see her shaking her head. She'd know. She always knew when I was lying. Did your Ma ever catch with you with Popsicle juice dribbling down your chin, ask you who ate the last one, and you say not me, Ma?"

"Mine was a mouth full of cookie crumbs. It seemed worth a shot. Try this, tell her the truth."

"As in I'm afraid? Wow. I never thought of that. Thanks, Lieutenant. What's gonna happen?"

"I don't know...son," I said, after a sudden and warming pause for the last word. I felt like a leader for the first time, a father washing away my son's fears.

His head tilted to one side. A smile grew after the word son and he said, "Thanks."

"For what?"

"I don't know. I just felt... OK when you said that."

"OK?"

"It's the first time anyone told me the truth. Back home they fed me all the we're the big heroes. Suddenly, I'm sitting here and it hits me. Dinks with the same bullets I have has an idiot telling him the same thing."

"Tell your mom exactly that. Maybe she'll worry less hearing the truth. Mother's always spot that OK B.S."

Sarge was right. I was learning that command was more than giving orders. It is listening to and understanding people. It felt even better saying son that second time.

"I will," said the Corporal. He looked less afraid.

I slapped him on the shoulder and turned to walk away.

Sarge smiled and gave me the thumbs up. I gulped my first breath in minutes. Confidence is delicious.

"Sir," said the Corporal. I turned.

He snapped a crisp salute. My heart leapt to my throat. I snapped one back. It was the first I'd earned, not expected. We froze in an instant of nervous respect.

Automatic rifle fire ripped over our heads. The Corporal and I got busy digging our balls out of the mud with our noses. Standing there with a smoking rifle, was a scowling Short Timer with rotation orders home., angrily shaking his head

"You cocksuckers just don't get it do you?" he lectured to the applause of my other seasoned killers. "If I was some homesick sniper with only one clear shot at any asshole here, who is my best target that gets me to momma quicker?" he yelled.

"The clearest target," I said, commandingly.

"No," replied the meek Corporal. "The leader getting saluted," he added, waving a finger at my nose.

The Short Timer let rip another angry blast over us. We dove in the mud again. Our missing dignity had to be down there somewhere.

"Wrong, you sorry shits. First off, Dinks got crap aim. Most times they hit the short time sorry bastard they've seen before dumb enough to wander by you saluting idiots, like me! Shooting new idiots like you two bothers no one. More new idiots arrive tomorrow. Killing one Short Timer ruins everyone's morale. You got it now, you bozos? Salutes kill!"

"Got it!" gagged the Corporal and I.

"One salute targets all. And it puts a bull's eye on an Lieutenant's forehead. It'd be nice if one lasted long enough to get his head out of his ass. No fucking saluting!"

We thought his last rifle blast finished the lesson.

"Think we can get up out of the mud yet, Sir?" whispered the trembling Corporal.

"When I finish pissing in my pants."

When we turned over, he was standing over us. He clicked off his safety and rammed his rifle between the Corporal's eyes. The kid froze and prayed with silent trembling lips. Teacher looked me in the eye and pulled the trigger. The empty chamber clicked. The Corporal and I gasped like virgins the instant they became women.

"If I was as stupid as you, there'd a been a round in my magazine. The next time you two fucks salute, there'll be two," he said, sauntering off, laughing, scratching his nuts, and lighting a cigarette.

"What's your name?" I asked, still stunned.

"Your worst nightmare. Don't! I know who you two are already; Stupid Shit and Fuck Up. Remember, it's easy to throw a dead body on a chopper but a name is too heavy."

I turned to the Corporal needing a name to stay sane.

"I'm—"

"Don't, Lieutenant. He's right. Damn him. He's right."

The Corporal and I shared the quiet of war; where boys bury this hell of names so men can survive the life of memories. The price boys pay is the sadness in men's eyes when they turn away from wives. Love never heals war.

Later that night, I was lost in the daydream of the day's lessons. I was in the middle of the single file line moving quietly along the foot wide rice paddy earthen dyke. The night air was sticky skin humid. The line of march stopped and worried whispers went man to man bringing the danger back to me. My flesh suddenly slimed with fear.

"Sssh. Toothless Freddie says he kin smell 'em."

"He can what?" I asked, incredulously.

"Not so dang loud, idiot. He kin smell 'em."

"No one can smell a man. Ask them what's wrong?"

Nervous whispers went up the line and back. All the while, sweaty trigger fingers twitched.

"Sir, don't court martial me for this. It's a direct quote from Freddy. He says, "Tell that sorry ass Lieutenant to get his chicken shit Yankee nose up here an' wiff hizsef!"

"Sarge, can Freddy really smell Dinks?"

"Ain't missed one yet, Lieutenant."

"I can't see my hand in front of my face. I can't even smell your stinky old ass."

"I love you too, Sir," he said.

There were stifled giggles of anger and nerves to our Laurel and Hardy moment. As I bumble mumbled, Sarge pulled my ass up the line like he was dragging an unruly child.

"Kain't wait no mo', you Yankee fuck!" Freddie's full magazine blast of red tracer fire lit the sky with panic.

I was a calm, well-trained, and efficient Audie Murphy. I dove in the paddy water and manically flailed about searching for my radioman. My tactics were screaming a Punk Rock version of, in my head, Chopin send all support fire here. Sarge managed to shove stumbling kids desperate to find their helmets, rifles, and balls into a quickie ambush line: dive in the mud and fire everywhere.

Names I Can't Remember

"Big Poppa, Big Poppa, this is Snake Six, over!"

"This is Big Poppa, over," my CO said calmly.

"FIRE!" I blathered, shoving the wrong end of a magazine into my rifle. The John Wayne coup de grace, yelling blam.

"Fire what, Snake Six?" was my cool CO's acidic snipe.

I couldn't read my map with my defensive fire plots. It was upside down. "Shove an A-bomb up John Wayne's ass and fire that cocksucker!"

Sarge somehow got my acne blizzard of assholes, elbows, and egos firing at the enemy instead of at each other. This was amazing since my orders proved my head was still three feet up my colon.

"Don't fire 'till you see the whites of their eyes! Damn the torpedoes. Full speed ahead. Set up a cross-fire and send out patrols to determine enemy strength. Fire!"

"We could shoot at where the Dinks are shooting at us from, Sir," Sarge grumbled.

"That's good. Fire!"

I was sure I was Patton liberating Bastogne. In truth, I was the banana peel tripping the Keystone Cops with their faces buried in the mud and blindly firing over their heads. My screams begged the CO for any bomb ever invented.

The velvet night sky was an eerie glow of daylight from the illumination rounds the CO fired from his artillery base. It looked like Silkie's eggshell white teeth set in her coal black face. It was over in a minute. We outnumbered the rice-stealing bastards ten to one, and fired cannons at their slingshot tactics of shoot once and run. Terrified kids with moist eyes and gasping for breath shivered the night away with nervous fingers on triggers.

Sarge and I lay in the mud feet from the dead enemy boy doing our own Who's On First. He yelled the body had to be checked for booby traps. My oatmeal brain drowning in adrenaline kept feeling my balls to see if they were still there. He was trying to teach me reality. The small enemy units here to steal food, would not stay and fight. There was never time for their comrades to take their dead buddies with them. At best, they would pull the pin on a live grenade and shove it under the carcass. The plan was stupid Americans would roll the body to check for maps or trophies and die. Sarge also knew these brave dying boys sometimes pulled that frag pin and hid it on themselves with their last breath.

I crawled through mud trying to find a long branch to push the body over with. Sarge was giggling. I said we could toss another grenade on the fresh kill to explode any traps. Sarge yanked the pin on a waterlogged grenade. While I scrambled away yelling, he belly laughed as it fizzled out to nothingness. When I suggested we call a chopper to drop a line to turn the body, he nearly split a gut asking me how I'd get a pilot to hover over an explosion. My dignity fired me. My guys were trying not to laugh.

"Hello? I'm so glad it's over. Do you hear me?"

We set up a small perimeter for the rest of the night to protect our position and guard a dead boy, my first murder, and badge of combat honor. Sarge and I tried tossing a loop of Claymore mine wire over his wrist to turn it. We argued after each failure.

"Listen. Tell my father I am sorry. I won't be there for the planting."

Sarge swore, grabbed the fresh kill's arm, shoved his own face in the mud, and yanked. After no explosion, I took a breath after I pissed my pants and opened my eyes.

"Hello. Did you hear me? He needs to know, so the rice is ready for the rain. My little brother is ready to help."

We guarded my virgin kill until dawn. Sarge made me search the boy for documents. I didn't find anything in the mangled and rotting flesh. I puked while he forced my hand into swarming maggots and mush guts. Face slaughter as it consumes you.

"That letter's not a secret plan. It's to my mother. Send it to her, PLEASE! It will help her accept—I'm dead?"

At sun up, the Virgin Ceremony began for the freckled face Corporal and I, virgins that had not yet killed. The ritual was a marriage of respect, savagery, and necessity. Our Generals had struck a deal with local Asian Generals. Even a dead enemy was still Asian and the body could only get the proper burial respect in traditions known to Asians. It all included incense, incantations, shrouding the body, and burying it in an upright fetal crouch in a circular grave. No

Names I Can't Remember

GI drooling revenge would do this. All bodies were carried back to the nearest village. Grizzled combat vets like Sarge evolved a brutal lesson. To survive, punk virgins who had not killed must confront death lustily before they crawled off and cried their life away in locked wards. Sarge waved the Corporal and me over to the corpse. The men who had suffered this christening looked away.

"You look so young, too. I didn't hate you, either."

My jaw dropped. The stench of sun-rotting flesh didn't matter. What I saw was a squirming black hive of flies feasting on jellied eyes. I couldn't see what color they were. The gooey muck popped and buzzed like dead kernel popcorn on a funeral pyre fire. Voracious mother flies bloodied each other with their wings. They gorged on vile puss fighting for space to lay their oozing mass of maggot eggs in a moist nest that meant survival. The brave punk's guts flopped to one side didn't convulse the bile into my mouth for it was his eyes that hypnotized me. They begged me to slaughter the black hoard frenzy spreading to his nose, ears, and anus. It's not his pale boyish skin caked in thick cracked blood that haunts. It's his eyes begging for one last breath. It's not his bare, callused feet, nor worn out clothes so flimsy from a thousand mile march to defend his rice and rain that transfixes me. It's a shame the horror comes after death.

"Why can't I see anything? Can you see my eyes?"

The Corporal and I said nothing. We couldn't look away from the life beginning on our first slaughter. We were gasping anguish.

"Look at me! Tell me what's wrong with my eyes."

Sarge bellowed the strangest eulogy.

"Listen up! That dead asshole is your ticket home, his grave, not yours. From his ass, they swallow the cool and sweet Cling Peach juice he would have gutted you for. From his ears, they guzzle your daughter's wedding wine his bullets would have made you miss. From his eyes, they gulp the future that Dink would have severed your head to steal from you. Flies seek the easiest points of entry to your life that dead Dink wanted: ears, asshole, and eyes. This will be on the test, shit heads! It is the eyes, repeat the eyes, the flies go for first. The greatest amount of food is in dead Dink eyes. Flies mass and lay thousands of eggs there seconds after his final daydream. Feeding maggots swarm and wiggle to life on the jellied mass of dead Dink eyes. I CAN'T hear you!"

"What's that noise? Why can't I feel anything?"

"Flies feed on jellied dead Dink eyes, Sergeant!"

"You maggots say something!?"

"FLIES FEED ON JELLIED DEAD DINK EYES, SERGEANT!"

"Was I brave? Did I honor mother and father?"

Behind the Corporal and me, the men of nineteen carved a sturdy pole from a nearby sapling. A soldier that refused to look at us brought the pole to us. The Virgin Ceremony continued. The pole was dropped at our feet. The Corporal and I knew what to do with it without guidance. Silently, we tied the dead boy's wrists together and the end of the line to the pole. We did the same for the ankles. Each move and touch was soft, tender and done with warriors' fear and respect. Carrying a hero like a slaughtered hog was the same indifference victory entitled us to he would claim.

"Why do you look at me so? What do you see? I know something is happening. Tell me."

"How old are you?" was my last boy's question.

"What, Lieutenant?" Sarge scowled.

"Nothing, fuckface," was my boy growl delivered with a man's first kill glare and anger.

"Sergeant hard stripe to you, dickhead...Sir," grumbled my platoon sergeant with sorrow and a watchful knowing eye.

"I'm seventeen. And you,' roo-tenant'?"

The Corporal and I looked at each other for the only time. Who would carry the front end and who the rear? The kid and I fumbled the decision looking at each other.

"Jeez! Seventeen? I just turned twenty," I said looking at the flies in his eyes and his nostrils.

"What, Lieutenant?" Sarge grumbled to fire the anger I needed to survive this maggot mass for mothers.

"Shut your fucking mouth or I'll salute your cocksucker ass."

Sarge spit at me with pride and disgust to finish his job. While we virgins did nothing, he checked the wind with a wet finger. The virgin on the back end would have it worse. He'd smell the stench of guilt being downwind and would have to look at the shredded dead boy guts and head flopping like a broken toy. It might be easier on the virgin in front. He could try to write a letter in his head to shut out the ugly weight bouncing on his shoulder. Sarge ignored my mumbling he remembered from long ago.

"Jeez? What is jeez, roo-ten-ant?"

"Jeez is ah...what's your word for 'wow'?"

"Wow."

The Corporal and I silently decided by flipping a coin. He lost. His chin dropped to his chest as he began to move to the rear end of the pole. My man in command lesson came swiftly. Sarge snatched the coin and turned it over for all to see.

"My brother was that old when you guys killed him."

"The Corporal won, Lieutenant." Not knowing or caring for Sarge's logic, the Corporal sighed in relief and picked up the front of the pole, smiling at his goulish luck.

Sarge whispered, "You wanted the fucking bar, son. Earn it in front of them, damn you."

The bastard was right. On the rear end, I carried the eyes oozing maggot-massing flies through the gauntlet of men saluting with their eyes tightly shut.

"Did you kill my brother too?"

"No. But I'll remember his eyes too."

"Me too. I remember one, from roo-eez-iannah."

Is walking the gauntlet of silent salutes by my own men happening? I don't know. I am earning their respect inhaling the shit stink of bouncing bloody guts. I wanted to plunge rusty knives in their backs for not letting me skip home to get my ass kicked playing chess with Scotty. Are the Corporal and I speaking on that long walk back? I don't know. I am proving my dead soul courage to men who had to trust me with their lives by staring at feeding maggots and choking down bile I puked with every step. I wanted to rape their cunt mothers to death while they watched for refusing to let me crumble in Reverend Dave's arms and beg him to fill me with God gas. Are we groaning along the way from the weight of the man we killed? I don't know. I am earning their courage to follow my orders and die by never taking my gaze off the jelly mass of flies devouring the last drop of compassion in me. I wanted to rip their cocks off with my teeth and spit the bloody mess in their yowling faces for burying the best years of my life in this hell of responsibility.

With every step along the narrow, slick, and muddy rice paddy dykes, the Corporal, and I stepped surely. Our silence said to each other do not fall. This boy we honor can't be dropped in the mud. When there was a no kill night, the walk home was loud and noisy. The men bellowed who'd kick whose ass at spades. The best chefs yelled and shared hot sauce recipes that made the C-ration puke in a can palatable. Sleep hounds yawned and moaned. Without a Virgin Ceremony, soldiers sing their anthem, bitching. If the food was hot, the mail was too late. If the mail was on time, the crappy food was cold. Bitching calms a soldier's fear. Luckily, our mail was never on time, the food was never hot, and the walk home was a bit like this.

"Hey Sarge, when's Lieutenant gunna' get our fucking mail?"

"When your girl stops fucking long enough to give her time to write, shithead!"

"Hey Sarge, when's Lieutenant gunna' get us some hot food sent out from the rear?"

"When the mess Sergeant figures out how to cook a dickhead ass like you with mashed potatoes and gravy!"

On Virgin days, guilt was the only silent scream.

"Should we say our names?" I whispered.

"Ahhh! I, names I can't remember. Why can't I?"

"What's your fucking name?" I mumbled, angrily.

"Does it matter, Lieutenant?" said Sarge, with a father's tender firm hand on my shoulder. You still would have killed him if you knew."

Did I just hear the dead boy? I don't know.

At the village, no locals, or coke kids came to stare at our pale white, olive, red, and black faces. We'd come home quietly as the bouncing pole groaned the paces. The Corporal and I were in step. Disgust was

Names I Can't Remember

the melody of our march, the oos, ahs and whispers.

Finally, we got to the highway near our Rice House base and stopped. The Corporal and I tenderly put the pole down. He headed back to the Rice House without a word or looking at me. It was the last moment I saw the boy on the pole. A passing warrior seeing my boy's arm crook, fingers stiffen, and rise, jerked forward to stop my arm. Sarge grabbed him admonishing him to let it be son. I saluted the dead warrior.

"How did we get to this? I want you to know I didn't hate you."

"I know. I didn't hate you either."

"Hold my hand, please."

I knelt and held the warrior's hand in mine.

"What's up, Lieutenant?" asked one somber man passing by.

"Nothing," growled Sarge, shushing the kid along with a go on nod to me and shielding me from prying eyes..

"Can I ask something?" I begged the fallen warrior.

"Sure. I'd like that, roo-ten-ant," his spirit sang.

"What's your name? Try hard, damn you. I need to know," I sighed.

"Quan Liau. It means morning sun. Yours?" his cracked lips fluttered.

"Doug. It means... stupid. What went wrong here?"

"I know now for my journey is over. Yours has just begun. Bye, Roo-ten-ant. I hope you make it."

"Goodbye."

"You say something, Lieutenant?" asked one of my men.

"I said leave him alone," barked Sarge.

I slouched back to the yard in front of the Rice House and wandered among the noisy, snoring, and belching boys. Later, I sorrow shuffled to the road. Villagers were doing nothing but watching my brother warrior rot in the sun.

"He stole the rice they broke their backs in the rain for," Sarge said.

"In time, forgiveness overcomes the hunger of vengeance," Quan Liau said with a last gasp from somewhere.

"Maybe he was starving," I sighed.

It was the last thing I said that day. Turning towards the Rice House yard, I saw the Corporal was wandering lost in the same virgin regret I was. Our stares were a filibuster of agony. I felt the same fear I saw in his eyes. We were running from the same truth. We loved every sweaty fuck moment and would revel in the incest wantonly again. Combat is a high I shoot up after every rush of regret because the horror is I love being hooked.

I did not look back. Did a single tear hit the ground? I do not know. It is the eyes I remember.

First day limp dick jitters,
Fifty lives balanced on my butter bar,
In battle command ambush first fright
What do we do Lieutenant?
I don't want to die.
We look to you Lieutenant.
Can we trust you not to lie?
Brautigan help, was it i-DEATH or IDEA-th?
Koo-koo-ka-choo Lucy in the Sky,
Slept through the class which to choose?
Mrs. Robinson slinks dress slit to thigh,
Killers cum we thee fuck me sucked, I lose.
Will I survive shit shiver some way to get them through?
Kid twenty cocky's all I got, God what have I gotten in to?

Endless velvet sky and moonless night,
Single file boy killers faces fade,
Hillbilly, spic, Lieutenant, nigger and white.
Behind fury written I love you letters laid.
Silent boots squishing paddy mud,
Rustle bump shuffle ssshhh care and prepare.
Is the one ahead or behind asshole or bud?
Stop come here whispers front toothless Fred.
Quiet; I kin smell 'em get ready lest ya'll'r dead.
Radio now; a class said what and that one why?
Can't remember just lead you, fuck no time to learn.

Names I Can't Remember

Cant wait Freddie fires, panic screams and tracers fly.
Will I survive shit shiver some way to get them through?
Kid twenty cocky is all I got God what have I gotten in to?
Dink kid man enemy died,
Soldier hog slaughter slung,
Wrist and ankles tied,
Pole tip to tip.
Belly blood n' bouncing bowels flop left to right,
Combat virgins carrion carry a trophy of the night.
So brothers bury others in dignity,
Corporal and I choke puke designed reality.
Squirming mass of birthing maggot flies,
Dance, feed and fight on oozing anus ears eyes.
My bar of glory gold,
Ain't worth never taught lies
Fifty lives to spend, save have damned
Jesus fucking Christ, I'm in command?
Will I survive shit shiver some way to get them through?
Kid twenty cocky's all I got, God what have I gotten in to?

Forward march the pimpled Corporal and I.
He won the toss carrying the front.
I shouldering the bouncing pole behind,
Through a silent kid killer gauntlet
Chins down and eyes desperately closed.
Heartbeats call cadence for the riderless steed
Yo gotta go home when yo le-oft, your righ, soun aww!
It's only rock and roll your soul, three foe!
I must look but he must feel.
Who has it worse Corporal kid or Lieutenant me?
Le-oft right bring it on down, heart horror cries?
Or flies feeding on maggot jelly dead Dink eyes!
The dead father mother brother husband between,
Inner tears quench fires in a hell horrored heart.

Miles to got with every step,
I see and see again oozing eyes,
Swarming masses of maggots birthing lies.
No hate to feel just volcano sorrow,
I he, he me respect killed all enemies
First, last and only boy man tomorrow.
Squeaking pole cadence left right left,
Guts flop here, guts flop there so where's the soul?
Squish mud steps gimme that ol time rock an roll.
Bring it down, one two three four, one two, three FOUR!
Silence, no screams, no laughs or words,
Of letters home, beer or spade trumps ace.
Soldier boys nineteen silent in sorrow
Our enemy dead brothers no more tomorrow.
Thinking, walking so little time but all has changed,
The night before all laughed and giggled,
Stood afar and swaggered chests puffed with pride,
The butter bar six month Lieutenant so stupid arrived.
Fuck you fuck an-aay so stay away,
Blood buys respect bar means shit no more.
Shove the rank up your ass. What will ya do Lieutenant,
Send us to the fucking war?
Insult blood shoved in my face,
Lessons learned last for a virgin whore.
New meat scum just last night.
Glory boy dreams all are gone.
Corporal freckles and punk Lieutenant carried dead from
     the fight.
No words, no looks yet we two virgins knew
We were now men glorious war had pissed upon.
We smiled weak in sorrow and turned away.
Losing virginity the face bloody now sudden way.
Last night, Fuck you fuck-an-ay stay away,
Shouted old timers their killer hearts in blood wades,

They wander up to whisper, "You play cut throat spades?"
Will I survive shit shiver some way get them through?
Nineteen hard-on dear God what have I gotten in to?

Jim Lipka aka Cat Man, 1999

Cat Man, 1969. See Mees the Cat on his shoulder?

The real Cat Man and Mees.

Names I Can't Remember

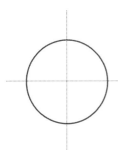

Store Bought Teeth

December 1969

"His wisdom was the poetry of common sense. Hillbilly Freddie turned a hello into a novel full of giggles and lessons for life. It was easy. Kill first or breathe last for a hero's just a coward more afraid of doing nothing."

Freddy's toothless smile was the Santa Claus in all this Gladiator gut carnage garbage.

It was a sleepy morning after my first honor and glory night in command first kill. I'd led terrified boys into the midnight, brought home crying men at sunrise, left a punk kid, and returned a murderer with a brave boy's rotting carcass tied to a pole. I was no longer exuberant boy or romantic virgin but an impotent and weary old man with acne bleeding reality. Getting drunk enough to blackout sleep, Sarge grabbed my scruff of the neck like an alley cat,

157

and kicked my ass out the door.

"What the—"

"Shut your mouth and run, Lieutenant!"

Cowering behind the Rice House, Sarge put a finger to his lips and pointed at Freddy. He stretched and greeted the morning with a toothless grin and yelled, "Ooo Eee what a good Lord mornin'! What a mighty fine day. Once I get the skunk outta ma mouth and the porcupine outta my ass, I will smite the Lord's enemies."

"Still no teeth," he scowled so loud it woke boys who scattered. "Lord, when I find that diddle dang draft board Yankee who promised me teeth, Iz gunna feed him his balls, rip out his heart, and feed it to hogs. When he begs mercy Lord, let my fist deliver it. I got no fucking teeth! I wan-em today! Oh Yah Lord, kiss Maw fer me an a spit a rain fer the crop would be right nicely of Yah. Amen."

I laughed. I thought Sarge tapped me on the shoulder to share the fun. What I saw was not a good sign. Sarge's flabby, chicken shit hero ass was running for his life. The shoulder tap came again. I turned. It was Freddy, sounding like heaven, looking like hell.

"Morning, Sir," he said in a smiling whisper. "Do I get ma' teeth I was promised today?"

I couldn't answer. His fist strangling my nuts had something to do with my shortness of breath.

Freddy was a kid who loved his Maw, possum pie, and his bottom-land. His toothless grin was a peaceful lullaby. Despite the nightly killing, his boundless happiness put us all at ease. Freddy didn't cotton to lies. His hell was the draft man that promised him the store bought smile. He was an ignorant kid with a man's Ph.D. in survival. His wisdom was the poetry of common sense. This cunning son-of-a-bitch could kill first because he smelled the enemy with his bloodhound's nose. It was easy. Kill first or breathe last. He was our out front, point man scout that faced death first to save lives.

I hated and envied his smile that confused the shit out of me. The guy was happy even with boys betting their lives on his ability to smell the enemy before they pulled the trigger. Why wasn't he sad and afraid like me? Why didn't his face reflect the same pressure and worry? Many smiled to break the tension of combat's eternity of boredom interrupted by orgasmic seconds of manic and ruthless terror. Freddy's smile was his heart. Ours masked fear. He didn't give a damn for the war. The Army was his chance to finally get the dang store bought teeth never in the only copy of the Sears Wish Book in Possum Pie Kentucky.

The insanity of Freddy's happiness was he risked his life the most. He was part hillbilly and all bloodhound. He could smell enemy a half mile away. Night fights were bump into the other panic explosions. They never were movie screen Waterloos seen and heard miles off while drums thundered last heartbeats. Point men died most because they found battles first. The job was rotated but not with Freddy. The nut loved it and we liked living. Why interfere with a man's happiness? He knew enemy with brains and balls let point men go by to kill the larger main body. Point men were the first to die or the last alive to carry the dead. Keeping us alive got him a day closer to his Army teeth.

"Lieutenant, y'all may hate it but there be livin' and dyin' so best get to the killin' 'er git in the grave. I be the best," was his homespun homily of common sense.

The boys made jokes about his lack of schooling and uncanny sense of smell like he was all nose and no brains. I laughed too but hid it. Freddy never angered at any taunt or joke. He wore the attention like a Medal of Honor for the ultimate risk of others who trusted him with their lives. When Freddy was with the squad you went out with, he had earned that respect. Maybe his toothless smile was tears of thanks he hid from us.

Our gladiator's trust was the ritual of the letters.

The moment came at dusk just before we went out to set a night ambush. The squad member whose turn at point it was, went to the boy he thought the unit trusted most. The quiet stare was the request to save their lives. If accepted, the man so offered would hand over his letter home should he die in first contact. That man then gave back all the letters in case the point man was the only one alive. Words, salutes, or handshakes weren't needed. Others were shown the same trust and respect when Freddy deserved a rest. Last letters is how we became men saying I love, trust, and goodbye without words.

No one had the guts to ask Freddy why he took on all the extra insanity. I had the gold bar that gave me the stupid for the whole platoon. My gut said someone had to listen.

"Life sings a song of its own, sir. I go to listen."

"How does that help, Fred?"

"When death comes up the holler, the hymn's the same as living just the tune's a might off. It's my job to know who ain't singing. Change in the tune, pucker time's coming. I got to spot when."

"How do you do that, Freddy?"

"The living has the wind in his face. You always pick spots for us to go an' wait for Dinks. Right, Sir?"

"Right."

"Pick spots that keeps us walking with the wind in my face so I can smell 'em first. The dead have the wind at their backs."

"I'll keep the wind in your face, Freddy."

"Much obliged," Freddy said, with his black hole grin as he walked away. "Dad-blasted army promised me, LT!"

Freddy then made his daily radio call to HQ to yell about his ever pending dentist appointment. Only generals got dental appointments. Freddy couldn't figure out why generals had such rotten teeth. Getting that appointment would be a breeze if it was battle related. His grandest plan was sticking his ass in the line of fire. He figured if the government believed the Warren Commission that one bullet could turn ninety degrees, he could claim the very same shot in the ass blew out his teeth.

Watching Freddie yell into the radio, I knelt at Sarge's side. He had some soap and water in his helmet. Together, we were washing off the mud we got covered with the night before. Failing with every attempt to turn the dead enemy's body to check for booby traps, Sarge and I buried a lot of fear in that mud. Every time we tried turning the body, we dove deeper and sucked a last breath waiting for the explosion that never came.

"Mud don't taste half bad does it, Sir?"

Names I Can't Remember

"Never knew how great 'till now, Sarge!"

"Any ideas how we can help Freddie with that teeth thing, Sir?"

"Thinking," I sighed, at that smiling hillbilly.

"Funny, Sir. It's easy to die. The hard part's being frightened and a leader. Pass me the soap. How that ignorant kid got so happy and wise I'll never know."

"It's amazing isn't it, Sarge? Coulda' gone blooie. But you were the hero that turned that body over."

"Huh? I was shaking lots. I figger a hero's just a coward more afraid of doing nothing."

"Sarge, that sounds like Freddy."

"Damn. Was it the figger that clued you it was his, too? I'm losing my touch stealing lines from the only kid that wants teeth more than he fears death. What's say we help him? In this sweat hell, we owe him a cool breeze."

"I guess we better keep the wind in his face," I said.

I couldn't figure if Freddy's grin let all the joy in or the horror out. The twinkle in his green eyes made life simpler. Despite his dental tirades, it was impossible to not enjoy being with him. With a hillbilly drawl, Freddie turned a simple hello into a novel stuffed with giggles and lessons for life. He'd deliver them with a devilish grin.

"An ig-or-ant man knows he don't know but a stupid man thinks he does. Like the city fella needing help. In the time that big city boy a rambled on about how he followed that map, I could have slit a hog, pit cooked it, and been a picking my teeth 'tween belches. When he took a breath and finished a yapping, the log I were a whittlin' were a toothpick. I spat a chaw and looked him in the eye a sayin' how come I'm the only one that knows where he be? I swear, give a Yankee enough rope, an he'll hang hiz-sef!"

Freddy's smile was his joy for life no matter how tough. It was in all his stories. Once he had us hooked, he took out the dreaded piece of paper that the recruiter had given him promising him his teeth. He always did it with such gradual charm; you never knew you were the stupid coon gladly setting your foot in his bear trap story.

"Damn Yankee recruiter seen my toothless smile a mile away 'fore

I yelled howdy. His snaky charm turned a live yes into a dead maybe. Son, how'd y'all like sparklin' n' spankin' showroom new Uncle Sam store bought teeth fer nary a nickel ner a dime? The slimy bastard had my mark on that paper in a eye blink. Says all I gots to do is drop into the clinic a stone's throw from some big city Saigon."

Freddy was hell bent to find the clinic. He showed the useless form to any jerk who'd listen. He'd been promised teeth and teeth he'd have. He didn't need a gun. His plan was simple; gum us to death with persistence. Later, I saw him carving on a thick hunk of tree. The bits of wood flew but the stick just got smaller.

"What is it, Fred?"

"A stick, Lieutenant."

"No, no. I mean what are you whittling it into?"

"Nary a thang. It is what it is an' jes' tells me what parts to carve away, what parts to leave it be."

"But it's just a stick."

"I reckon that's what it's a mind to be. Beautiful?"

"I suppose it is just that, Freddy. Mind if I ask you a personal question? Just between you and me?"

"Ah, a preacher question."

"Yes. A preacher question."

"Yes, I have, Lieutenant an' I didn't go blind. Kinda' liked it I must say. Still do."

"Huh? Oh! I didn't mean that. I was just wondering. All the other guys are so worried and nervous. But you are so happy. What makes you smile so much?"

Freddy got a twinkle in his eye and he thought. All around us, he winked at his buddies. They all smiled behind me waiting for his charm truck to flatten me.

"Jes' got hungry fer skunk."

"Huh?"

"Ah. City boy, huh? It's like this. All day long, I got a powerful hunger for possum pie. When I got to the trap, danged ifin' I didn't find skunk. So, I jes' got hungry for skunk. Don't make sense to starve for possum like these boys with a trap full of a skunk do it, Lieutenant?"

"No. No, it doesn't Fred.

Freddie reached in his pocket and all those nosey soldiers ran off. Gingerly, he unfolded the crumpled paper from his pocket and rose to stand nose to nose with me.

Freddie clicked off his rifle safety. "I really want ma' store bought teeth." He chambered a round. Card games stopped. Beer belches were stifled. As his finger twitched on the trigger, he directed his pinched eyes seething anger to me, "You ever live in the South, the shoot now ask names later South, LT?"

"Li— li— lived in Nashville a while, LONG while!"

"Up the holler by me an' Maw in Possum Pie, Nashville is a pit a Yankee snakes shot fer pig slop. Where y'all from?"

"Chi- Chicago, ah Windy City, friendly Windy City!"

"That'd be a might north a Nashville." Freddy scowled and spat some slime tibakie chaw on his finger to wet his rifle sight for a dramatic and threatening tad of Kentucky windage. He raised his rifle and pointed it at my nose.

"Fred, getting an elective dental appointment at a front lines unit is—well, it's all but—"

His shot singed my nose clean of hair. "Crap I done heard makes me miss only the first time. You was saying, Lieutenant?" he said, slamming another round in the chamber.

"I'll work on that appointment right away!"

"Be that ma' dang twitchy trigger fanger dancin?"

"Tomorrow, OK?"

Freddie clicked his safety back on. He smiled. My heart moved from my throat back to my chest. All the guys behind me smiled too. Then the laughter started.

Freddie slapped me on the back while all the men laughed. He said I was the only one to fall for the joke so bad. Freddie and I shook on the promise. I'd do my best to get him those store bought teeth if he promised to let me keep my nuts.

Fred wisely accepted his ignorance and was humble. He'd lived more library books than any of us would ever lie about reading. When guys kidded him about where he was from and how he spoke, I tried

Store Bought Teeth   *163*

to step in. His big brother look stopped me.

"No need to be hard on 'em, Lieutenant. I ain't bothered. Some folks won't ever learn how insults just show how stupid they are. Let 'em make fun of me. Just pity 'em like I do. Some a ma's learnin' is how to deal with them. 'Sides, when my learning runs out, a shovel full of dirt's going to smack me in the jaw."

"Life's a journey, not a destination," I whispered.

"Right nicely put, Lieutenant. Them boys got to learn the cut of a man is what he does not the fancy words he kain't say. They remind me of the teacher that goes to his dumb friend's house to make fun of him. He pokes fun at the dumb friend's laundry on the line 'til he spies his missus' naughties hanging there."

"Thanks for the lesson, Freddie. Much obliged."

Fred walked off with a smile and a wink. It was the same grin he had when he walked away from every toothless taunt and hillbilly crack. Our Possum Pie Galilee man overflowing gentleness and fury wandered over to some boys angrily playing cards and told more soothing yarns from a Bible with a hillbilly twang.

God, I wanted him to live. He alone among us deserved it. I laughed aloud for the first time because he alone among us would care the least about being dead.

Despite his toothless grin, Freddie was bilingual. He spoke amity and savagery fluently. It was all backwoods wisdom to him. Eat or be eaten without remorse or anger. His life in the backwoods taught him all the tricks he used to know where death was before it found him. The best of it he learned from other Point Men that came home in the morning. Oddly, they never talked to one another. They spoke rituals and tricks that kept them alive.

Before marching to that first battle that night and every night after, I watched Freddie get ready long before the rest. It was a survival high mass of Point Man stuff.

He walked around, his nose high. A sniff here at a bush, a tree, mud, water, animal dung, human feces, and so on. Like a lion with a limp and the oldest, deepest scars, he brushed against it all. He would know every scent of the jungle and use them to mask his own.

Names I Can't Remember

He roamed with one ear leading. I saw a Maestro hearing every note of the deadly night symphony. At the sudden sound of each insect or bird, he jerked and listened. He listened to the sound feet made crunching the earth and the whisper of cloth against a branch or leaf. He memorized every note. He knew death isn't in the melody of the night but in the sudden note of a stranger, the crack of a limb or squish of mud, out of place, and never heard before. He knew what notes the jungle never sang.

Point Man tricks helped him see in the nights so black his hand disappeared, and hear what shouldn't be there. In the barrel of his rifle, he placed a thin branch. It felt first what he could not see so he could feel death before it shook hands. Noisy bootlaces were tucked to prevent any sound. Mud was slapped on every metal surface and inch of skin to quiet any screaming shine. He stomped his boots in dung to kill the fragrant aroma of leather. His rifle strap had long been replaced with a simple string that had no noisy metal clasp. He flicked bits of mud and froze listening as it hit everything listening for any reaction.

After I first watched these rituals, I got drunk. The second time, I got drunker. I was the coke kids best beer customer. I couldn't handle it. I was den mother to a pack of killers writing Mom. The drunker I got, the lonelier I got. After the handshakes, I was no longer one of them. I could kibitz at card games, take in their bitch of the day, or throw a dirty joke on the pile of laughter. I was tolerated not welcomed. They had each other to bitch at and share the fear with. All I could do was yell at my gold bar. Sarge helped as much as he could but in the end, I was the officer not him. As senior enlisted man, his job was the mission and protect the men by keeping me from killing them with stupid not make me a better man. My gold bar said I'd learned that. Yet, he knew sapphires don't make a skank a starlet. Sarge had to be a teacher priest in a past life.

One night early on, I drank so much they left me at the Rice House. They had every right to shoot me. No one wanted a drunk plotting artillery. They didn't know what a true drunk I was. To boost moral, I traded for seven quarts and hid two for me. I was the happiest killer there, hung over but happy.

The night they left me back, I stumbled out to piss. That's when I first saw the man with a cat on his shoulder. In my drunken haze, I ignored the quirky stranger. A floppy leather hat hid the eyes of the lean man with a bushy beard. A curved meerschaum pipe snaked out of his mouth and filled the cool night air with the aroma of Latakia that smoked cool but stunk. He wore a tattered leather vest, faded jeans, and a tie-dyed shirt. Beneath the whiskers was a wicked grin. He stood casually slumped. The oddest of it all was the black as night cat curled around his neck purring in his ear.

"What the fuck's going on here?" I mumbled, with my cock in my hands and a boozy grin.

"You're pissin' away lives you don't own," growled Mees the cat.

When I turned back to yell again, they were gone in the night. I swear I heard Cat Man's hearty laugh and the sound of purring echoing far off. The next instant I think, Sarge shook me awake, poured some water down my gut to soften the hangover, rolled me back over to sleep it off, and mumble my loneliness to a Cat Man.

On my own, I would have stayed a stumble drunk every damn day. They could fight, argue over cards, brag about bravery, strut, intimidate, and read mushy letters from home to burn off fear and anger. All I could do was get drunk alone. When the hookers on scooters came, a poncho was strung up as a curtain. I was invited to get in line with cash and wait my turn listening to the lifeless groans of ecstasy with an accent. I didn't. All I could think of was a grimy trailer in Georgia where two limp dick kids blushed at each other. I got drunk over love lost in the passion of cash from embarrassment not lust. There was too much happening to guzzle beer constantly. The coke kid thieves had supply problems and booze was a rare scrounge.

Another afternoon close to sundown, I watched him again. Freddy wasn't grinning his usual toothless smile. It was a sad look. In his hand was an opened letter from home and a sealed response.

The reason officers exist is to have someone to blame. To my men, I was the outhouse where they shit every bitch. It was the cost of my new silver bar. I'd been promoted, not for honor or bravery, but because booze kept my ego from babbling enough stupid to not drop quicker than a hillbilly, nigger or spic. Freddy's look sent a shiver of terror through me. It was time to leave for the night's ambush site. I couldn't spot his problem. I sat on the Rice House stoop at his side trying to lead not panic.

"Ya'll got a minute, Lieutenant?" Freddie weakly whispered.

"Sure. What's up?" was my firm but worried response.

 He fumbled with his letters.

"What's in your letter, Freddie?"

"Ma' teeth."

"Your teeth?" I asked incredulously.

"Not 'sactly, sir. The words is from Maw. Sarge read me what I couldn't cipher. She was a sayin' how proud she'd be to see me with my store bought teeth."

 Suddenly, I saw it. There was no mud on his face.

"I don't get it, Freddie. You don't have them yet. How'd she get that idea that you did?"

"Well, Sir, I'm rotating home not long from now."

"Ninety days. You are an official Short Timer now."

"I figgered I'd a had 'em by now an' I reasoned—"

"Tell her but you couldn't hold back the exultation."

"NO! I always hold my wind till I'z in the out house!"

"Brag, Freddie, Brag."

"Never served at Ft. Brag, Sir."

"You perjured yourself, you ignorant jerk," I cajoled.

"No, Sir! I'm a savin' myself fer marriage."

"OK, you were a bit economical with the truth," was my last try at humor that had no effect.

"Naw. It was an all cash lie," he sighed.

 Looking down to laugh a bit, I choked on fear. His bootlaces were untied, able to make noise. Noise Kills..

"A little lie to save hurt feelings is OK, Freddie."

"Maw's a real Bible lady, Sir."

"Thou shalt not kill and eye for an eye, Freddie. She knows that confusion and will forgive you. What's wrong?"

"I, I..." he tried with moist eyes. "I never, and I mean NEVER, lied to Maw. It tain't Bible right."

"Ohhhh."

"When I was knee high to a sow belly, she slit the hog cheek to jowl but let me dig out the entrails. All the while, she was sayin' what the Pastor had said, that the poison in them was all the lies on God's green earth. She made me swear I'd never do such an evil thing to her. I lied to Maw, Lieutenant, and jest don't give a damn no more."

He shoved his letter home in my hand in a disgusted way and shuffled off, rifle and chin dragging.

Freddy was dragging his cherished rifle in the dirt behind him. There was no feeler stick in the barrel. Walking away, he looked back at me. Sarge and many of the men stood with me. It was the only time we saw fear in Fred's eyes and no toothless smile on his face.

It was nearing sundown, almost time for the letters ritual. This usual moment of pride, trust, and honor was now a funeral for a kid's puppy. Freddy's despair had infected the unit. No one wanted to collect the letters. The duty fell to a New Meat replacement. He'd seen Freddy's letter sadness and ignoring his point man rituals. After the new guy collected all the letters, he paused. You could see his eyes fill with brightness as he got a brilliant idea. With the cock sure swagger of a punk who'd never wondered which guts go in what belly, he'd decided to boost Freddy's self-confidence. He gave the letters to Freddy with a smile. Then something happened that wasn't part of the ritual and had never happened before. One by one, every man walked over to Freddy and took his letter *back*. The trust was gone. I saw Freddy slump and his spirit sink into deeper despair with each angry retrieval. A sigh of agony flooded out of Freddy when he looked up and saw Sarge and me last in line. I couldn't look him in the eye. I just took my letter and slinked away. It was the only time I was a kid, one of them, not the asshole with a silver bar. I should have loved being one of them finally. I took a big slug of booze. I heard Oleanna in my head. That chorus of glory angels sounded like graveside moans. I hated myself. The cocky New Meat who'd had the bright idea finally saw this was a killing place not a kegger. He crumbled to the ground and trembled in heaving sobs.

Freddy looked at his own letter and stepped forward. I grabbed him by the arm.

"Don't. I gots to do this. The wind's at my back."

Freddie no longer trusted himself. When even he slammed his letter into Sarge's hand, I heard a collective gasp of horror. Looking at Sarge, I could see the anger and fury in his eyes. Panic had set in. His children were crumbling and he had to stop it or we'd all die that night. Mother Hen Sarge kicked into high gear. He grabbed Freddy by the scruff of the neck and pulled him aside. Near a tree and out of earshot, we all watched them argue. While Freddy resisted, Sarge was scribbling on paper.

The sun was setting when Sarge and Freddy returned to the center of the wake.

"Sarge made me tell Maw the truth. He says that what all Maws does is, understand and fergive," he said, sliding a feeler stick in the barrel of his rifle.

The men gave their letters back to him. With each, he tucked boot-laces, smeared mud on his face, and his toothless smile returned. I was last one to give my letter.

"Wind's in ma' face, Lieutenant," he said, with moist eyes.

I saluted him.

Sarge yelled "saddle up." Frightened boys transformed themselves into killers again. I watched that line march into the dark night led by a swaggering hillbilly. I swear I heard that cocksucker whistling Oleanna with a drawl.

So alone again, I guzzled booze, felt sorry for myself, and hated my guts, a normal day.

Sarge was a maniac the next morning leading a gang of insane boys. He got on that radio and ripped every officer from the captain to the general a new asshole. He motivated our scrounger to borrow a jeep for Freddy's transport. Our unit poet with a record for bad checks suddenly discovered transit orders from the division dentist. Guys worked in shifts to teach Freddy how to read and write far better than his Dick and Jane plus X signature ability. He excitedly cyphered the articles in Playboy all were shocked to learn even existed. I held out my steel pot and asked volunteers to contribute cash for his dentists', ahem, fees. Sarge was my hardest sell. I told him he had to stimulate cash flow. He cried like a baby tearing up all those poker IOUs. We made a deal. The night five cases of T-bone steaks vanished from the generals mess and wound up at the non-commissioned officers club in the rear, ah, I was AWOL from the platoon and couldn't account for my time. Freddy's dental appointment was the next day. He picked up his store bought teeth a week later. When he and Sarge drove up honking and yelling to the applauding guys, Sarge winked at me while he was picking steak from his teeth and belching. Freddie stepped from the jeep and bowed to his clapping and yowling buddies. The kid with a Polaroid took a picture and gave it to Fred. That hillbilly rose proudly to show off the whitest, biggest, toothy grin ever and walked off with the snapshot, paper, and pen to write Maw.

Forgetful drunk that day every after, I remember a store bought teeth smile bigger than any sorrow.

Possum stew n' rabbit Sunday pie,
White lightin' yowls oh ya-hoo!
Down the holler hear firey preachers spunk
If'in the trap be a empty, sweet 'tater stew.
Stop a droolin' fer possum n' get hungry fer skunk.
It's so dern simple livin' wind in yer face.
Lordy keep me downwind of the hate race.
Diein's so dern damn dang easy,
Livin' makes ya white lighting sweat n' tired queasy.
If'n I go, if'n I stay
Makes no mater any way.
Killin' skunk there same as here.
Maw jes trust me back in a while.
Ain't no lies in this toothless smile.
Warm fire blaze'n high dancing angels in yer eyes
Yonder one makes ya shiver cracklin' maybe's n' lies

Hard to cotton killin' fer hate I ain't got.
Paw kin y'all tell me what I gots ta know?
Son, aim true fer his hate's yer heart spot.
Maw'ill cry n' yer traps ta check 'fore next snow.
I'll be home last moon Maw nary first leaf,
Draft man promised me store bought teeth

I never saw the billowed breath icy mountain air
While wood song sings each blue and fire sky dawn,
When the trap is cleared and prey struggle to breathe,
The rocked edged stained knife at it's throat.
Just one last cry from the evening meal.
There are no furry smile tears when hungry cries,
Just one long swift and bloody cut cheek to jowl
And the putrid steam from spilling guts warmed his
    hands.

I never saw him wipe his bloody hands
On well worn wish book jeans torn and patched,
When he sliced, chewed and smiled so good
The fresh kill prize I was not there.
I missed the proud walk home the hound begging
For a tasty prize of what buzzards would not eat.
When he smiled and held the prize high to all,
Dinner would be a long absent feast of plenty yells,
I didn't see them rip the flesh from the meat.
Can I hear the story songs they sang,
Stomping dances to entertain,
Stories told white light'nin colored
Of strangers new and coal air sucked?
Did I see the bones tossed to critters
And hides set aside, what was it alive?
No matter the stew is gone and smiles abound.
He'll hunt again to quiet the belly growl
Without me there while he slaughters life.

I never saw him teach the youngin warrior,
Smell the meal this way, slash and cut that,
Bash the head and kill it quick
For slow blood death spoils the prize.
Gut and trash the entrails for scavengers,
Yet keep the severed head prize to boast.
You now will hunt and feed for I am gone,
To hunt and slaughter what I will not eat.
The toothless grin no longer smiles.
I never saw his I must go Maw sadness.

I saw the boy man to whom killing came easy
When hunger and fear started every day.
I saw the man who smelled it coming,
Bet his life saving me and all who never lived his way.
I saw, I saw, did I ever saw the man at all?
Just that toothless grin so happy wide,
His soul dripping out of all that smile,
Something surely saddens him.
But that I never knew as he left his maw in tears.

Who will slaughter stew for you,
Gut the belly and scramble for the bloody flesh,
While flies fight critters for putrid scrapes
And the rotting smell fills the air?
I never saw the sorrow over who will kill.
For those he left sad behind,
To slaughter so easily what he would not eat.
Save my life and boy men lives given me.
Such glory and adulation I owe one I never knew.
I hate me not knowing what saddened him.

Thanks Freddie for my, our lives you did bequeath
Thank God for those fucking store bought teeth.

Names I Can't Remember

Brothers look out for each other.

Doofus in training

Names I Can't Remember

Doofus

JANUARY 1970

"Forced to help him, our Doofus was the best failure for the worst fears. He was hope. An angry boy became a proud man when forgiveness welcomed the worst and weakest I into Us."

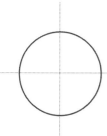ne quiet morning, I was staring out the Rice House window watching the accident-prone kid trip over the laughter behind him. I turned to Sarge.

"Who's he?" I asked, looking at a kid alone.

"The Doofus?" he giggled, while cleaning his rifle.

"Why Doofus?" I asked, cringing.

"Look at him, LT. That kid doesn't walk. He stumbles. Why, he has no business being in combat," Sarge said, insultingly while punching me in the arm.

"Doofus, sounds like a Fudsy trying to grow up in a whore house," I sighed, remembering heaven and hell angel Silkie.

"What's a Fudsy, Sir? Hmph, maybe a Doofus without an ego or commission?" Sarge whispered to me alone with the fatherly stare. "Guys have to make fun of something. I think he likes it. Look at the goofy look on his face. He bumbles just to catch himself with every step. Awkward is a compliment to him, the poster child for Uncle Sam Doesn't Want You!" Sarge said, laughing loudly.

Everyone could hear Sarge, even Doofus. He looked through me to Sarge like a deer trying to get the guts to run from the headlights. The best he did was trip while guys taunted with pointed fingers. Only I felt the hurt and anger beneath the smile on Doofus' face.

He was pale, five six with a large nose and bucked teeth. Despite our efforts to tie things down before going on ambush, his utter lack of coordination and confidence made him sound like a bouncing sack of cowbells and fingernails on a blackboard at a librarians' convention. He didn't write home to Mom. There was no joy in telling her you're the punch line for every insulting joke. His glasses were always on the tip of his nose. The weight of the thick lenses and endless sweat made sure he constantly poked himself in the face to push them up. His head and chin always tilted down. I guess it was his way to show a defiant smile and hide the hurt at the same time. No one wanted to be near him. He never talked. He constantly whined, his tattered flag of surrender to ineptness. Yet, he never stopped trying. I hated looking at him and myself for quickly looking away. Before I found the angry and self-righteous drunk in me, we were the same kids stuffed in wastebaskets and never picked to play. I didn't want to remember. Remembering the weak is the fear of I and death of you unless survived as we.

Our brilliant General decided every patch of jungle shown as a thousand-meter map square needed an emergency, helicopter-landing zone cut in it. The duty to hack them out rotated from unit to unit. Most had to be cut in enemy areas since we stayed in the flat land near the highway. These L.Z.s had to be cut fast since you'd be out of the range of the most quickly available artillery and too remote for instant helicopter or ground rescue. Ten men dropped in by helicopter spent two frantic hours chopping jungle. Speed was life. Chop fast and split before Dinks got there and killed you. The far out chopper ride was fantastic. In the sweaty stink, card games, beer belches, and fart contests weren't fun. There are only so many ways you can write, "I love you, Mom" or "I want to fuck your brains out, babe." The distracted who accidentally mixed up their letters got strange answers.

When my platoon got the duty, I decided to lead the ten men that would go. to impress the hell out of them all

"Sir, it's the third squad's turn for this duty, without Doofus?" Sarge asked sharply, to make a point.

I looked at the goofy kid falling over his happiness as the rest of the squad packed their gear. I wandered over to a card game on an ammo crate to break the bad news. Doofus' squad members saw me coming. The taunts and insults started again.

"Son, lemme' talk to yah over here," I said to Doofus.

Although I held him up, the kid clanked and stumbled.

"I ain't ever had the door seat—," he squeaked.

"Listen, I want you to hang back here as my... radio commander," I lied with a phony smile and slap.

"Sir, your R.T.O. sleeps most of the time. The only radio traffic we get is about no toilet paper, lost mail, cold food, and dead buddies. LT, don't reassign me. Screwing up is what I do best. If you take that away from me too, I got nothing left but the laughter," he begged, looking me straight in the eye.

We prepared for the two to four hour jaunt it was expected to be. We didn't take our normal rucksacks with 50 plus pounds of water, ammo, socks, poncho, and goodies. An ambush pack would be less than half that just water, ammo, butts, and fear hidden under BS.

On a bright sunny mid-day, we hopped in two helicopters and soared off over our dilapidated Rice House. The flight was high, cool, and a grab ass blast. Even Doofus had fun. Some had stripped down to bare chest or just a T-shirt to make the hot work easier.

For an hour, the jungle fell to create a circle on the top of a no one wants it hill. Boys hacked while swapping stories of hard-ons never had and well-fucked girlfriends never kissed. Beetle, Beach Boy or Lynard Skynard lyrics were butchered. Water was guzzled under the hot sun, even a can or two of beer. All was happy in pimple land. No one was cracking jokes about Doofus.

Ten boys were deep in enemy territory of tangled jungle green stretched to the horizon and beyond. We were isolated and alone but no one gave a damn. Out there, somewhere was hundreds or thousands of Dinks talking on the jungle grape vine. The helicopters were surely seen and the change in the jungle song surely gave them our exact location. We'd be long gone before they could do a damn thing about it. They probably left us alone on those stupid missions because we did work for them. L.Z.s never patrolled and seldom if ever used, gave them camps or gun positions that they could use against us.

Instantly, the hot, sunny, and cloudless sky was gray. B.S. ceased. Chopping got frantic. Eyes looked up. Sun gone, the blackness rumbled. Humid hot turned to shiver cold. Pea soup clouds sunk lower. Could the chopper get in to yank our stranded asses out of this fog? It began to rain. We thought we heard the helicopters. The soggy sky drowned their rumble to a faint pitter pat. All I heard was the heavy breathing of frightened kids. I guzzled booze and breathed the heaviest. The darker it got, the heavier it rained. I let the men see me coordinate our defense and extraction with the old man on the radio. I told HQ we would hunker down for the night and wait for a morning extraction. There was no one on the other end not even a hiss. Maybe I became a leader then earning the cocky Oscar for making my men feel safer. The lie worked. It softened some of that we're surrounded terror I saw on my kid's faces. We set up a night defensive perimeter. That meant, we're surrounded here so point the guns everywhere. We built jungle hooches to escape the monsoon. Even hope and fear didn't keep us dry. After great men fail, weather ends every war.

In the morning, the where's my nose rain and the fog would make a Russian writer ecstatic. We shivered in drenched clothes. The radio wrapped in plastic was soggy. The hill was oatmeal slop and metal rifles gurgled. Being isolated and cut-off made us shiver more than the cold rain. Dinks knew we were trapped and would soon attack.

I gathered the men. There were no captain's glory bars, colonel's honor eagle, or general's courage stars to save my ass. I was a punk on a hill surrounded by people who wanted to kill the ten boys whose lives were in my hands. I had no chips. I must bet eleven lives on a hand of bullshit. We could wait for better weather, rescue, slaughter, or hack our way out of enemy infested territory. Running was no safer. In jungle this thick, we could stumble into an enemy general's poker game. Where I lead would kill or save us; command hell. Eyes begged me to get them home to mamma.

"What's the order, Lieutenant?" asked the gutsy one, coldly.

They pleaded silently. Doofus' soggy booted feet about to stumble asked for help. The kid who had picked his fingers bloody from worry was screaming at me to be brave. The one with the drenched pulp letter home in his hand cried out for my honor. The boy with his hands clasped prayed for my glorious leadership. Those eyes bore into my gut and hacked me apart. I looked down to avoid their eyes. I didn't have the guts to tell them I had no idea what to do or where to go. After a slug of courage from my booze canteen, I laid it out. I hoped my booming voice would hide my knocking knee call for a vote. No one spoke. The silence was a Hiroshima panic.

"Pissing your pants yet, LT?" cracked the spokesman.

They had the right to shove my bar up my ass. I was.

Staying to defend our mud hole was not an option. We were the steaks surrounded by hyenas just released from Auschwitz. In the Dink's backyard, we were outnumbered a thousand to one. The risk of leaving was our side would be looking for us in the wrong place. I decided we would cut our way home. Running was the advantage of leaving where Dinks knew we were to lower less foggy ground and a shot at rescue. I argued it was better than waiting for the bullet marked To Whom It May Concern to arrive. Reading my ten-year-old map didn't matter. I'd slept through the class. Moving was a gigantic danger. Americans were noisy in the jungle and we had Doofus, a goofy noise champ.

As we hacked and slashed our way down the mountain in the fog, boys looked up, and strained to hear if the thump of a helicopter was in the fog yards above. The only sound was the Doofus. He was clanking, bumbling, falling, and whining to himself. We ignored him at first. We were used to his uselessness.

Later, we rested at an open level spot. Socks were twisted from drenched to soggy. The radio was taken out of the plastic to see if it worked. It crackled once but our pleas raised no one. Lost and alone, we needed something to blame. When one pacing boy bumped into Doofus, he kicked the gawky kid out of frustration. The rest did too. A defenseless lightening rod had been found. Doofus shivered from the fear of punches not cold rain.

We hacked further down the mountain. My impeccable navigation stumbled us into a ravine. Glaring at the old map I could barely read seemed to inspire. They smiled while kicking Doofus. I guess they figured I knew where we were. Maybe the V shaped ravine was less tangled and lead to a flatland stream. Brilliant. Water flows down hill was my Medal of Honor strategy.

It had sheer ground on each side, a shooter's alley. Unseen enemy could slaughter us like Carny targets in a line. Boys shared last water and booted Doofus' fallen ass. I guzzled sour mash courage. We tried calling HQ. The soaked radio didn't even hiss. Soggy asses rested on mush ground. Canteens were filled with diseased muddy drops. Chests heaved last gasp courage. The anguished eyes of empty souls looked up for chopper mirages. We fired illumination rounds. The foggy shroud yards above sucked them into oblivion. Doofus whimpered and sniffed for all to hate.

In dead humid air, hacking and slashing was the only misery left to breathe. Doofus was losing it in the thorny tangle with each fall and noisy clank. The men dumped fear and anger on him. He didn't fight or lash out. It made him braver! He demanded his turn to cut point. Suddenly he was three inches taller.

Doofus flailed at the jungle. His exhausted body bounced off it and fell. An odd thing happened quietly. One kid helped Doofus to his feet and took the machete to take his tired buddy's cutting turn. Everyone watched in wide-eyed surprise. An angry boy became a proud man when forgiveness welcomed the worst and weakest I into Us.

A collective gasp jerked the line of march to a halt. I moved up to see what the men were looking at. The gently sloping, rocky ravine had ended. The ground fell away at a sixty-degree angle to a slick rock face for a few hundred feet. Ninety degree straight up ground was on both sides. There was no option. We had to traverse the dangerous rock face. It was the only way down.

"I can't make it," Doofus sniffled.

"How's it going, private?" was my idiot brilliance.

"Could be better, Sir," he mumbled, not looking at me.

In his eyes was the sparkle of a gentle man that sighed hello, help me please showing his cheery look I'm a failure lonely eyes.

"No way we can carry you down this, kid."

"I know, Sir."

"Can I ask a question, kid?" I asked feeling confused.

"Sure, LT. What's on your mind?" he whined.

"How did you get in the infantry?"

"I failed at everything else, Sir," he said frankly.

I heard belly laughs being stifled by the rest.

"Can't type unit travel orders?"

"They said they'll find that company any day now."

"Cook?"

"The battalion will be out of the hospital soon."

"Supply clerk?"

"Sent the desert division goose down parkas."

I grabbed the coke bottle thick glasses off his face. With a scrap of a torn T-shirt, I fashioned a strap that held them firmly up in front of his eyes. "Better?"

"Yah, Sir," he beamed. "Gosh. I can see now. They slip so much, you know? Thanks bunches, LT."

"I know," I said pushing my glasses back up.

"Private, how'd you pass all the infantry physicals?"

"I ran so slow, no one noticed I was laps behind not yards behind. I only did two laps. They were so busy watching strong guys do chin-ups so fast I started counting at ten. I couldn't make eleven, my one, but eight was passing. How could I fail being a lug nut grunt? Even a monkey can carry a rifle or scream fear."

My knife blade glare cut off the laughter.

"How did you pass marksmanship? Did you hit the proverbial broadside of a barn?"

"What barn, Lieutenant? When we retrieved targets, I poked holes with a bullet.

We all laughed at the idiot with brass balls. It was the first thing we did together.

"Can you do anything?" asked one laughing soldier.

"Hell no, guys. I stink... at everything!? I am the funkiest stink bomb in this whole fart factory!" he said, bowing with glee at the laughter and applause he'd caused.

Doofus threw his steel pot down. Like Frankenstein over a cauldron, he looked for the ingredients to his recipe of immortality. We watched amazed as our wizard of inept gathered spices. Doofus smashed a useless radio battery and threw the smelly mess in his pot. He squeezed in sweat from T-shirts, gun powder from bullets, mud, a candy bar, hot sauce, smelly socks, and the gelatinous canned puke the Army called Ham and Eggs. To cook the stew, he pissed in it. The only thing missing was eye of newt. After stirring fiendishly, he poured the stench over him. Boys patted his back, and ran holding their noses. We hacked happy. If HQ couldn't see or hear us, they could smell us. If his cock-eyed scheme worked, Doofus was a hero. Even if it failed, our Alfred E. Neuman was the best failure for the worst fears. He was hope. He was one of us.

"Look where you are going, not at your feet."

"Here's my last TP. Keep those glasses clean, shit head," laughed another, slapping his back.

"Use your rifle like a cane to catch each step, man," suggested the next, laughing as he passed.

My booze finally tasted good. Doofus, the stink bomb, bumbled down that sheer rock face like a kid at his first surprise party. We inched down that slippery rock face picking him up with every fall. Everyone giggled waving their arms to clear away the stench that had monkey's moaning miles off. When he whined, we shot him the

Names I Can't Remember

finger. When he sat on his ass and complained, someone grabbed him by the scruff of his neck nearly strangling him to stand and walk tall with the squad.

Hours later and exhausted, we rested in a low patch of open ground. One by one, eyes squinted and ears turned skyward. Boys circled trying to find something they seemed to hear. The thumping was no longer a desperate mirage. Weak at first, the sound grew. Was it a helicopter? Guiding it, we fired illumination rounds into the dense mess. Slowly, some chopper jockey with brass nuts and a death wish felt his way through the clouds. Try swinging a flaming torch while holding an open gas can in the dark sometime. That puke green, butt ugly, dragon fly chariot emerging through a hangover gray sky, centerfold beautiful.

The chopper landed and out popped John Wayne! He was dark, swarthy, five-foot nothing, and chomped on a cigar that should have tipped him over. Only the ego stuffed in that puffy chest and gold leaf on his collar stopped it.

"Who's in charge of this stinking mess?" he bellowed, holding his nose and strutting about.

It was a group smile and a shove that pushed Doofus.

"PFC... Doofus Stinkbomb reporting, Sir!" he beamed, snapping a crisp salute and widest grin.

He was Major somebody from Battalion. His after-shave was equal parts olive oil, garlic, and conceit. I shook hands with this Italian Mighty Mouse. It isn't often you see starch stiff fatigues with a crease and spit shined boots so deep in the jungle. This blustery Major, bucking for a colonel's eagle and Medal of Cocky, spat tobacco juice. The chopper door gunner nervously eyed the jungle.

"Where's your gun ship escort, Sir?" I yelled.

"Grounded. I got tired of bad cards and filthy whores," he snorted with a grin. "When my boys are stuck out here, time to kick ass and take names air fucking mobile!"

I knew he'd make general for attacking every useless hill firing with bullshit and boys for a Custer body bag victory.

"How'd you find us, Sir?"

"West Point you ain't, son. Even an OCS jackass Lieutenant doesn't head higher and to the enemy," he said slapping, my back. "The fog turned us back over and over. Then the weirdest thing, some God-awful smell! Might have missed you without it."

The guys slapped Doofus on the back so hard he fell stunned and got up a hero with a big ass grin.

"It'll take two loads to get you all back, Lieutenant."

When I turned to select the first load, the chopper was already full of snickering boys. They flapped barren collars and saluted middle fingers to the bar on mine. I went to the Huey and got our heavy machine gun. The chopper groaned and shivered skyward. My last sight of it was the best. While the boys slapped and grab assed, Doofus was saluting. It was the crispest and best ever. Then it hit me. I was surrounded in the middle of nowhere, with a machine gun so soaked it might never fire, and a Mighty Mouse that thought balls could be fired from a gun.

"Sir, we should set a defensive position," I offered.

"What the fuck for, son? We got you, that M-60 machine gun, my 45 pistol, and the meanest ass cigar these Dinks ever saw! I could slaughter a Division with this sucker."

Back at the Rice House, I'd gotten a large goody package from Mom. In it were all the homemade cookies she'd baked, frozen rock solid, and wrapped in tin foil. There were cans of cherished fruit with that sweet cool juice and candy galore. The men got most, but the best was for me. I had asked her for a Polaroid and thick green sweater. Even in the sweaty sex humidity, monsoon season was shivery cold. Someone took a picture of us ten standing around a smoky fire and drying off. Shivering, we laughed, smiled, and devoured the goodies. No one mentioned we should have died that day. Ten boys came home one man. Our arms were around each other. I stood there stripped to my green boxer shorts and that warm green sweater. Doofus and I pushed our glasses up at the same time and smiled.

"What the fuck went wrong there?" I sighed.

The silent answer was a boyman ex-Doofus proudly beaming a ground-pounder warrior's smile.

What's-his-name made that big touchdown.
Who's-it was queen of the whatever prom.
Oh yah an' So-an-So the leader of lambs
To protest that thing we hated so.
Glory great remembered for what 'they' did
Yet all remember Doofus never picked to play
How healing his wounds saved us all that day

Weak whimpers whispered at every dance
Da Doofus, made us laugh, forever prance

There is no fear when you know you can't
Failure's the taste of shit you learn to love
When water is far in a blazing sun
Strong thirsty elephants return
For the one unable to run

Tinker toys lay in piles
Lincoln Logs askew in dust
Prom tux creased and never worn
Shoes and jersey virgin white
How did weakness win the fight?

Weak whimpers whispered at every dance
Da Doofus, made us laugh forever prance

In the cool crisp breeze of autumn life
Such blazing color I miss the black and white
Rainbows only gray in one shade's strife
Leaves one hole of fear in every fight
One potato two potato who's potato three
Herds of able leave the weak to die
I was he, thee is me the deserted lie
Mamma mamma can i play today?
Did the children pick you?

Hanging head he walks away.
Ahly ahly unson free,
Don't nobody wanna' play with me?
Geeky goofy flail trip fall,
Left alone at the ball.

Weak whimpers whispered at every dance
Da Doofus, made us laugh, forever prance

Weak whimpers whispered in the wind,
Red is red no matter who we bleeds,
Thee is we, you are me a desperate favor,
Weak is mightys' stinky glue savior
The warrior geek never picked to play
Saved the strongest one foggy day.

Grandma, What a Hard-on and Big Blue Balls You Have

FEBRUARY 1970

"Tell your Moms I refuse to let you die," said our Apollo from his winged chariot. Expert killers were boys scurrying for pencils. Drunk or sober, I wanted to suck his cock. Command was less lonely with another drunk at my side."

The day God stepped off the chopper, I couldn't tell which got out first; his square jaw, ego, or cock. My new CO was tall, rock hard, and ready to chew Ho Chi Minh's nuts off. His Green Beret was a peacock's plume flowing prick peak low over one ear and brow. He glared down at me over his raised nose with coal black eyes. He stood there with his chest ballooned, hands on hips, and one foot forward. His Caesar granite stance before his bloody and victorious legions screamed, "Worship me." His uniform was starch armor. His insignia weren't camouflaged. They were full color targets that growled, "Aim here shithead," defiance. Mortals lower their heads below the slashing chopper blades. He strode erect. His leather jump boots gleamed like an intimidating black stallion pounding the earth. Mud desperately tried to dry out rather than face a slow death of agony for soiling those diamonds.

His violent attitude erection was a sword that killed with its look. The end of its grip was at his highest rib. The balled end of the sheath was below his knee. The brass grip was wound with rich leather darkened by aggression oozing from massive hands. The scabbard was curved slightly and nubbed at the silver tip set with emeralds. The hand-guard tang was a gleaming silver skull delicately etched and scrolled with inlaid ivory and gold filigree. The sheath was exquisitely etched leather the color of richly creamed coffee. A closer look at its red star tattoo convulsed bile into my mouth. It was hand sewn human skin.

His icy silent stare froze our gaping jaws in awe. He exhaled carnage and looked at his sadistic disciples for the fiercest warrior. Nigger parted geek river wearing his foot-long ear necklace hard-on and stood balls to balls with the captain. Each knew no pride could have two alphas. They nodded imperceptibly with bloodthirsty contempt and respect oozing from their pores.

The captain's eyes scanned Nigger's gleaming black chest slicked with sweat and crossed by polished brass bandoliers of heavy machine gun ammo. He grabbed Nigger's razor sharp bayonet. We killers ready to run gasped. No one fucked with Nigger's stuff. The last idiot that did wouldn't be out of the hospital for a month. His claw like hand mashed the captain's and flung it off his bayonet. He took out the blade and placed it under the captain's chin at his throat. The sunlight dancing off the gleaming razor blinded the cocky officer. The captain reached down for a hunk of wood as thick as a man's arm, held each end, and presented the target. The black stevedore's massive blade severed the wood cleanly with one mighty blow. We

Names I Can't Remember

murmured our respect and fear of the warrior defending our honor.

The captain held his blade high with Stradivarian respect. My eyes pinched as the sun exploded off the diamond-like steel. The nearly translucent blue steel was far stronger and lighter than it looked. It could only be the rarest of Samurai weapons. It was pounded into thousands of mighty layers by wrinkled artisans guarding the Shoguns' secrets with severed tongues. The captain took hold of the blade tip and swiftly bent it to the opposite tip of the handle. He balanced the blade on a finger where he knew its center of gravity was. It didn't waver. He flung his silk scarf in the air. It floated across the gleaming steel and drifted away in two pieces.

"There's ten outside of Japan. Where the fuck you get a Diwahki in this rat hole?" asked Nigger in awe. It was the first thing our Goliath had said in a month.

The captain sliced his palm and Nigger's. Neither flinched. Mingled blood sealed the peace in their war of balls. A crisp salute dropped jaws further. Nigger's only show of respect was the finger to a general.

God then turned to us.

"You will write your mothers. Say I refuse to let you die," he said, in an ice-cube tone.

As our Apollo mounted his winged chariot to Olympus, last night's killers were boys scurrying for pencils.

"Oh-lee-ANNA
Oh-lee, oh-lee-ANNA"

Drunk or sober, I wanted to suck his cock.

Our Moses flew off to deliver his tablets to each platoon. The next day, a squad leader told me the ammo chopper was the old-man's. My Patton sure he could rescue Bastogne alone had been spotted at the far edge of the village. Referred to as walking the kill zone, he was alone staring at the jungle a few hundred yards away.

I grabbed my rifle and a snoozing radioman and rushed to meet him. Even with his ability to leap tall buildings in a single bound, he was New Meat. Having a new CO shot in my area would get me busted to private dick head KP king.

He glared stiffly waiting for a salute. I snapped one.

My short timer RTO ducked and jumped away.

"At ease, Lieutenant."

I wanted to angrily ask how a Special Forces god wound up with mud grunt mamma's boys. His scowl made it clear he wanted to sharpen his blade on my neck. I handed him my private whiskey canteen with a smile. Even an impudent drunk can save his ass spotting another one. We were both equal parts alcohol and ego.

"Measuring me for an Arlington plot, you sorry ass?"

I wanted to scream "yes." We wandered the far reaches of this small valley near Highway 1. The scenery was too beautiful to wonder about this out of place special ops Captain. God graced this valley with rice, rain, and a serene dignity. We were blowing it up with indifference. Morning sun gave my pale skin hand the pink, orangy glow of a crackling fire.

The white beach yards off was stained with blood and brass shell casings. Kids that should have been in school or the fields were collecting the valuable metal turned into trinkets sold to GIs. They fought over them despite finding the arms and legs of a competitor they'd argued with yesterday in this sandbox full of live rounds. Kids no older than eight fumbled with sticks and crude knives to remove the explosives from live shells.

One of the shells caught the captain's eye. He froze and stopped us with his arm.

"See anything different about this casing from those?"

"Nope. Just trophy junk," I said matter-of-factly.

"The others made a ridge of sand when they fell."

"So? That one has no ridge."

Gingerly, he swept away a thin layer of sand. The hidden string led to a grenade in the scrub. After pinning it, he probed under the casing with a feather light touch and found the primary trap. He pinned the frag like a surgeon bypassing my heart valve about to explode.

"Walk out of here in the same footsteps you walked in," he demanded. The RTO and I did. Then we breathed.

As we walked away from the bay, we entered the checkerboard

of small rice paddy plots that separated the ocean from the village. In perfect rows for a few hundred yards, dozens of them circled the tiny village. Foot high earthen dikes edged the small wading pools forty feet square. Cone-shaped hats worn by the peasants bobbed up and down as they planted seedlings and weeded. There was a gentle rhythm to this back breaking chorus sung by old men, women with babies slung on their back, and kids that never played hop-scotch or hide-and-seek.

The village was dying one rice bowl at a time. No battles were ever fought. Small Dink raiding parties stole rice and conscripts at night. Surviving was constant planting and having children to work in the fields. All they wanted was an evening meal. All we outsiders force-fed them was freedom pamphlets. No matter who won this war, they starved. Rice and rain filled bellies not ideas.

On the North end of the fields were two hills three hundred feet high. They curved in a graceful arch from the highway to where the fields met the beach. We stared at the lush green beauty. Cutting our way to the top to survey, I learned how deadly triple canopy jungle is. The bramble was a thorny mess that cut my skin bloody and blocked the sun. Hacking fifty yards is a good day's work. Jungle is a distant beauty. Up close, it strangles any life to death.

We struggled along the slope back to Highway 1. Its two black-topped lanes were an artery of life and commerce, a movie theatre of sorts. Black French cabs leftover from the colonial days raced from Hue to the north, to Da Nang to the south, through the torturous Hai Van Pass at Monkey Mountain. They were a whisper of all black running board mystery, in a loud war. Their snouts were long and low with gleaming chrome radiator covers. The front wheel wells were tall, curved, and sporty covers for white-wall tires with spoke rims. The trunk end was short and angular with a tiny oval window. They were expensive cabs imagined full of black market dealers, dope pushers, whores, and spies. Riders smoked slender foreign cig-arettes and leaned out of the windows to show off their colorful silk clothes bought in Saigon. Villagers with crinkled faces wondered why anyone would wear such fanciful stuff that would never last one day in the mud. There were the buses that groaned along. They were very old school type buses dented to ugly with a primer coat. All were loaded with the poor, sitting on the roof or the bumpers hanging on for life. They groaned and sputtered by daily, giving farmers time to giggle and get the kinks out of weary backs. We said little during the captain's inspection trip. War has always been the silent poetry in peasant smiles and killer's eyes.

The captain froze again on the dirt footpath. He was gazing at the pebbles telling him something.

"How far is it to your Rice House? Don't tell me."

My RTO and I hunched over my map.

"Two hundred ninety yards due east," the captain said.

"Bingo, Captain! How the—"

"Pebbles ground in the dirt. Not these. Two here, seven, and six there. I bet my balls if we sighted their line, we'd see your HQ. One farmer here knows more about mortars than rice, the one with the fewest calluses," he said, stroking his saber like a hard-on ready to ejaculate. A sadist smelled blood and smiled.

The noisy life of the village broke our somber mood. Among the thatched roof huts, venerated mammasans too old to work the fields chased laughing, running and naked babies. Narrow paths separated the rows of huts on both sides of the highway. We watched women sweep at the dirt walkways, stoops, and floors in the single room homes. With short brooms of dried rice stalks tied together, they swept dirty dirt off clean dirt. I was confused but their dignity, simplicity, and pride knew the difference.

Outdoor rock mound stoves were boiling the rice with a few vegetables that was every meal. Proud papasans held high a valuable chicken, piglet, or rare game animal. Meat was a treat to celebrate an old one's birth, honor the chief, the harvest, or religious day. There was a constant hum of a small generator bought with communal funds. It ran the ice machine. That ice cooled the beer and soda sold to GIs by the coke kids carrying plastic bags. It gave the village hard cash for better seeds, Western cigarettes, and highly valued radios to blare the twang of Asian folk music and Saigon war news.

Names I Can't Remember

We walked the clean dirt path from the highway to the open field in front of my HQ. To our right was a tall stretch of tangled bushes at the edge of the field. To our left were the rows of huts on this side of the road. The area was football field size. Before we appropriated my HQ, it stored village rice and must have been a meeting place. Villages hearing their chief's news trampled its yard, never farmed, down to dirty dirt.

Day boredom was lively as usual. Boy-men shaved out of steel pots at the earthen well. Kid-sans yammered at them trading cigarettes they'd stolen from an idiot's C-rations for the chocolate stolen from the gullible and vice versa. Punks constantly wrote letters home fending off coke kids with a loud di di mau. Letters home are bandages. They calm fears, fill lonely, and remind us we are more than killers. We never told Ma or Betty Lou how frightened we were but they always knew. Even the Dear John ones had great purpose. They proved home was still there, that killers could still cry.

No one teaches how much fun war is. The camaraderie is joyous, for the men. You can order men to die or go less nuts in a group, not both. I joined in getting drunk from afar. No one had to teach me that. The captain and I had the same fragile smile glued together with lonely and desperation, the command distance you must keep between you and your men. They were snapping cards in flowing moves like ballet dancers. Two guys were hunched over a steel helmet with a fire underneath. Julia Child and the Galloping Gourmet were guffawing over how much hot sauce to add to the pig slop C-ration crap they were turning into gourmet goop mélange. A jokester was stuffing a match book between the toes of his sleeping buddy. Scrounger was adding homey touches knocking together chairs, a shower, and a private latrine out of ammo crates he rented for a handsome profit. Stateside TP was extra! One kid managed to bang together something that looked like a soapbox racer. After giving all village kids a ride, he finally got a chance to laugh and race it. Histories never record the smiles of war. Only soldiers know laughter or defiance is how to fake Disneyland in friends on meat hook nightmares or terror talking about all the tears.

The Rice House was no more than a crumbling pile of mud too afraid to fall to dust despite having the crap shot out of it. Only three walls remained. The tin roof was half gone. In a rural village, window glass is an expensive sign of village pride. Here, it was fragments of shattered humility. The stoop steps and tiny porch were gravel piles more than structures. Inside were our rucksacks for weather and security reasons. The small stage area to one side was where my HQ group hung out; the platoon sergeant, RTO, and I. It was curtained with ponchos for privacy when teenage pimps with whores on Hondas stopped by to sloppy seconds to sixties fuck blow everyone for twenty bucks American, each.

The soul of this village was the small orphan home church. A few Catholic Asian nuns and a circuit Asian priest rarely there ran it. It looked like a dollhouse cathedral of serenity slapped together with ignored. The Mother Superior kept a small garden out back. The church was the peace diamond in a junk jewelry war. Villagers and soldiers were always gazing at it. Ugly as it was, we saw beauty and sanity there. Every hut had an incense temple for the local faith of patched together Eastern thought. Still, the Catholic orphanage was revered. It reminded us that rice, rain, and God kicked every general's ass. Today's hunger defeats any war for tomorrow.

"Beautiful. Shame there has to be a war," I sighed.

"War is beauty, Lieutenant," growled my CO.

He noticed my amazement. In all this muddy swelter, his spit shined combat boots still gleamed.

"My feet never touch the ground, Lieutenant," he said grandly.

"Why Grandma, what a hard-on and big blue balls you have. Doesn't it hurt to walk on them?" I blathered.

"The last jackass that made a crack changed his mind."

"How'd you do that, sir?" squeaked my radioman.

"I made him watch while I skinned the live fuck's arm for my sheath," he said, in a dead whisper. My RTO fainted. The captain smiled. The memory was giving him a hard-on. "How much do you fear me, Lieutenant?"

"What scares the crap out of me is you think orders and vengeance

Names I Can't Remember

are the same. You crave bodies more than victories"

"Keep the fear, Lieutenant. The killing will hurt less next time," he said, with a guffaw and a slap on the back.

His scars terrified me. They covered the back of his hands, forearms, and cheeks. My platoons' ol' man enjoyed seeing the color of every man's eyes he slaughtered, skinned, or dared to defy before dying.

"It's my twentieth sheath, I think, Lieutenant. I'll get it right the next time," he salivated. "Drink?"

"Yes!" He disgusted me, but I wanted to learn his survivor depravity so I'd make it home.

We drank his single-malt scotch ambrosia. It slid down my gullet in a silky warm flow that warms like a crackling fire in a blizzard before carving my innards like a hot poker. We got to know each other better the drunker we got. I was able to forget the crazed killer I hated and love the drunk in him. That part of him made me feel safe. Command was less lonely with another drunk at my side.

He babbled about West Point, the infantry, and Special Forces. He had Patton's glory in his veins; "to lead many brave men in a desperate battle." Captain Balls wanted to slaughter alone and didn't need a war to love killing.

"Everyone looks away in disgust. The old shamed by yesterday's blood they asked you to spill, the young spit at you to hide the joy you, not them, will fill tomorrow's body bags. Medals mean nothing to them, Lieutenant! It's a damn shame. A warrior with no war is—"

"Alive? All I wanted was a soft bed and hot food," I sighed, thinking of a quiet kid suffering for a beard.

"A messiah drowning in atheists."

He was a happy killer. I was convinced he'd make a fine poet laureate of a private glory, cigar, sherry, and snore club one-day. He'd be in a room with mahogany walls, game skin leather chairs, stuffed trophies never shot but bought off the rack, the elusive perfume of rare cognac, and Cuban cigar smoke. With the truth, sorrow, and agony lost in the haze of lonely, he'd tell exaggerated stories of medals never won and blood never spilled to snoring drunks. He'd survive this slaughter unless the enemy stabbed him with his own hard-on or he died charging up Hamburger Hill alone convinced he could defeat a human wave sapper attack with brass balls. He never explained, and I didn't ask why an elite Special Forces and West Point Green Beret grad got stuck with mud grunts. He must have screwed up big time. Any combat command is a must to this or any career man. I didn't see the need to question his judgment and have my left arm become his new sheath.

I got to know what mattered about this papier-mâché Patton a drink at a time. He would toast a deep breath or a great crap. It never affected the hollow leg bastard. He got more intense and friendlier. His smile is how I knew how blasted he was. It was the only time he had one. Booze helped him forget how he craved killing.

He had three other platoons and his HQ unit to inspire with his smile, slaughter, and salute approach to combat. He'd be at a far off firebase. I'd only have to deal with him on the radio for battle orders that seldom changed; protect a village whose only assets were pride and hunger. My war was small units of teenagers on both sides. Our average age was nineteen. Dinks were younger. Most kills and killers never shaved and had acne.

I found peace in booze and God's arms beyond midnight. Darkness was my lover ready to slit my throat after fucking her silly without knowing her name. Only night knew what a guzzle blackout drunk I was. The sun was too much time with children that hung on my arms as the brother and father they'd just dug graves for. Night was God's grace, a velvet black blessing and forgiveness for my sins, "You are safe. Your anguish is mine." Night was God's last gift of dignity and distraction to a drunk.

It was a monsoon so dense, erections and fear collided before blue eyes. The squad I'd lead on ambush had set a kill zone near the steep bank to a ravine. Some Dink and my point man, store bought teeth Freddie, bumped into each other. I swear I heard the clank of barrel on barrel before their tracer fire lit the sky with panic. My idea of precise defensive artillery fire was scream in the radio for any bomb they had, even ones in crates. I was a quantity not quality chicken shit warrior Lieutenant. With our heads hidden in the mud and firing wildly, the only thing we killed were the dive bomber mosquitoes stupid enough to choose us for dinner.

After less than a minute or two of my tactical brilliance, my radioman said blue balls, was on the horn.

"Snake six, this is Viper one. Be advised, muzzle blasts outside your perimeter observed from four sides..."

We John Waynes paused our swat flies with A bomb firing to let this sink in. Dinks outflanked Americans? We were surrounded and taking fire from all sides.

Gun smoke smells like fear whipped with panic. We shot every round, grenade, mine and pimple we had. After a minute, the Corporal I'd gone through the Virgin Ceremony with was the only one with ammo for his hand-held grenade launcher. I saw his hands tremble, his eyes flood with fear and his chest inflate with the pride of a man concrete sure of his duty. He was everywhere firing that piece of crap that shot mostly dud rounds. Later, I put him in for a Silver Star. Me getting us surrounded might be why all he got was a Bronze Star with V for very afraid.

The battle ended without death. My frenzy defense worked. I called for permission to move my unit to friendlies or they to us. We were defenseless with no ammo. A night march would risk starting a major battle between friendly units so many had small ambushes set in this area. Helicopters can't, shouldn't, and don't fly at night, unless a general is out of pizza, beer, or hookers. It's impossible to see, find, or fight anything. In a driving monsoon rain, generals go thirsty, hungry, and horny. The Chopper jocks are insane men that will fly through massive enemy fire to save a bleeding man. Flying in a pitch black, driving rain is threading a needle with an elephant's cock.

Thundering through the night monsoon downpour came the tiniest needle stuffed with the biggest cock. Drunk Captain jock too tight had hijacked the battalion commanders chopper. My soggy flashlights gave the pilot no light. My Woodstock was jittering hands flicking a Zippo lighter and soggy matches at the noise I heard but couldn't see. Loaded with ammo, Captain kneel before god me forced the pilot to land the in the middle of our small, muddy perimeter.

Things quieted down as we all tried to find ways to stay warm and dry in the sheet heavy rain. The irony of war is that the best peace treaty is rotten weather.

"Lieutenant, where's the old man?" asked my confused RTO.

In the light of a fading illumination round overhead, our glory nut CO was alone in the distance. Brandishing his sword, he was hunting for new sheath donors. He didn't even have his side arm out. It made me angry that boys die but glory gods never do.

Some guys and I plodded through the mud and rain going out to protect him and get him back in our perimeter. On the way back, we found a dead enemy. In escaping our massive and aimless return fire, he ran along the bank to the ravine at the wrong moment. Not one of our tens of thousands of bullets killed him. Pellets from a mine guarding the ditch, fired in panic killed him.

My *imagination* heard the "Meow." Was that him again, the man with a cat on his shoulder?

"Funny isn't it?" the whimsical stranger asked.

"What?" I asked, annoyed.

"A man's guts and a boy's stink the same."

"Fuck you. It's happiness, you cocksucker. Happy they're not mine," I growled, slugging some booze.

"Happy? Just shame in disguise," he snickered.

"Kiss my ass. Get your leather vest, floppy hat, fancy pipe, and that nut cat out of my fucking life!

"He fought for his home. You were fighting for a soft bed and a hot meal, Mr. Popcorn and Hot Tea," he giggled.

"What went wrong? You gunna' tell me now you bas—"

He was gone. He was right. The guts I cared nothing about stunk the same as my Virgin kill boy I cried over.

It was a good kill. He was a man that chose to die, not a boy ordered to. He was a leader with papers and trophies. I gave the Red Star belt, holster, and pistol to the Corporal who defended us. Crying, he proudly wore them.

Captain the guy on the cross is my son, scowled with envy. He and I talked, smoked, and drank from his flask for the rest of the night.

The talking was welcome distraction. I had killed again. We were two drunks spewing bull and running from shame.

"Poor country? The whore houses and dope dealers here have more customers than any fire fight. We're making these Dinks rich," he blabbered loudly and proudly.

"Except the orphans living in the garbage dumps."

Drunks always peel bullshit down to truth but never remember their genius. War used to be weeks old news punched up with glory by censors and historians. Mine was the first where video tape got the truth on the air before the ink was dry on the lies. Had it been February Sweeps at Valley Forge, Bull Run, or Normandy, the Union Jack would fly over the White House, the Mason Dixon Line would be a national border, and Paris would host Octoberfest.

In the driving monsoon rain still drenching us, he stunned me again. He got up, took out a bar of soap, and began to shower with his uniform on!

I laughed. It was a drunk's laugh. My head was back, my mouth was wide open, and my contempt for him roared with belly loud derision. His cold low tone cut my balls off and shoved them up my ass. I shivered and got goose bumps.

"I live and die for this uniform. You should be as proud of it as I am. This saves water you'd kill for to give the men in the dry season, Lieutenant. Sometimes, nuts is paractical."

He killed my laughter, even the echo. He was right. He drunk mumbled, I guzzled ignore, a perfect marriage.

"War is raw, son not seasoned and barbecued lies. Just nigger, spic, kike, wap, hillbilly, potato farmer, and honky boys dying for D.C. power freaks whose only balls is spending our blood on their ideas. I'd French kiss the fuckers if I could. Without glory, I might as well be a god damn teacher," he said slobbering and passing the flask. "War is the only thing that makes the winners' slaughter the loser's fault!"

"Air fucking mobile, Sir!" I yelled, guzzling and passing the booze to him. I had no idea what garbage he'd spewed.

"You bet boys for their profit, power and promotion. Cowards are promoted spending lives from inside a deep bunker. A warriors' memory is fears and tears because he bled the same blood his men did. Rank and medals only prove how good I am at kissing ass. Men's respect, I have to earn," he said, drooling scotch and nodding.

"What did you say, Sir?"

"I was speaking?"

I was too scared to say anything. I wondered if the Baha'i would ever cry because fate or fear made him kill. Remembering him with his beard made me know how wrong Captain-I-can-suck-my-own-cock was. The warrior that saved my life was a drooling, snoring drunk. I was looking in a mirror.

Our last drunken escapade could have cost the lives of many men. Our company was transferred to the rear for training, and be the division emergency action unit. We invaded a barracks and inspected the troops. A pissed off major signed us out of jail. We were two lucky drunks this time. I knew then why an exiled elite captain lead mud grunts. Some other time men died while he was drunk. It didn't matter he was a racist butcher. Ten kids and a punk Lieutenant were happy a Gung Ho killer saved their lives whether he remembers it or not. Maybe booze was his bravery and biggest fear.

In the cool and cloudy mourn,
On the heathered moors afar,
The lonely piper cries and wails
Singing the song of sorrow for
Not the mighty that deserved to die
But sandy haired boys with lives,
Lovers and mamma's who'll cry
Glory's tears each and every lie.
God's with no congregation
Beat tears and fears with fury
That echoes in one man canyons.
Glory is but whisper in an empty room
When no one volunteers to die,
God's whimper with empty pews,
When well worn bibles gather dust.

In crumbling churches of worn out lust
Thou shalt not covet thy neighbors wife
Unless boredom strangles a lonely life
Thou shalt not steal
Unless the hunger's real
Thou shalt not kill
Unless the other will.
Warrior's bleed God's confusions
Choking on force fed glory allusion.
Why pray to gods that refuse to answer
And give us fear coated bloody blades
Body bags, dirt and spades
When we worship whirl, the only dancer
Shedding meaning light on faith is the cancer
All the kings horses and all the kings' men
Couldn't put Humpty together again.
Now I lay me down to sleep
If I should die before I wake
The drunken God gets all the cake
When brave boys go in bags to mamma's wake.
The ittsy bitsy spider crawled up the water spout
Down came the rain and washed the bloody guts out
Out came the sun and dried up all the ooze
The itysy bitsy spider crawled in the eyes again
Some drunken god saved my life today. Amen.

Is My Name Lin Yan?

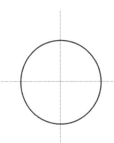

MARCH 1970

*"There is no war in his sandbox eyes
that remind us all of home. He is
a cool breeze in the hell swelter
of our sodden souls, the Lone
Ranger, the best hustler of all."*

He is the cool breeze in the hell swelter of my sodden soul. I now call him Lin Yan. Names I can't remember. Sitting on the Rice House stoop. I'm too drunk on eighty-proof self-pity. In the front yard swarm of kid thieves hawking stolen goods and begging candy, his swagger is more confident than the rest. His bold smile, pouty pushiness, and needy brown eyes close every sale. He struts in front of the others with his cash nearly falling out of the pockets of his threadbare clothes. There is no war in his innocent, sandbox eyes that remind us all of home.

On the steps to a crumbling building in this useless village by the sea, I'm hanging out with my only friends. Whiskey, binge, pass out and I are bloody stumps gushing command loneliness. Humming Oleanna, I smile at cheering legions only my bloodshot eyes see.

Looking for sympathy, I trip off the stoop into a sea of black pajama clad papasans in cone shaped hats. I teeter over a no teeth farmer with mud and dung ground into his crooked fingers, calluses, and creases in his neck. He rests his hand on his back to ease his stoop work agony and looks at me. I see fear and confusion in his weary eyes and defiant scowl. He is the beaten kneeling refusing my M-16 might with the pride and poetry of the poor, his growling belly. He shits to nourish the paddy he'd planted moments ago. He offers me his musky scented hand to seal his insult. I shake it to impress with my strength of stupid.

I wobble among my serfs waiting for them to bow. Kids kick mud on my shined boots in frenzy for my greenbacks, Hershey Bars, and cigarettes. At a card game on an ammo crate, I throw back a beer and sway waiting for their envy eyes. Hillbilly slaps down a king and "wha-hoos." Nigger trumps viciously with a duce and wiggles a cock and ass dance. Spic sticks his ace back in his hand and picks his nose. Worshiping me is surely next.

"Get out of the fucking sun, Lieutenant. I can't see my hand!"

I stagger back to the Rice House. The stage end HQ area has a poncho liner as a curtain. Behind it, are the grunts and groans of a pimpled Lothario getting his rocks off with some teenage Honda whore for five bucks. A line of anxious gigglers with cash in their fists waits patiently, their belts unbuckled.

"Hey, Lieutenant! You gonna get fucked today?" one yells.

"No thanks, grunt. You've fucked me enough."

My HQ looks like a cow town bordello on payday Saturday night. My lonely sees me alone at a wake.

"God fucking damn! What fun this is, you fucks!" I bellow, toasting my warriors, my canteen high over my head.

"Drink it down, drink it down, Lieutenant," they yell.

"I AM the kick ass living Lieutenant!" I scream, wobbling.

"And guzzle again," they repeat.

"I give you beer, booze, and butt fuck me cunts!"

"Go, go go! Guzzle again, da da da dum!"

No worship. They return to cards and I slump away.

Lin Yan is one of the Coke kids selling cool sympathy in this steaming shit house. Blatz is beer that tastes like rusty piss with a vinegary twang. Fanta soda wrinkles your face with its rotten lemon taste. This shit doesn't sell in the States because it is all here. Coke, Dr. Pepper, Budweiser are here but goes to generals and better thieves. There is a Chinese brew we call Tiger Piss. It gets its name from a horrid taste akin to a jock strap, the large brown bottle it comes in, and the fierce yellow tiger on the dark brown bottle. It is illegal to drink it. It comes in capped bottles, not cans. Enemy agents put ground glass in it and re-cap it. We drink rivers of Tiger Piss. Thirst, boredom, and who gives a damn beats fear. We can get soda and beer free, filling out pounds of forms, and waiting for JC's delivery after his Second Coming.

Out of the corner of my eye, I see the Spic sergeant shaking his head, chomping on his cigar, and heading my way dragging a kid. The kid isn't resisting. Sergeant Spic probably caught the kid making off with a can of ham and eggs. A crime, yes, but no one cares. Ham and eggs is tuberculosis in a can that even hot sauce can't save. Fingernails or nose hors d'oeuvres taste better.

"He says the nun is a spy for the Dinks, LT."

Whispers ripple from ear to ear. Waiting for me to act, the men share recipes on how to barbecue the kid they rough housed with, and bought soda from, moments ago. The air stinks of hate. Enemy soldiers slaughter each other but share respect in the open. Spies slit throats in private betrayal. The boy's horror eyes start my panic Oleanna hum at double time.

I strut like a god. My glance is steely. My brow is furrowed. I stink of scotch and serious. Lin Yan cowers. Locals move away. My guys watch and whisper. My gold bar worship at last. Moses is about to explain his time on the mount without a drink.

A smart-ass man with a cat on his shoulder is giggling. "You groveled for the bar. Earn it," he sneers.

Names I Can't Remember

I manage to hide my panic and act like the man the men need to see. Taking the boy aside assures them I will deal with him decisively and viciously. It doesn't matter what I am doing just that it is me not them. Lin Yan shivers. I speak softly to calm him. My skin is bumpy and dead cold.

"What's all this crap about the nun?" I ask quietly, looking right in his wide, teary eyes.

"Sister been helping VC. She walk distance to your guns on hill. She give dem food and toll dem where you bang bang at night. Cross my hot an hope to die, Roo-ten-ant!"

He fearfully yammers on. He breathes in gulps. His nose is running. His jet-black hair gets more tangled as he shoves it aside. The whites of his deep brown eyes flush with the manic red accusing causes. He points everywhere. On a rare cool day, he too is sweating profusely. He stares defenselessly and nods, begging for forgiveness.

The villagers chatter like popping corn. My guys tilt back their helmets, whistle and wow. Fingers resting on bayonets begin running along razor sharp edges as pinched glances turn from the boy to the church and land on me.

"Wanna buy a gold bar cheap?" I whisper to Sarge.

"Don't look at me. What ever you do, it better be damn good LT," he says, with a cold, sarcastic smile.

"Call the 'ol man," is my brilliant leadership.

"Wish I'd a thought of that," grumbles Sarge. "Did you think I'd leave this can of worms in your drunk hands, you silly prick?" he snarls, shaking his head.

"You drink as much as I do, Sergeant," I roar.

"Because I want too. You do because that's where your nuts are," he seethes. "You got dumb lucky saving them on the LZ thing, Captain God, and they trust you. I need my platoon to stay calm. Now, LT, grumble and wave your arms so they don't lose that. Do it!" he growls. "And make 'em believe it."

"Ah, you scare the piss out of me, Sarge" I say, in a decisive whisper and animated way to fool the men.

"I'll ram your nuts up your sorry ass if you fuck with my... your men, Lieutenant," he says softly. The men see Sarge with locked heels and a nervous look as if I'd just dressed him down. His acting deserves an Oscar and an Emmy.

"Now, get some truth out of that punk before the higher ups get their hands on him and we lose the only chance to know how deep in shit he's got us."

"He's just a kid, Sarge."

Sarge growls and yanks up his shirt. On his beer belly is the Grand Canyon of hard and ragged edge pink flesh; the ugliest scar on an angry man who forgot one of his own rules.

"I got it from the last strange kid with a wild story I thought was just a kid. When I turned my back, he slit the other grunt's throat, nearly gutted me before I could smash his nose with my fist, and drive the bone in his brain. I still wear that grunts dog tag. Read it!"

"Lieu- Lieutenant James Lipka," I whisper.

"The trusting jerk you replaced. Son, no kids here, just dead men, and brave boys writing home about dead buddies. What do you see?"

"Nothing. It's quiet for a change."

"Exactly, stupid! Quiet, no screaming card games, no brave warriors scribbling letters home, no grab ass chest thumping, no teenage whore fucking, and no beer guzzling. When a grunt doesn't brag, fuck, and drink, he is one screw up from a body bag. I could cut their fear with your limp dick. That's how bad this kid's story has messed up this unit. Stop moaning about command crap and... command like the Lieutenant I know is under that hangover some God damn place," he says, like a caring father winking and leaving.

I look at a trembling kid who's special to me. He lets me remember the boy I no longer am. On his tattered shirt is a toy star, shaped like a sheriff's badge from the old West. I am about to interrogate the kid known as the Lone Ranger, the best hustler of all. I nervously giggle.

I remember our first meeting just after I took command. The kid swaggered in my Rice House HQ like he owned the damn joint. His shirt pocket was stuffed with markers for the debts my guys owed him. It was payday and he was there to collect. Sarge, Hillbilly, Nigger, Spic, nervous nellie RTO, and Doofus were there. When the kid sauntered in, they hid their wallets from the slick thief and readied their complaints about his useless crap.

"Keem-oh-sa-bay! Da Wrong Ranja here, Roo-ten-ant. Money talk an' boo-shit walk. Soda, one buck. Beer, two buck. Ice, one buck. Cup, one buck. Cup dat don't leak, two buck. Dope, four buck, hot fuck, five buck." The kid coulda been a carny con-game barker.

"I oughta wash your mouth out with soap, kid," scowled the fatherly Sarge, yelling in his face.

"Soap, two buck. Hot Honda mamma? Boo-koo dinki dau!"

"You shit. I paid you fifty bucks for Cuban cigars," growled the angry Spic, chomping his last soggy stogie.

"Captain God, jack ass steal em back from me. Bummer. Can't trust no swinging dick in this rousy place. For ten buck, I steal em back boo-koo fast, Spic Sarge."

"That dang watch I bought from you stopped the day I bought it. I want my cash back," yelled the hillbilly

"All sales final. I love A-mell-i-ka! No refunds!"

"Smoke me, kid. Kools," seethed the nervous RTO.

"You got da bread?"

"Pay ya' next payday, kid."

"See ya' next payday radioman. Me old timer. I no new meat just fall off da freedom bird from da states."

"Can ya' change a fifty, you little thief?"

"Gimme. You got two twenties for dis ten?"

"Here."

"Your butts. One more satisfied customer."

"Hey!? My forty-five in change?"

"Too slick for me Pelly Mason. Here, three fifteens."

"You must think all Americans are stupid," I said.

"Na, roo-ten-ant, just the live ones."

"What?"

"Nothing, SIR!"

"Better. Stick with me. Guys kick ass for no change."

"Three fifteens?" he whispered. "I let him outta my sight, I go broke. Honda mamma fuck you good!"

"Sure."

"But not as good as me."

"What?"

"Nothing, Doug-san, new hot mamma. Boo koo dinky dau. She oil your dip stick. One hundred buck."

"A hundred!? My girl ain't worth that much."

"She a virgin, roo-ten-ant?"

"Forget it, kid. I got cla— ah, gonor—, I ah broke my dinky and can't dow for boo koo payday."

He was so busy counting all our money he had no idea what was coming next. I had him right where he wanted me.

"Maybe you better scram kid, back to the church before Sister Nuyen reads me the riot act."

"Step back, Jack. Let's make a deal!"

"Anybody! Do I still have my watch, my hands?"

"You owe me, Rootenant."

"What?"

"Five bucks, ah... chat charge."

"Chat charge?"

"Ess-penses. I got ober-head!"

"Anything you don't sell, kid?"

"Peace, bad for business. War big bucks! Later. Hi Ho Silver, away!" he yelled taking my cash and running.

"You got to deal with Sister Nuyen first. She's coming to get you," I say sweating. "Hmm, why do I want to smoke?"

Sister Nuyen was one of the hand-full of Asian nuns that ran the dilapidated Catholic Orphanage and church-ette in the village with the help of a traveling priest I'd never seen. I politely nodded to the Sister in her billowing habit. I hadn't met her yet. Her scowl said this was not the day for that. I couldn't help but notice how cute she was. Gold bars make horny boys stupid men.

"Lin Yan, Mon petit choux. Get that fishing lesson?"

"I ah— Sister Nuyen!? I, I just coming to see you. Why da roo-ten-ant so mad at little cute kid like me?"

"You steal everything and sell it back. That and the lying must stop. Fish with a pole. Grenades kill too many fish and there's none for next week. Remember Lieutenant's lessons and bring the fish to the church. Don't sell them!"

"You think hustling is easy, Sister?"

"The commandment doesn't say, 'Thou shalt not steal except when God says you can or you're not treated fairly.'"

"Papasan prayed. War kill him. Fair to me, Sister?"

"No, son. No, it isn't" she sighed, unable to heal his honest anger. I saw Madonna and Child in her soft tone and tenderness to the weary child hiding in her lap. Her milky soft hand brushed his hair aside and stroked his forehead. In the shade of a weary tree, I saw the glow of God's light on her serene face as she disciplined her confused warrior. Her scowl was more tender smile.

"I just do what all the roo-ten-ants guys laugh about, Do unto others before they do unto me again, and split."

"Oh my, Lin Yan. You are... the beauté de diable."

"Huh?"

"Forgive me. Ah, the beauty of the devil, the freshness of youth... who speaks a harsh truth. What do you do with all the money?"

"Buy stuff. I put some in poor box."

"Thank you for that."

"But Sister, everyone here poor. Why not we keep it?"

"Forgive me, Father. I agree with him. Lin Yan, there are people poorer than us. What is it you buy?"

"Eb-ri-ting! Soda, beer, soap, and butts. Doug-san's men pay big bucks. Dey pay good for boo koo dinky dau. What do dey do with hot Honda mamma, Sister?"

"Later! What ever happened to Lincoln Logs?"

"Ring-kong rogs, Sister?"

"When did you get so old and used up?"

"Me brand new, think Ah-mel-i-can! You cry Sister?"

"No. I forgot how. You can't buy peace, son."

"Soldier spending not shoot, Sister!"

"Yes... My Lord, this has got to stop."

"What all these soldier want, Sister?"

"The same thing, all of Vietnam as one country."

"Why fight if all want same?"

She turned away to mumble an angry prayer, "All this country is the same green. The dung stinks the same. Only the VC and Lieutenant's maps have lines. Only the uniforms change color. Father, forgive me, but how the heck do I explain to a boy that strangers in marble buildings decided to carve Vietnam with treaties for cheap labor, navel bases, and vacation resorts?"

"No one winning. What makes losing war so good?"

"Slow darn news day. Forgive me, Father. After Dallas and LA, Cronkite needed a hot item."

"Klong-kite?"

"Go. The Lieutenant's waiting for you."

"Roo-ten-ant Doug-san nice. You like Fuzzy?"

"Fuzzy?"

"Roo-ten-ant's hair, short—"

"Ah... you call him Fuzzy," she smiled.

"Him cute?" said the con artist, changing the subject.

"Fuzzy? Yes... no! Go!"

Today's dilemma ends yesterdays' memory. A kid shakes in fear at my side. Had I ever been sober enough to teach him fishing like she asked? My hands are turning a branch into a fishing pole. I motion the boy over to the narrow stream with muddy banks dividing the village.

"The secret is never touch the bait. Fish can smell the sweat, the... blood, from the other fish, on your hands."

"Fish got noses? Amel-i-cans got funny fish."

"Pay attention! Hold the hook and snag the bait. So, the Sister is a spy for the VC?"

"No 'bout a doubt it... maybe."

I smile at the little brother I never had to teach stuff and be worshiped by before I left home. He smiles at the brother or father he barely remembers in graves he can no longer find. He is shuffling his feet. For the first time, we are brothers in blue and gray with pinched enemy eyes full of suspicion and wariness.

"Be careful with that hook or you'll rip your finger. Through the bait's gills and out the other side."

Names I Can't Remember

"Ahhh. Dat works great, Fuzzy. Thanks."

"Fuzzy. Feels nice. What makes you think she's VC?"

"She always asks too much, roo-ten-ant."

"Just jerk the line a little and drag it through the water. The fish think the bait is food."

"Wow! I feel a fish. I fool him good, roo-ten-ant.

"Stop calling me that!"

We smile and stare quietly do I dare trust you?

"Did you ever see Sister with a map of our places?"

"Never said I saw her. What up, Fuzzy?"

"You got one, see?"

"Hey! Gimme the pole. That's my fish, roo-ten-ant."

"Stop talking like a gook."

"But I am a gook."

"Couldn't ya' just be a kid?"

"Me no kid! Like Nigger Sarge say, war make you smart ass or dead kid. What I do wrong, Fuzzy?"

"Call me Lieutenant, damn it!"

"Yes, Sir Roo-ten-ant damn it!"

"Di di mau!" I yell, as he runs off.

Sarge says shaking his head. "Is he a kid or a spy?"

"All I know is I need a drink."

"The Ol' Man says he's kicking this higher up and will get back to us. He says you should talk to the nun."

"Me? How do I—?"

"No, no, Lieutenant. I keep your head out of your ass but I don't make your decisions. That leads to blame. Sergeant's never get blamed!" a worried Sarge says leaving.

I jerk from side to side looking around for any answer or support. I'm alone. The noisy card games, Lieutenant butter bar jokes, aggressive coke kids, and begging locals are no where to be seen. My normal and casual cock-sure gait is a head low shuffle to the church. Gulping from my whiskey canteen, I drunkenly start rehearsing my lines.

"Screw with my guys? Mess with my war, bitch? I'll slam you against the wall, cunt. Spill it or I'll cut your tongue and eyes out and ram them up your pretty ass."

"*You bully shadows well, kid. How are you in the sun?*"

"*Meow. That's how you interview a nun?*"

"Let me be right or home. What the fuck is wrong?"

I am gasping for air and answers the bottle doesn't have. The panic building, my eyes dart side-to-side looking for enemies in empty shadows. Beads of sweat form on my quivering lips. I angrily start kicking dirt. My knees give out and I stumble to the ground shaking. I start to whine.

"I should know what to do," I snivel, remembering.

"*Ohleanna...*" echoes in my head.

"*Do you surrender your command?*" yowls the wolf pack of OCS officers at the bridge.

Radios useless, alone on the LZ, and my tiny force surrounded by massive enemy units, I stare at a map I can't read. In drenching rain, I lead my men home with fear, confusion, and dumb luck.

"*I loves dem mens when dey needs me,*" Silkie sighs raising my head to her breast, softly stroking my hair.

"*I gots ma store bought teeth!*" Freddie smiles.

"*The only thing that drops quicker here than hillbillies, niggers, and spics is Second Lieutenants!*" laughs Hillbilly, Nigger, and Spic.

"*Break one heavy load into small parts so you are stronger than it, and carry it many familiar miles,*" whispers the boy with whiskers he refused to shave.

Looking at a sunny sky, I feel the dark clouds and cracking thunder in my soul.

"God, what do I do now?" I sob, closing my eyes.

"*Bummer. Why doesn't anyone pray when things are groovy?*" says the booming voice from above.

"Who's that?" I ask, startled.

"*God, silly. You did ask for me.*"

"God!?"

Villagers hearing, to them, my one sided chat, move away from me, giggle and make a he's koo koo sign.

"*Sure. Would God lie? Watch.*"

Names I Can't Remember

"Yeow!" I scream, grabbing my balls.

"*Damn. I zapped balls with the clap not a thunder cloud clap again? Clean the damn seeds from the weed, Peter.*"

"Yes," I wince.

"*Ask your booze.*"

"Hey! Don't knock it. You get high."

"*That's the far out thing about being God. If I sneeze, dive under a rock and grab your ass. Escapism was my best work. Screwed up on those damn Crusades though. Faith made fanatics, my God or else.*"

"I gotta do something."

"*Do you have any idea what you are about to do? Either she slits your throat because she is the spy or you offend me and burn in hell forever. That makes the kid the spy, but a kid?*"

"I'm a kid too! Got any suggestions?"

"*Eternal peace is my bag. I don't sell answers. You aren't supposed to know. That's why I invented faith. Believe, my son, not beg the booze.*"

"One of them's telling the truth."

"*Hmmm. Solomon had the same problem. I thought his resolution was far out. You ain't Solomon and scotch is no solution.*"

"Am I supposed to know?"

"*Son, war is all anger and agony, not answers. Just look around you. Work and hunger are these people's only meals. It's hard to believe in me when these plain people pray up to their asshole and elbows in muddy clay, water buffalo crap, human shit, and urine year after year. The only faith they have comes with an extra spoonful of rice.*"

"How the hell do they survive?"

"*Why can't it be how the heaven when my tribe does something extraordinary? Jesus! Cancel that. I got it, boy. Damn kid sticks his nose in everything. Son, the old cling to the simple, ancient ways of spirit, myth, and meaning. The singsong, off-key, teeth grinding, hymns whined in the fields to pass time echo Buddha, Taoism, Cao Dai, and Hoa Hoa. Happiness here is gruel of equal parts cow dung and hope. French Colonialism tried shoving me down their throats. All that wealth made the message rot like too many crops. I've been tolerated for what I bring to the village. The old too weak to work the fields sweep my*" *church steps. Babies too young to work are left with my nuns rather than break their mother's back in a sling. My church has candles for light and is a dry place to complain when monsoons fill the rice bowls with starvation. Saving souls is slow work. The wealth of memories is all I can give their poor lives. My nuns listen, the diamond in their life of coal. Being listened to is a soothing rain and rice in their desert lives. When the crop fails again and the belly growls too loud to sleep, I am the only meal they have. Son, soaked in scotch, you save no one. Faith is the only answer to fear."*

Opening my eyes, my prayer is over. I sigh. I'm there with no answer or forgiveness. The rundown, sad, small church wears its humility like a robe of silken gold, the quiet gaze of its small steeple lowered. The gray crumbling stones are mortared with simplicity, sweat, and calluses. Mud brick steps rise to a one-room school size sanctuary winged by a tiny residence. An ancient humped woman with beetle-nut blackened teeth holding a hand made broom of tied stalks leftover from the fields immaculately sweeps the steps. The tired sound of the bell rings for Mass only because the work in the field is done. Here, God waits His turn behind hunger and survival. The hungry and tired file into God's gas station Reverend Dave spoke of. Inside, defiant souls sigh hymns of survival.

"Mommy?" Looking for sympathy, I drink.

I walk up the steps to the side residence and find my way in. I wander down a narrow hall just wide enough for one pair of shoulders and stumble into a large open room that looks like a kitchen. The walls are large cinder bricks, pale white, and smooth on the interior side. The one large table in the center is roughly hewn wood covered with stains and gouges. A narrow counter runs along one wall that is a checkerboard of miss-matched planks hammered together. One large window lets an angled shaft of Godly light slice through this non-electric room. Half of a ragged edged, fifty five-gallon drum serves as a basin. A metal bucket filled with water is the faucet. Both are OD green in color, marked U.S., and named as only the military can invent language; one each, OD in color, individual, multi-use, product, metal conveyance system, handle enhanced, and general utility receptacle. The refrigerator is a ramshackle junk pile of wood and tin banged together as a place to keep food in the only dark cooler place in this jungle. It doesn't matter if it works or not. It is empty except for roaches seeking shade. The stove is an Army, junk pile reject. The heavy black steel thing isn't connected to any gas line. It reeks of carbon stench from wood burned in the oven to make cooking fires for the burner. No matter. The rough wood cupboard shelf is bare and the dry wood box is empty.

Across the room with her back to me, is a nun, habit shoved high over the elbows, filling the silence with the gentle rhythm of scrubbing. She hasn't heard me enter and keeps working. Even though she is covered by dusty yards of plain, black cotton, the rhythm of her work gives a shimmy and shake that runs throughout her body from her head down to her cute and brightly bouncing bu—

"Watch it!" God cracks, thunderously.

Hearing my boots on the rough floor and stammer cough, she turns. Sister Nuyen's oval eyes are deep and dark. They sparkle with serene happiness despite the deep work and worry lines. Her pale yellow skin wears the smudges of dirty work like make-up highlighting her inner glow. Then there is that smile. It is an arms around you, sit and be comforted smile. It stops me in my steps, wraps itself around my heart, and quickens my pulse. Her weary slump from hauling hundreds of gallons of water five at a time doesn't matter. Sorry children there's no rice tonight wrinkles crevasse her prime of life face. Yet, she smiles knowing God protects these families that struggle in the mud because they cant eat prayer. My gut is a knot. I scan every twitch seeking an assassin about to explode. Am I looking in God's mirror or a killer's eyes?

"Hello, Lieutenant. I'm happy to see you. Work is so lonely. Please sit down. A moment à deux would be nice."

"Huh?"

"It's hard to let go of my past. I still dream French fairytales. À deux, a private moment for two, a chat."

I tilt my helmet and shake my head. My shit isn't weak, it's dead, and the funeral was last week. I grab her by the wrist and yank her body to mine. My sweaty hand trembles as my mind wanders and I babble. I'm not sure I even see the men.

"Ma, I had to steal the popcorn and tea."

"What?"

"Oh, lee, anna... I'm only nineteen."

"Lieutenant? Are you OK?" she asks, trying to take back her wrist from a distance.

I tremble, holding her wrist, and watch my shuffling feet while trying to make up my mind what to do.

"Lieutenant!"

In a daze, I look at her. Sweat pours down my face on a rare cool day. Like a nervous virgin, I kiss her. I stand there looking at her with a cold stare, waiting for any reaction. She staggers, manages a nervous smile, turns away, and crumples, grabbing the edge of the table to keep from falling. Her head is bowed and she whispers a prayer.

"Congratulations, Sister."

"Cowards are heroes behind closed doors. The brave wear courage in the sun à la belle étoile, Lieutenant."

"You'll live a little longer. A woman would kiss me or slap the crap out of me. A spy would bless and forgive me."

"What does that make me, Lieutenant?"

"The most cunning killer ever, or a nun. Who else would show such revulsion and shame?"

"I'd always wondered what savage lust would be like. It's not a question the Monsignor likes to answer."

"What's so funny?"

"I finally have something to say when the other Sisters tell stories from the past about, how do you say, copping a feel? I... liked it." She is beet red.

Each of us finally gasps for air sorting out the humor from disgust. The silence feels heavy. She does the oddest thing that slows my racing breath. She walks to me and strokes my cheek while shaking her head like a mother.

"It's OK. War makes gentle boys such brutal men."

"What's it like?"

"What?"

"Being a Nun, in the middle of all this."

"After that, Father forgive me, I'm not sure."

We both laugh to break the tension.

"Today is my last day of kitchen duty," she says, to lighten things. "When the Father blessed me this morning, he said, 'You look bored. Get dressed up and go out to show off your nun-ness.'"

"So, you're a nun."

"I am a nun, Lieutenant. Who got... felt up."

"Sister!"

"Forgive me, but God does permit humor. Only secrets hurt. It will take a lifetime for me to get the guts to mention this in confession. Our secret. OK by you?"

"Oh? Sure. I ah, have to ask you... some stuff."

"What troubles you, my son?

She rises from the creaky chair and tenses. When she paces about like a caged lioness, my hand slowly moves to the trigger of my rifle. I don't know if she sees this but she stops and takes a defiant stance. Her eyes slice into me like a razor sharp butcher knife.

"We're trying to protect you from... them," I blubber.

"The VC and North Vietnamese steal our sons to fight and protect us from you. Crops and sons are survival here. You fill our land with garbage the orphans you beget have to live on and eat from. Have you ever seen a three-year-old beat the rats and two-year-olds off a scrap of rotten meat and devour it maggots and all?" she laughs.

"Sister?"

"These villagers were free until you all force-fed them flags that leave them starving. The French wanted us to work their farms on our land they never bought. You ever starve, Lieutenant?

"Yes. It's why I'm here," I sigh.

"We don't eat VC freedom pamphlets. American liberty doesn't fill bellies. Rice is the only freedom we know. No one gives a heck, forgive me Father, who sells the bowl!"

"Are you a spy, Sister?"

"Today, we plant new rice and sons. Tomorrow, the young will make war and the old will make do."

"Someone is helping the VC trying to bomb my Rice House. You've been accused. If I turn you over, your own people will forget the questions and use a rifle to make hamburger out of your chest, rosary or not. At least I'll listen to your story. Have you been making any maps of this area?"

I have no idea if Sister Nuyen even hears me. She is trying to muscle a large wooden spoon with nicks and scars through dense pasty rice in a gigantic, dented pot. The rice is winning but she refuses to give up.

"Hamburger, greasy, fatty, juicy red meat... One day rice and fish heads. Next day, fish heads and rice. Then rice with no fish heads..."

"Sister?! Have you been making maps?"

"I'm Sister Nuyen. Look at this cross and rosary," is her angry response that cools to spiritual gentility.

"Have you?" I insistently whisper.

"Yes, Lieutenant."

I yank the rosary from her hand. In the same violent instant, she pulls out a hand grenade.

Her hand holding the grenade flinches. Instantly, I chamber a round and click off the safety. The loud click stops us both. Gently and slowly, she hands me the grenade. The deafening silence is broken by the whoosh of two very frightened people taking a breath.

"A four-year-old was fishing with one of these. The pin was all I found next to scraps of American money."

"How'd you get that?"

"Here's the map that Lin Yan told you about. I use it to keep track of your ambush sites. Farmers that work at night or urinate don't get shot accidentally. I am guilty of trying to save the same lives you are. God forgive us. Everyone saving lives here is doing all the killing."

We both slump back in our seats at the small table made of leftover ammo crates. I take a sip from the booze in my second canteen and light a cigarette.

"How about me, damn it? Forgive me, Father."

Surprised, I pass her my booze and butts. In one smooth move, she knocks back the good, long glug of a barfly. She relishes the first drag on her cigarette like a sweaty lover who'd just had her brains fucked out. My suspicious eyes want to know if a razor sharp knife about to slit my throat is hidden in the folds of her habit.

"Truce. Just long enough to enjoy this 8-year-old Tennessee sippin' whiskey and American butts. Father forgive me, but this is Christmas. Thanks, Lieutenant," she says, with a relaxed sigh.

"Hell of a convent you attended! A nun slouched casually, with her feet spread, and leaning on her elbows?" I say, taking my finger off the trigger, tipping back the brim of my helmet.

"Lieu— "

"Call me Fuzzy!"

"Why Fuzzy?" she asks, sincerely.

"I want a name not a responsibility."

"Friends call me Phil. Are you my friend, Fuzzy?"

"I don't know, Phil," I warily sigh.

"Friendship, like life is told in the hands. That's what the gypsy in Marseilles says. Give me your hand. Wars end when people touch."

I jerk away. I reach for my bayonet. Her hand was soft. I had forgotten what gentle feels like.

"So tender, strong, and young. There is no hate in this hand, yet it trembles What frightens you, son?."

"Why are you here? I mean, you don't act Vietnamese..."

"But I am. My family is French, but I was born here, not far from this village on the family rubber plantation. Are all Americans Indians? Home is where you plant your heart not your history, Fuzzy."

"Where'd you ah, study to ah, get... nuned?

She laughs. Stupid sometimes gets lucky.

"Marseilles first, then Northwestern in Chicago."

"Chi-Town's' home, Phil! Weird, calling a nun that."

"It's weirder never seeing people's eyes. They stare at my cross and habit. They never taught us how much serving God makes the person disappear like I'm heaven's neon sign."

"Pretty. Your hair I mean, not fuzzy like mine, Phil."

"Thanks. And your eyes are so blue, not fuzzy."

"How'd ya' get from here to Chicago, then a nun?"

"Every French girl here goes to study Vietnamese history with a Paris accent. Paris was the chance to get out of this darn village. Father, forgive me. I couldn't get this church out of my mind. I played here all the time. Our farm had so many people coming and going. This was the only place I could be alone or not smell like a barn."

"The Eiffel Tower, Paris must have been—."

"I was mad! In class, they talked about French glory in the east without ever mentioning the Vietnamese I was, and grew up with. Everything was about France."

"Chicago's Magnificent Mile—!?"

"The best corned beef, cabbage and Glumpkies!"

"Getting nuned, so inspiring and—"

"And Uno's Pizza, the best! Forgive me, Father but supper is faith to a fish heads and rice kid from cow shit country. Oh my? That will cost me a day of Hail Marys."

I watch her little girl mood of excitement change instantly. This child falls in love with home and God all over again. Her hand strokes the beat up counter tenderly. Her face is the joy of a sad lover seeing Him in a sunset. Her sigh says home is the comfort of a lifetime that heals after over the rainbow leaves you lonely in days.

"It's called taking vows, Fuzzy. That took time. I got lonely for this church. I spent most days in the school chapel. The learning became less important. One day, I found myself asking God what she - what HE, wanted me to do. I was tired running from the church I loved."

"What made up your mind, Phil?"

"I was praying for the first time. I shivered. My heart went all a flutter, and our Father spoke to my heart. I looked up and said, I love you and give you my soul and life. That scared the crap out of me. I wrote Father Yin back home here, for advice. The sixty five-year-old priest walked fifty miles to get to the nearest phone. He said just four words, Come home, little one. I just knew. The Holy Mother needed me to help make life hurt less here."

God is in this woman. Even a pompous drunk's dreams can see it. A spy would be glib, convincing, and seamless. This nun jerks in her chair, loses control of her words because the passion runs so deep, and gets so lost in emotions that she has to stop and remember I am there. No spy could fake the deep river God in her soul.

It is good being a boy again. My chin in my hands and elbows on the table, I lean into mom's fairy tale.

"I remember one professor. He taught a woman that now loved crusted cheese and wine from dusty bottles about the rotten fish heads and pasty rice her servants ate when she was a girl. Our tribes have fought over food and outsiders since Christ was a kid and didn't know a politician from a parable. The hungry always give the poor land so they all starve slower sharing hope in the rice and rain. Victory gives us greed for a bloated belly every day even if it's another man's meal. Why should anyone starve on ideas?"

"Do you ever feel the weight of their lives on your shoulders, your responsibility, Phil?"

"Yes. The starving can't eat cranky. Faith is forever, not today's election promises forgotten tomorrow. Why the army, Fuzzy?"

"I was hungry, with no job. I slept in a vacated parsonage with no heat, water, or furniture. For two weeks, I ate popcorn and hot tea I stole from the unlocked cabinet in the church kitchen. I enlisted for three hot meals and a warm bed. Two years ago, I was a clerk, a bored clerk that had to shut up and take orders. Someone waived a gold bar at me. I hated following orders and wanted to give them. If they'd only have told me what it would be like."

"Being shot at?"

"Na. War gets ya' high. It's the boredom killing me."

"What about your innocence, Fuzzy?"

"I can't have any. I'm in command."

"You have to save him. No matter why he is lying. He's just a boy. Please... please, Fuzzy."

The Church bell rings. We both jump. Our nervous looks land anywhere but in the other's eyes.

"That means our truce has to be over. The orphans have to be fed. I'll be back here tomorrow. May I go, Fuzzy, or am I still one of your suspects that frightened boys must molest?"

"For now, Phil, I ..."

"Will you have more American butts and Jack Daniels?"

"Sure."

"Stop by for a talk. My ol' man's a good listener. You'll see who's really in command. I'll be busted to sister in charge of latrines if I'm late to Mass. Your decisions are today, Fuzzy. His souls are eternal. Make a difference. The boy deserves it," she says, rushing off.

"Which boy?" I ask, guzzling.

My walk to the Rice House is a boozy giggle. I can forget Phil's wisdom and make this spy shit a non-event in my lazy day. Whiskey sips mean more than the sorrow and war weary why I don't see in Lin Yan's eyes.

"Meow. It's simple if you'd sober up long enough to see it. VC raided Lin Yan's family hut. His brother had been beaten and forced to join their army to save his family.

"Didn't they tell Lin Yan and the parents the older boy would die and they would all be killed unless they helped?" the man with a cat on his shoulders asks in an accusatory tone.

"Prrr. Yes. The greatest betrayal was assigned to the boy. Accuse the nun, or his family would be slaughtered."

After a while, the rumble of a helicopter fills the sky. It lands in the open field yards away. It's carrying honchos who will handle the spy matter. The locals, especially kids, always rush up to a chopper arrival and this is no exception. There are new GIs to hustle for money, cigarettes, and sweets.

I see it all through my whiskey haze. I am the little boy on the Rice House steps fascinated by a firefly. Cat Man and Mees are in the shadow of the tree by the mud well ten feet to my left. The smirk on his craggy face and Mees's hiss are odd I think. No matter. My men are entertaining me. They scream about who got orders for the freedom bird back to the world. They argue like starving wolves over canned peaches in a goodie pack from home. The bidding for ten sheets of stateside toilet paper is up to twenty bucks. One boy shaves his hairless face in the muddy well water. Off to my right are Hillbilly, Nigger, and Spic playing three-handed cutthroat spades while guarding Lin Yan. The kid is stealing change from all three while they slap cards at each other and yell. Corporal Virgin is sitting on his rucksack oiling the Dink pistol trophy from the carcass we honored. Doofus trips his way up to a coke kid to buy a soda and falls as usual, but now with purpose and a don't fuck with me attitude. Toothless Freddie is near Highway 1 in a hot conversation with a crooked back mamasan that has no idea what he is saying. He has his store bought teeth in his hand and is pointing out their best features to the beetle-nut blackened mouth old lady. Her cackle laugh with her hand over her mouth draws a crowd, fascinated by the strange talking man with teeth in his hand. Skinny RTO is marking distance to make sure I am his ten feet away so snipers don't shoot him by mistake. Only Sarge looks at the chopper and shakes his head.

Over the hedgerow to my right, I see Sister Nuyen in the church's garden. Her habit sleeves are pushed up high over her elbows as she weeds the scrawny vegetables she'll add to the orphan's meager bowl of rice. Wiping the sweat from her eyes, she rises to straighten her aching back. Turning my way, she waves and smiles.

"Hi, Fuzzy!" she yells, winking.

"Lieutenant Fuzzy to you, Phil, or no American butts and Jack Daniels!" I bellow, happily.

Despite the noisy circus of life and screw you ego in full perfor-mance, everyone hears our exchange. Someone turns up the tape of Jimmy Hendrix's acid rock, mescaline overdrive Star Spangled Banner from loud to psychotic break. Everything stops and the tribal taunting begins with giggles and goofy dancing.

"LT and Sister sitting in a tree, 'K–I–S–S–I–N–G. First comes lick my balls, then comes roll the grass, then comes the devil fucking her ass', cackles the cat-screech chorus!"

I am angry and blushing beet red. Sister Nuyen is too busy with her weeds to care about sickening jokes. She smiles a blessing punc-tuated with a middle finger and goes back to work.

Out of the chopper steps the MACV officer, the political unit of our army high command, and an Asian officer of the South Vietnamese Army. I see them heading towards me and think nothing. Lin Yan has not looked over at the chopper. His nerves have calmed and he lolls his time kibitzing with the guys at the game of hearts.

Like a languid cloud lolly gagging its way across the sky, the horror is an oozing, slow motion lullaby.

"The itsy bitsy spider went up the water spout,
Lin Yan sees the Asian officer,
The boy's horror washes out.
Rock-a-bye baby in the treetop,
When the wind blows, the cradle will rock
His little arms reach out begging,
"Don't let him take me. Save me, LT!"

Oh-lee-anna, Oh-lee, oh-lee-anna!

He's dragged away,

No one sees the pistol come out.
"Don't you ever ask them why,
You just look at them and sigh,

"Where are you, Mr. Bergman? Please try and calm down, yells the therapist trying to survive my flashback."

I am leaving, I am leaving
But the fighter still remains."

"I should have ... I couldn't ... If only I had ... Dear God!"

For the times they are a changin."
"Nice tunes. Anyone wanna' a drink," I belch seeing Lin Yan. "Where y'all running? What's wrong with—? Why are, What the—?"

It's just a boy I am a   kid fuck you
I am not guilty   mother fucker   mamma
I love   Sister Nuyen   save me LT
no one   was the spy   VC   fuck sister
made
me lie   to buy
some peace here
                             God
                                        please
save me lieutenant please   take me
he will kill me send   to heaven   everdead
                                        for a rest
I was beaten   my brother was taken   forever   we were
all threatened   fuck sister or die
with death   if   didn't   too
                             we   lie   we
would die
            all we ever   and the rain
                    wanted was the rice
                         mamma
Is my name Lin Yan?
                    Why don't   you know?
        Give me back my name   butter bar up your ass
                                 Or drown in tomorrow.
            Tell Mamma-san you sorry
To get back her sorrow.   ego asshole
                                    Be-ah soda Coke-a-Rock-an-Rola
        Roo-ten-ant cold I gots   guts for you.
                        In my bag   balls shiver n' shake
Soda one buck, fuck or Be-ah but two
                        Green back own-ree or choc-oh-rot
    Hot fuck five   cold gimme life ya got.
Dat ARVN Soldier's pistol is a lot— **"Click!"**
        The last thing I see is the why in his eyes.

Junkie hooked on dream not paychecks with suicide notes on the
back
Running out of God gas **A** so he lies alone and coughs in his room
B names I can't remember   gimme booze I must get drunk
Names are crucifixions **M!** on the long lonely winter I remember her
ohleanna   **L** suck me fuck me in we thee   ma what color are
your eyes
Lieutenant's drop quicker   saddle up
              jellied dink eyes **A** smile store bought teeth
savior doofus never picked to play
                  save me **B** can I suck your blue balls
cat man what happened here
          meow fuck you don't ya know **I** fuck me sister
god   where's   my   booze **R**   popcorn
may I piss   one last   time on your picture ma   tea **N** one warm bed
oleanna oh-le-oh-le-anna mamma
                  what the fuck have I gotten into? **S!**

    I kill a 10 year old boy with stupid today.

Is this Monday or next week?
I know I am drunk, mommy.
Did I kill anyone else today?
The engineer of the train
From Warsaw to Auschwitz,
Was he on time or was he hanged?
Are you proud of me, mommy?
I didn't cry today.
Son my sorry son
Don't you know?
Lolli-pop innocence kills no one.
Little boy lies are always true.
Only parent's angers do.
I failed the first quiz.
I know the answer now teacher.
Asians are to Asians
As beating is to death.
I had the glory gold bar.
It's my job
Cat Man yowls
Mees meows.
Is my SAT, Satan asks today, better?
A boy's lie deserves no man's death,
Fuck you mother fucker he yells at me
He was a boy and you should have known.
It's my job I cry?
Was I supposed to know the lie?
Swat his ass, smile and send him bye?
Too late the test is over.
Your grade is his brains on your memory,
See his horror eyes forever.
Where's my common sense?
Who stole my humanity?
Why did war get in the way?
Ohleanna, Oh-le-oh-le-ANNA!

Did I ever know his fucking name?
It's your job echoes tomorrow.
Is my name Lin Yan?
Don't know I
Cry today I not, why?

Endless fields of grain
Stretch from today to forever
Back to Chokio Minnesota.
Fragile stalks sway
One next to a billion
A mighty relentless amber ocean.
Alone dancing so tenderly
A pas de deux of passion.
Wind crashing symphony of simplicity.
Sky rumbles rolls an angry gray.
Immense blue gray warrior gives way.
Clashing slashing hot white streak
Slices the sky to death with fear.
Tsunami summer rain shafts swarm the skies
Beating to submission amber waves of lies.
The mighty ocean of grain sways no more.
Beaten down to a sodden carpet
Rotting death flies
Thoughtless maggot lies
Gutless passion of blood
Of glory gold bar heartless will,
A warm summer rain devours me.
Soaks and shivers my blood soaked soul.
Such an invincible castle I have built,
It's mighty walls fall to mud.
The drenching forever rain must be guilt.
I hate him I with every sigh.

It's my glory gold job.
Today didn't cry I... why?

Is my name Lin Yan he moans.
I have no answer.
For a lifetime he has begged
As his eyes begged that day.
Still I am silent.
The horror of that day
Froze my heart
Made me strong
To eat the shit
Like the taste
Make it through every vodka puke night
And pillow soaked in scarlet tears
Each day still he asks.
I am silent now as then.
Guts yearn to go back,
Kneel at a gray mothers knee,
Beg forgiveness
Say I am sorry
Yet I am here willing
But afraid to go.
I want to know his name
Give him his peace.
I am here.
I have no answer.
Please whisper soft so strong
The echoes of a guilty life.

Is my name Lin Yan?
Why don't you know?
Give me back my name
Or drown in tomorrow.

Tell Mamma-san you're sorry
To get back her sorrow.

Be-ah soda Coke-a-Rock-an-Rola
Roo-ten-ant cold I gots for you.
In my bag it shiver n' shake
Soda one buck, fuck or Be-ah but two
Green back own-ree or choc-oh-rot
Be-ah soda cold gimme life ya got.

Teach me one potato two potato
Ahly alhy unson three potato gore
Why you never teach me hide-n-seek?
Frag fishin' all yah got in your fucked up war?
Rice and rain were dreams and dragons
In my weeds out back now my sister's your whore?
My mother told me to kill you.

Soldiers I've killed with no regret
We share warrior blood, what's respect?
Who they were, what were their dreams
Has never been a thought or pain.
The mellow nun says life's but rice n' rain.
Yet the boy so pure begging me for life,
Lashes me with relentless, what is shame?
He flails my soul raw with gentle cries
Bleeds me full of self-disgust
Taking my life for not knowing his name.

Bullets blood and bodies fly
Battle can't resist commerce coke kids
Smiling the crimson soaked greenback lie
Fuck you schmuck you Rootenant now
I own your happiness while you just survive.

Your gentle moment and quiet smiles are mine.
I begged a symphony you refused to hear
I died at the horizon yet you feel me so near.

Leave home for home,
For a joy shattered life
Guilt is the patient glue.
I am he, he is we
It costs a name to free you.
Please set me free
You took my boy
I your man, do you see?
We must go home
Me to rest you to life
Give me my name
Ends the weary game.

Be-ah soda Coke-a-Rock-an-Rola
Roo-ten-ant cold I gots for you.
In my bag it shiver n' shake
Soda one buck, fuck or Be-ah but two
Green back own-ree or choc-oh-rot
Be-ah soda cold gimme life ya got.

Is my name Lin Yan?
I didn't cry today.

Marion Shelton presents Shelton Award,
named after her POW husband Charles, to Al Chiola,
who called the chopper that saved my life.

Names I Can't Remember

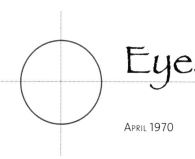

Eyes

April 1970

"They see a big man fall, broken and giving nothing but tears, desperation, and help me. In my men's eyes, I see the shame a kid feels when a bully beats up his father."

Save me!" *scream his terrified eyes as his tiny trembling hand reaches for me. BLAM! Brains. I gasp for air trying to shake hot bloody head mush off my face.*

BLAM! My bloodshot eyes snap open. Feeling my head pounding from another hangover, I stare at my clean hands as my jeep backfires again. Bouncing down the rutted road, I choke on dust and confusion. Driving me somewhere, Sarge's cold stone stare says "don't talk to me."

"Sarge, I gotta give Lin Yan his fishing lesson."

"Lieutenant, the Dink officer blew his brains out last week," Sarge says in a frigid tone, pointing to the back seat.

I turn around and look at the pile of empty bottles.

"Last week? What have I been—"

"Charming, drunk, and so creative!" he grumbles. "What do you want me to do with the General's chopper you stole?"

"When did I learn how to fly?"

"The day you attacked the PX with your tank."

"I tenderly stroke the brown, crusty stenches and stains of Lin Yan's blood and brains on my shirt — hot, wet, and fresh to me.

Sarge sees my trembling, shakes his head, and passes me a half-pint. I daydream as the countryside whizzes by.

"Silkie's sweet, soft tits for you, my mans. I love dem mens wit cash, and when dey needs me."

"I'm so tired. Let me rest, Silkie."

"Come to Silkie, baby."

She tenderly brings my head to her massive breast and feeds it to me. Suckling with my eyes closed and sighing, she hums a lullaby. Her giant breast, my pillow.

"I should have known the kid was lying to save his family. My stupidity pulled that trigger and killed him!"

"Doug, you're here, not there. Doctor! Get in here!" yells the social worker on his knees desperately trying to mop up the pools of sweat flowing off my drenched shirt.

"Save me!" BLAM! Brains.

The Jeep backfires as Sarge slams the brakes.

He brim tips his leather hat, scratches his whiskers, and puffs his meerschaum pipe. "Has he changed, Mees?"

"Meow, just a drunk gorging cocky cookies by the carload. Will these new guys hate him as much as he does?"

They laugh and wander off to into the jungle.

"Where are we, Sarge?" I ask, opening my groggy eyes.

"Where an old soldier cries for the boy he gave away so long ago," sighs Cat Man.

"Your new unit, Lieutenant," Sarge says, laughing.

"My new unit?" I ask, getting out of the jeep.

"Yah. Go figger the Army. Since you ain't dead after couple a months in the bush, you get a cush job, promoted, and some new punk with a head up his ass gets a combat command," Sarge says, slamming my rucksack in my chest.

"I got promoted?" I say, noticing my new silver bar.

"You could have sent my kids home braver and better. But, you get drunk when the first kid gets his head blown off. You taught 'em how to worry. They still gotta fight. Rifles don't fire fear. What do I do with them now, LT?"

Sarge slams me with his fist. He jumps in the jeep and drives off without waiting for the answer I don't have. Adjusting my jaw, I count fifteen men ambling about this radar unit command post near a stream. A generator hums feeding electricity to the fan and lights in my new command bunker. Looking inside, I see a bed with a Commanding Officer sign on it. The mattress is six inches thick. Behind me, shirtless boys play basketball near a backboard made from scrap lumber. Naked soldiers dive off the home made board into the stream. Charred beef sizzles on the barbecue fashioned from a gas barrel. In the throne room, a cushioned seat and stateside TP!

"What are these two jeeps for, soldier?"

"Who the hell wants to know? Oh! Sorry, Sir! You the new Lieutenant?" he says, saluting with a limp wrist and a smile.

"They haul the radars but that never happens. Last Lieutenant just bombed up and down Highway 1 for kicks. I'm Babs, Sir."

"Babs?" I query.

"I do a great Striesand imitation, Sir."

"Babs has the biggest ear collection here, LT."

"Pink bullets make 'em just as dead, Sir. Why don't the Army get it, Sir?"

"Get what, son?"

"I wanna go home more than get a date. 'Sides, these jerks can't coordinate colors to save their ass!" he winks.

The guys all shoot him the moon and laugh.

"Why no wire around the compound?" I ask.

"And keep out coke kids? Can't stop the rockets, LT!"

Days later into my vacation, I lean out the bunker door daydreaming. The fan, whiskey, and ice have me dry and smiling in the jungle swelter. Looking at the hills across the highway that borders the beach on the South China Sea a few thousand meters off, I hatch a plan out of boredom.

"Troop, wouldn't these radars track more Dink movement from the top of those hills?"

"Sure," says the crew-cut kid at the radar. "How do we get 'em there?" He whispers to the boy next to him, "Can't they just give them the bar without a mind? Lieutenant, doing the job too good pisses Dinks off. Rocket attacks get worse. Why make our pool party a war?"

I grab the radio mic. The HQ officer I get is angry.

"Warrior 1, you wanna haul costly and temperamental, night vision radars up a dirty hill, over?"

"Yah Four Star 6. Here, we see the village. Up there, a whole damn valley to see thus kill more Dinks, over."

"Kill Dinks? Why the hell you wanna do that? X bombs times Y bullets equals Z bodies squared, numbers not carcasses! Enemy bodies...the paperwork dem gooks require is— hey, you hustling me for replacements? I gots plenty of boys fresh from the States to trade for dead ones. Hell, that's a zip an' ship no brainer. But, you bust that radar an' they'll shit can my ass, over!"

"What does the general want, a busted radar or a few dozen Dear Mrs. Jones letters to write, over?"

"Damn Warrior 1! Sure I can't get you a soft ice-cream machine. Stuff ain't too runny if yah lick fast, over."

Later, I get a radio message saying transport will arrive soon. I figure one busted down Huey making a pizza or hooker run for the general will limp by eventually.

One Huey has a distinct, low drone, rumble. The thunder that fills the sky today is badass face chewer real. A Cobra gun-ship thunders through the sunlight. My spine tingles. Another Cobra screams by. My cock twitches. As two Hueys rage overhead, ooze drips down my balls, and a satisfied moan escapes my lips.

"Warrior 1, pop smoke for your attack group, over."

Assholes and elbows scramble for guns, gear, and beer. After popping smoke, I bumble my ass into a flight commander seat. There it is; a shinny black flight helmet decorated with skulls and two radio

Names I Can't Remember

mics attached. I hocked every birthday wish for the cocksucker.

"Sir!" barks the Captain that out ranks me, "One's for your channel direct to battalion command. The other is your mission commander's channel to me!"

My cock is so hard; I don't want a drink.

I wear the radio helmet like Caesar's peacock plume in my chariot passing my Legions. The radar operators throw themselves and the units in the open cargo bays and we rage into the air. Cobra hell hounds swirl, dive, and thunder through the sky like winged devils challenging Dinks to a sword fight. Ego pushes my chin high and mists my eyes.

"Warrior 1, this is Body Bag Charlie," the flight commander garbles in his mic just feet away from me.

"Warrior 1, go," I snort, my chest inflating.

"My Cobra cowboys, Cock and Balls, haven't oiled the guns in a while. Request permission to ... secure the LZ."

"Permission granted," I squeak, hearing, "Shoot the bastards between the eyes!" in my Patton imagination.

Last year's touchdown and cop-a-feel kings unload a crap load of boredom on that useless pile of weeds. We could have frightened everything off that molehill with a scream. In slum schools across the land, five kids share 1 book so we could spend a million killing a few dozen rats, gay sissy rats at that!

The radar stays on the hill for a couple of days. My guys spend their days walking down the hill to swim, play ball, and body surf in and on the white beach ocean breakers. At the bunker, we sleep, belch, fart, and swim. War's a mile DMV line, then a kick in the nuts.

Sweltering days and nights pass filled with brain death boredom. I start looking forward to the rocket attacks. Poet turns his sleepy eyes from the static radar screen to me. My hands fumble pushing ammo magazines in my bandoleers that have a clumsy cloth flap on the open end. Drunks always want the easy way.

"Those are such a pain in the ass."

"Yah. The flap makes it so hard to get the ammo out and loaded in a firefight. Maybe if I..."

"Another smartass Lieutenant wants to kill quicker. He who fires faster fights again," moans the Poet.

"Oh-le-anna..."

"What is that tune, Lieutenant?"

"I have no idea. We sang it in OCS."

My hands keep shoving magazines in and out of the clumsy bandoleers. My mind is back on the fields of green. The Poet read aloud from his journal.

> "Gods in starch stiff green,
> Virgin angle white scarves,
> Mirror black boots,
> Sky blue helmets singing
> On vast fields of Georgia green.
> One boy killer prays at the altar
> Of soulless, scarlet wanton glee,
> Smiling smirking evil's smile.
> Kill, maim, carve guts Follow Me!"

> "Oh-lee, oh lee-anna."

> I'm the God in starch stiff green,
> Virgin angel white scarf,
> Mirror black boots,
> Helmet singing sky blue,
> Blood stained conceit brand new.

> **"OHHH-Lee, OHHH-Lee, ANNA!"**

The new Lieutenant meat grinder runs out of fresh carcasses again. Desk jockeys at Division decide to assign me another jungle grunt combat command. I am so drunk and bored, I love the idea.

Before the orders arrive, my kick ass killer Audie Murphy Ammo Vest is done. A local seamstress took two shirts, removed the pockets from one, and sewed them on the other. With the sleeves removed,

I have a vest with many pockets. I wear it over my regular one and load the pockets with ammo magazines. The fourteen magazines normally worn in two magazine bandoleers are now thirty or so magazines in eight, easy to access pockets. I model the vest waiting for the chopper to fly me to my new unit.

"LT, warriors' survive, not assassinate grins the Poet. "Can you handle all the extra weight?" he yells.

In the swirl of chopper noise and dust, I hear nothing, hopping in the cargo bay. The extra twenty pounds from the vest makes me groan but I smile and wave.

The Poet shakes his head. "That bastard thinks cocky hides stupid. How do you tell an ego idiot his strongest enemy is in the mirror?"

The chopper drops me off on a hilltop HQ deep in the jungle. I will command the platoon that travels with the captain's command squad. Home is a fifty-foot circle hacked out of the weeds. Foxholes dug around the perimeter have two or three men assigned to each.

The CO is a crew cut, career West Pointer of fair complexion, foul mouth, square jaw, and toothy smile. I shake his hand and snap the rigid salute his glare demands.

The downpour begins after the chopper leaves.

Hunkered down in mud holes covered with ponchos, I get to know my gang as we fight to stay merely drenched. The cards are wet, letters soggy, food muddy slop, socks twisted from sopping to drenched, and TP is shitty mush.

"God damn monsoon! Three spades."

"Pass," gurgles a kid with a mouthful of rain.

"Four hearts. Any you dicks gotta' dry—"

"NO!" they all yell.

"Pass," I say. My spades hand is full of trumps but I know enough to lose big bucks as the new meat Lieutenant.

"I hate fucking rain," growls the CO.

"Why, Sir?" I ask, sucking up.

"Can't fucking kill Dinks," whispers a kid acidly.

"No body count, no major's oak leaf," boils the captain. He chews acid whisper kid's face off with a glare.

It's an angry distant look in the CO's eyes. I know that look. Finally, I have an officer to share that command loneliness with that's choking my sanity and making me drink more.

"At least the rain cut's down on those 'Dear Mrs. Jones' letters we have to write," I sigh aloud.

"You ever write one?" growls the C.O.

"No," I meekly reply.

"Then shut the fuck up," he blasts.

"So, sending boys out to die doesn't hurt you unless they get killed, maimed or captured?"

The CO crushes his cards so fiercely the men gasp. I'm the only one that sees his other trembling hand closing his pocket flap over a fistful of letters. "There!"

We crawl out of the mud hole, gush, and glop through the mud. He leads me behind a five feet tall bush crushed to three now in the heavy rain. With pinched eyes and trembling with anger, the CO grabs my nuts.

"You wanna' keep these?" he hisses.

"Yes, Sir," I gulp with popping eyes.

"Don't you ever mention their deaths to my boys again!" whispers his butter soft voice cutting steel.

"Yes, Sir," I gasp.

"I like the rain too, Doug. These letters..." he says stopping. His eyes flood with the words in those letters dumping hell on the heaven of mothers' lives he just met.

We stand quietly in deluge rain shivering. The drench washes away our only brother moment. Even together, we are unable to share the crushing weight of those men. Weary eyes secretly hoping this peace treaty rain lasts forever say it all. We walk back to the game, crushed by weary, but faking for the men.

The weather breaks on the fourth day. The sun burns hot and bright on the thick, tangled mass of green that surrounds us to the horizon. The radio crackles to life and the CO grabs the mic.

"Saddle up!" yells the platoon sergeant.

"Well, Lieutenant, ready to kick some Dink ass?"

Names I Can't Remember

"Airborne all the way, Sir!"

"Just what is that weird ass shirt you got?"

"Ammo vest, Sir. Custom made."

"Hacking bush kicks ass. Heavy ain't it?"

"More dead Dinks!" I scream, my back killing me.

"Can the OCS crap. Keep my pimple warriors moving."

"Yes, Sir," I whimper in soggy rock humidity.

"A moment, LT," asks the crew cut career NCO.

"Yah, Sarge. What's up?"

"Two guys are on sick call. We have to divide up the junk they were supposed to hump."

"Give me the radio and one of the ammo cans, Sarge."

"How long since you humped bush, Sir?"

"Couple of months. Why?"

"My bush grunts hump fifty pounds every day and still get their ass kicked. You gunna hump twice that, out of shape, in a hundred degrees, and hundred percent humidity?"

"Give me the extra gear, Sergeant," I yell, so the men hear. Their approving grins stiffen my stupid.

"Snotty prick," Sarge mumbles shaking his head.

I don't hear him. I am busy winning the Jack Daniel's Medal of Honor with guzzle clusters.

The single file line starts hacking down the hill into the thick of the jungle in the cool sunny morning; eighty with 75% humidity. Each man is spaced a few yards apart but in sight for security. Fifty lives and my COs' HQ unit strung out over a hundred and fifty yards in my hands are the axe man's razor sharp massive hatchet rising above my neck. I march a third of the way back near my radioman. The CO is mid-line for safety. The jungle thicket of grass, bushes, and small trees from ground to over our heads is a tangle. Every step is hacked with a machete. For the first hour, the going isn't bad. The men are fresh and the arms are strong. They spell each other each few minutes at point where the hacking is done. A man with his finger on the trigger guards the hacker. After a few exhausting minutes, a new cutter takes over. We maintain a slow march through the jungle.

Like a stateside fresh, combat virgin, I swat the first B-52 mosquito sucking my blood. Watching the next land on my arm, I raise my hand to swat it. Suddenly, I feel my wrist being crushed in a vise like grip.

"Noise makes body bags," hisses a puny private.

I see it in shut the fuck up steely eyes. My bush grunt killers covered in bite sores endured quietly slaughter my glory attitude with that another idiot rookie glare. Nodding my apology, I remember forgotten jungle rules, bitten men live longer not always. The stupid punk Patton irony of all this was that hacking jungle was a noisy mean shoot here sign anyway.

The morning cool swelter gives way to suffer. Stopping to devour some water, men pass me by.

"Save that water, Lieutenant," says one, sarcastically.

"This is the easy whacking," says the weakest.

I stop glugging and turn. While moving, these combat hard vets stay fresh sipping, unzipping, and pissing.

"Nothing's coming out," I mumble looking at my cock.

Stronger backs and mightier arms march by silently.

The next hours hacking moves us no more than fifty yards. The more I adjust and fight the extra weight on my back, the heavier it gets. Invincible, I rush up to the point and take my turn. Hacking and slashing with fury, I move us inches until I stop and stare.

"Why y'all staring at yer leg, Lieutenant?" yawns a hillbilly.

"I want it to, but it won't move," I stammer, as sweat streams off the tip of my nose.

"Stop breathing so hard. Y'all 'er kicking yer own ass thatta' way," he says, taking the machete, indifferently.

I cover my embarrassment staring at a map with sweat blurred eyes. The more I beg my legs to move, the more they twitch in pain. Humming Oleanna sucks my wandering mind deeper into silly smiles and shattering sanity

sing ye glory gods   in powder blue

suck it up,   be out front ... popcorn, tea?

Names I Can't Remember

make your men's lives easier,
    carry more than them,
        push harder   never weaken.
    hack a step, just one more.
        I am, I need, I feel, I fear,
tossed out of my rucksack   one by one to carry them.
    Thighs, butt crack, arm pits, and feet   rubbing
    raw. Jungle noises gone.   Did my prick get hard, Silkie?
Bugs are resting watching   an idiot kid plowing on.
    Man boys labor breath trying to fill our lungs
with silent cement air.   Speaking's too hard. Slurping
    sound men sucking sweet juice fruit
cans opened walking.
        Commander, not person,
        Guzzling water at last
    Can't piss a drop.

    Winter dream mind meandering...

        I scream,   you scream,
    We all scream   for ice cream,

    Sleigh bells ring,
    Are you listening?"

    Will   somebody move the elephant
        Out of the fucking pool!

    Lin Yan why cries every step.

"Hey asshole!"
"Who's that?"
"It's your body, stupid."
"What do you want?"

"You're a Lieutenant, not Superman."
"Follow Me!"
"Well prick. You are going to have to without your muscles. We've had it and we're ready to give up."
"Keep moving! That's an order, body. Oh lee anna..."

At point, my rubber ego arms bounce off the jungle. After seconds that seem hours, another takes the blade from my trembling hand. Men I should be leading pass me again.

"What's with LT?" swaggers Nigger, sucking sweat, a cigarette, and sweet hot water.

"Huh? Something's wrong?" asks Spic, mindlessly honing the machete and hacking mightily.

"Don't meeeeann nuttin'" moans the pissing Corporal.

"Kicking... names... taking ass!" I babble.

"He OK?" yawns another passing by.

"He who? You hear Spade got cookies from home?"

An angry whisper order comes up the line.

"The old man wants to see LT."

"The old man wants to see LT."

"The old man wants to see LT."

"The old man wants to see LT."

"The old man wants to see LT."

"The old man wants to see LT..."

Glory runs my dying body back to him.

"What the fuck is wrong up there, Lieutenant?" he scowls, wearing his sweat like medals.

"Nothing... sir... just... rough... jungle," come the words separated by gasps for hot, wet, lead air.

"Dinks can hear us. Unless you get them moving faster, they'll have time to shit rockets on us. Kick butt up there! Something wrong, Lieutenant? What's the problem?"

Names I Can't Remember

"No Dinks to slaughter!" Then, my rubber mind babbles.

"Whenever trouble tries to come around, you can hear that mighty sound. Here I come to save the day! Means that Mighty Mouse is on the way!"

"Lieutenant?"

Mush brain manic panic runs my limp burning body back to the point. My bowels let go.

"You're the problem, solve the problem!"

How many men pass?

I don't remember.

Becky's giving me a hand job.

Does any man speak?

I don't know.

I'm stealing popcorn

And hot tea from,

"Help me?" screams my body.

"More weight?" yells my glory silver bar.

I don't remember.

In the   coffee   house play.

God... !!!!!!!!!!!!!   I was brilliant that night.

Ma gives   great   head

Swallows every drop,

The last   she shares kissing   me.

'Oh, lee-anna.   Oh, lee, oh, lee-anna...'

You're the problem, solve the problem.

Save me, Lin Yan's eyes forever cry. Blam! Brains.

One by one, my men pass me, enter the shallow stream, and cross. On the opposite bank, they huddle to squeeze socks dry, drink water, and smoke. No one sees me enter the stream until my body gives out, falls, and I begin to crawl: one hand and knee then the next as somewhere sings the Bhai's soft lullaby of soul.

"Break your load into small parts so you are stronger than it, and carry it over many familiar miles," says the Bha'i that refused to shave, vanishing into a shadow.

"Fuck, you!" I yell, crawling.

"Stub your toe, LT?" wonders the man passing by.

The slimy rocks are cushions. Cool water forgiveness makes me smile. I stand, wobble, trip, and crawl. Silver bar glory and last gasp dreams flood me with defiance. Another hand and knee forward through the cool water on my blazing dry skin. The water is Silkie's sweet nipple. Nothing I see, falling, rising, crawling, hand, and knee by inches three. Such cool, cool rest, fall in the water I wonder but don't. My dead body twitches beaten by lives never mine to save. My aching neck can't raise my head.

"Is something wrong with LT?" yawns one private.

I tremble in the cool water Madrid of my panic agony. I paw at the water. Razor sharp sand rips my flesh raw. My bull ring emotional mud soaks in scarlet agony.

"What's LT looking at down there?" wonders the chowhound, gulping jellied beef stew from a can.

My head sinks lower, hamburgered by picador steel Pride and Ego. "Let the proud beast live," cheers, I hear.

"Huh?" answers the unconcerned kid, guzzling water and jiggling his prick dry.

Slime snot bile gushes from my nose. I refuse to fall. I slash my horns snorting one last violent groan.

"Why ain't he sweating?"

My mouth opens to beg for water. Silence. My gut yowls demand my body to move. Silence. My mouth drools mucous no more. Desert dead muscles refuse to move. In my Satanic sanity, Manolete's muletta flourishes, his blade sinks to my heart, and I thrash my head high to the sun one last glorious time.

My men's massive daddy why eyes is all I see. They cut me screaming, "It hurts when you're not strong... I'm afraid... protect me, Dad." I see and feel their fear. Weakness and the desire to give up bleed me dead of the last drops of Oleanna glory. Shame beats me flat in the water.

"Did he trip?" asks one, scratching his balls.

My groveling soul reaches out my hand for victory my loser life never earned. I gasp in horror seeing eyes that surround, attack, and accuse. I see all that love, cherish, and admire my ballsy life of surviving everything and helping anyone crack from weakness, lies, and failure. I crawl a step and look. In my men's eyes, I see the shame a kid feels when a bully beats his father. In their looking away, I sense the wife beaten when the crisis weeps the husband she needed to lean on for strength. In their accusatory whispers I hear every family's death yowls as the man they expected to lead them from the burning house runs out to save himself and watches them burn. My head falls in the water. Rise body and lead them! It refuses. I moan. They stare. Afraid for their lives, they see a big man fall and crack giving nothing but tears, desperation, and help me.

Those soul carving eyes shove my face in the water. My mind manically races to any yesterday way out of the shame I feel. Damn your deaths just watching bullies stick my crying fat ass in the school wastebasket! Save your own fucking lives for watching Mom blubber seeing my drunk's piss covering her favorite painting. Don't look as I swallow the pills lined up in front of my volumes of pimple poetry loneliness or I run with his cumm in my mouth liking the taste! Can you see me drink myself black to forget every theft or hide behind costumes and smiles to fill the lonely and hide the anger? Were they there, at the bridge when I gave in to the OCS wolf pack demanding I surrender my command? Do they see me at Silkie's as my limp dick gets limper? No! I try crawling again but fall flat to see desperate eyes men beg me again to rescue them once more in bloody glory victories only in my mind.

"Tired, I guess?" says one smoking, robotically.

"Nah. Just filling his canteens?"

Those savage eyes are cocks ripping my ass as I yowl. I crumble in a scalding shower fully clothed. I clasp my arms around a bleeding heart. I choke on fear, anger, and bewildering violation shoulda' coulda' can't wash away. Rivers of me save them not thee me eyes drown me in failure shame of self-blame ego rape.

"Meow. What color is the rainbow?"

"What would you like it to be?" smiles Cat Man scratching his whiskers and tapping his pipe tobacco.

"Blue. I love blue," I sigh.

"Then dream the dragons in baby boy blue eyes."

"Ahhh. It looks so cool, clear, and calm."

"Drink today's destiny dry. Why is tomorrow's cry."

My eyes open. Feet away is another stream. My pulse pounds. What the fuck is wrong? I crawl out of this one, rise, and wobble stumble trip on to the next gasping, grasping, and growling confusion.

"You're the problem, slowing them down.

Solve the problem, risking their lives.

You're the problem, failing as a leader.

Solve the problem, weakness isn't glory or honor.

You're the problem... oh-le-anna.

Save them solving you!"

A desperate lie is the only solution I see. If I fake an appendicitis, I eliminate the problem, me, because the CO must Medevac me out to complete his mission. I fall in the stream holding my gut that doesn't hurt. The CO runs up the line to the edge of the stream.

"What the fuck is going on here?"

"LT collapsed and grabbed his side," yells a private.

"Jesus Christ. I got a mission and a puke LT wants me to call a Medevac in the middle of nowhere? Snap out of it! Get on your fucking feet and push on!"

"Sir... sir, LT is burning up. I think—"

"Aaaaaaaaaaaaahhhh!" I scream in no pain.

"Get him in the water to cool him," yells the RTO.

"Eagle one, Eagle one, this is Valkerie 6, over. Where's my damn map? RTO, where's the fucking map?"

"Ah, in your hand, Sir?" says his timid RTO.

The screaming continues. All the while, cold water is pouring over me. Men gather yelling "what the fuck," "what's wrong," shrug, and walk away shaking their heads.

Silkie softly sings, bringing my head to her nipple. Rest sweet rest as my wonder wanes, a big man fallen.

I hear the chopper thundering closer to the ground. Thrown inside like a bag of shit, I'm smiling. The shame doesn't hurt anymore. I pass out.

"The truth is I wanted to give up. A cowards' lie was all I had to believe that I was still leading and solving the problem, me. Help me beg my eyes. Not one fucker does a damn thing! Why do we all help the helpless but watch in wonder disgust when a big man falls?" I scream at the devastated counselor sweating my shame.

"Oooo ahhhh," I sigh, waking under cool sheets soothing my bare ass on a thick, soft mattress.

Keeping my eyes closed, I listen to the quiet snoozing. Over there, I hear the squeaky rubber soled shoes. Some kind of cart rolls by. Is that moaning or whimpering I hear? Who cares? A smile drifts across my face. I reach to scratch the itch on my nose. It still itches. Scratch again I say to myself.

My eyes pop open. My arm isn't moving.

"Aaaahhhh!" I yowl, in paralyzed horror. Sweat instantly drenches my face. My eyes bulge wide.

"Ssssh. Relax," gently whispers the angel in white, stroking my cheek. "It'll be a while before you can move. You're getting shot with the best dope we got and—"

"Shot!? Oh, my God!" I yell looking at my crotch.

"Yes. It's all there," winks the nurse, patting it.

"I've dreamed of this moment. You are supposed to have perky, melon tits and a grab that saddle ass."

"Don't knock it," lisps the bearded private. "You weren't shot. See that IV in your arm? Saline and water."

"Just what did you do to your body, son?" asks the stern doctor wandering over and looking at my chart.

The counselor puts a comforting hand on my shoulder. I lurch away and crawl to the corner for private tears.

"I had to carry more, make it easier for them."

"Can't lead anyone dead. What do they teach in OCS? You lead, not pamper them. Well, Superman, the body is ninety eight percent water. When you got here, that number was fifty at best. Your muscles froze trying to suck up what was left. Your brain was within seconds of being crusty mush. That's *third degree*, killing heat stroke. It's gonna be a few days before your body lets you move."

"Nothing wrong with my appendix?" I ask, weakly.

"Pink and perky. Let me make this fast and simple, you conceited punk. You came in here not bleeding with twice the gear of any two-stumps gushing grunt I ever saw. Whatever happened, you did it to yourself. While the heat stroke was killing you, you jumped in the grave suffering some weird situational anxiety."

"Huh? Speak patient, not god"

"Nervous breakdown! I have to tell real soldiers they have no face. I got no time to baby-sit a punk with more balls than ability. You nearly killed you. Got it?" he says, slamming my chart down and swaggering off, shaking his head in disgust.

"I solved the problem," I sigh, countering his insult.

After a few days of immobile re-hydration, I get a rolling IV stand. I hobble through the ward delivering Lieutenant cheer. Smiling, I defy my agonizing muscles.

"LT, my leg feels great!" smiles private delirium.

"Get your sorry butt here with me kicking ass and taking names, troop!" I bellow to the kid stroking a limb that isn't there.

"That you, LT? How's my face look?" a blond kid begs.

"Hollywood, that face is gonna win an Oscar!" I lie to the punk getting fresh dressings and massive morphine for his mangled hamburger mug beyond repair.

Tripping over my IV stand wheels, laughter explodes.

"Trip on that silver bar again, LT?" screams the carcass in plaster from forehead to four stumps.

"Nah. I keep forgetting to throw my cock over my shoulder, you fuck. When you get an itch, fuck yourself!"

Recovery complete, I'm transferred for re-assignment.

I sleep late, eat great, drink my memory drunk, read, and watch movies. One day, my hooch door bursts open.

"LT, the Battalion Executive Officer, wants to see you," says the private disturbing my mid-day hangover nap.

Throwing my legs over the edge of my bunk, I smack my lips trying to wet my sandy beach mouth. I rub my throbbing head to ease the pounding and scratch my whiskers.

"Bad night, Sir?" asks the smiling kid.

"It's day? Nah. It was a great Monday, I think."

"Ah, it's Tuesday, LT," giggles the private.

"What happened to Monday?" I ask, squinting.

"That would be when you ate the hooker on the bar."

"Hope I enjoyed it," I say, putting on my pants."

"So, you got orders back to the bush, Sir?"

"No way! Let some new meat LT earn his nuts. This is my time to get very laid, and very drunk," I say smiling.

"Ah, the Major pats you on the head and gives you that cush job to finish out your time," he laughs.

Throwing on my hospital shirt, I reach for the door.

"Good luck, Lieutenant. You earned it."

His words freeze my hand on the door.

"What's the matter, Sir?"

"Huh? Nothing," I respond worrying about what I had just earned. Dragging the kid down the dirt path to the HQ office my arm slung over his shoulder, I blather and babble my battle tips to the confused kid that types a hundred words a minute. At the honey pot burn station, two bare chested kids take a break.

"Hey, LT, give us a hand before you saddle up for the bush, will yah," they grin, waving me over.

"Not a chance, troops. This swinging dick is about to get his desk job and ticket on the Freedom Bird!" I yell.

"Oooo! Welcome to the rear WIMP, you Weak, Incompetent, Malingering, Pussie," they yowl, bowing.

In an explosive fury, I leap on the taunting troop. It takes four men to pull my hands off the boy's throat.

"I'm no wimp, you fuck!"

"Easy, LT. It's just a saying. We're all wimps here." "WIMP? No! Me... I'm a... WIMP not warrior?" I snivel.

"Kiss the Major's ass for the cushiest job!" they laugh, slapping me on the back.

"I'm puckered. I am puckered," I yowl, like a wolf.

We share a beer and some crude jokes for a while. The rest of my walk to the Major's office is nearly a jaunty skip and hop. I moon the jeep load of grunts headed to the jungle. At a roadside crap game, I win fifty bucks.

"This is your lucky day, LT," growls the kid with the beady eyes, empty wallet, and massive rucksack.

"My boy, that rucksack won't kick your ass now that I've lightened your load a bit," I grin, counting.

I slug back hair of the dog from their Black Jack bottle. With a puffed chest and a smile, I smell the cash and leave. On this sunny day, I take a deep, self-satisfied breath and knock on the Major's door. Nothing. I knock louder. Nothing. With whiskey guts, I bang on the door with a closed fist.

"Lieutenant Bergman, for the fucking Major!"

"Bergmmaaan" is the low, disgusted growl. "When I want your sorry ass in here, I'll let you know, Lieutenant."

"Sir, yes Sir!" I yell, my asshole snapping shut.

I bake in the sun for bullet sweat minutes.

"Come in," is the guttural groan.

I enter and cross to his desk in a relaxed manner. Sitting behind the desk is his tall and lean frame. The Major is hunched over some papers. He doesn't look up at me. He says nothing. I feel the room full of quiet, confusing tension. Wary, I try to relax and wait.

"You're at attention, Lieu... Lieu-tenant," he says, choking on a word he doesn't want to say.

My back stiffens. My heels snap together. My chest thrusts out and my chin shoves down. I feel his refusal to look at me. He shuffles papers breathing contempt. I stare at his head covered with regulation stubble short hair. I snap a brisk, rigid salute, and wait for him to return it. From crisp sound alone, he knows I've thrown one.

He doesn't look up or return it; a your shit's weak moment any soldier knows. Confusing scorn fills the thick silence. I stiffly stand until it melts away and my arm slinks to my side. His coup de grace growl tells me he relishes denying me dignity. Finally, his head slowly rises. A loathing look spits in my face and jerks me back. I gasp and my eyes snap wide.

"Save me!" BLAM! Brains and stream eyes scream shame.

"I've read Captain Coxs' report of what happened," he says, in a lifeless tone. "Bellyache. Not a shot fired."

"Yes, Sir!" I snap back.

"It's my job to assign, do something with you."

"Yes, Sir!"

"I could transfer you to another unit. I could keep you right here and grind you to dust. That, I would love. I'm not sure what to do with a spineless coward."

My stunned face screams, coward?

"You turn my stomach. It's right here in front of me. It simply astounds me. Under NO enemy fire, do you hear me you shit; you desert your men with the malingering act of the son-of-a-bitch you are! You disgust me."

My knees buckle.

"I can't stand to look at you. With no threat in sight, you fail your command responsibility for the mission and the lives of your men with massive disregard for the honor held dear by every officer in the infantry. If I replace all the enlisted men emptying piss barrels and burning shit with you, it would be an insult to the shit."

Every word is a sledgehammer beating my body and pride crawling in that stream. I gasp for a breath of disgust.

"I hate your fucking guts. I considered refusing to deal with this. It is the only time I almost refused an order in my entire career. I had to look at the chicken shit that crawls on his belly to get out of combat, even when the combat hadn't happened yet, and lays his sorry fucking ass down just to get Medevac'd out. You're the puke in my stomach I'd love to heave in your face."

He shoves some papers in front of me.

"Sir?" I whimper.

"Resign your commission for the good of the service."

My whiskey blubber gut seizes into rock. Horrified eyes see my assassin smile as he tastes the delicious agony of my dying suddenly. His throaty growl echoes in my ears as my eyes snap open. Beads of sweat explode on my quivering lips. My fingers twitch and my mind races. I see every bravery real and imagined.

"Give me the damn extra gear, Sarge," I yell.

"You're the problem. Solve the problem," I scream inside, flailing at the jungle and pushing through panic shattering me..

Crawling in the stream, I raise my head again and am beaten down by their eyes. I drag my dead body on, fall again, and scream while holding my gut.

"Resign" echoes pounding my head. I shake, violently.

"No, Sir!" I yell, in bewildered shock.

His pencil shatters in his trembling anger fist.

"Was there any firefight when you... you crawled on your belly?" he seethes hard enough to spray spit at me.

"No, Sir. The doctor says—"

"Fuck him!" The chair squeaks as he runs his hand over his baldhead. "Were there any Dinks anywhere near you?"

"No, Sir. I humped twice what they... They say I had—"

"You had no fucking balls!" he screams so intensely his face floods red and his veins bulge. "Resign!"

"But, I saved them from me... my job?" I whine.

"You prick. You turned Captain Cox's fifty brave boys into chicken shit kids with no faith in the chain of command. They watched an officer give up like a coward. Get the fuck out of my office, you spine-less fuck! God, I—"

"I did what I had to do?" I moan, my weak salute melting away. The Major turns away, refusing to face me.

Trembling and turning to leave in shock, I freeze in my steps. Cat

Man and Mees wink at me from the shadows.

"*What he saw in their worried eyes wasn't hate but nothing more than the shame he felt.*" Cat Man whispers.

"*Meow, a boy's excuse for a man's failure. He can't face that he wanted to give up, give in, and did. The appendix crap was just his excuse and guilt band-aid.*"

Oozing out of the Major's office, I wander aimlessly. Stumbling over dusty ground in my hospital gown, I pass a private fresh from stateside. He spies the Officer's bar pinned to my robe and snaps a crisp salute. At first, I begin to weakly return it until my arm falls to my side as I search for words.

"Don't do that. Only officers deserve..." I mumble.

"But you are one. Sir... Sir?"

At the end of the dirt path, I stop at the ravine near the edge of the command compound. Looking at the lines and lines of latrines, I stare at the swirling smoke and suck in the stench of the gas burning the shit and piss in the honey pots. I stop near bare chested soldiers with lit cigarettes hanging from their jaws while slopping gas into one of the halved barrels. Nigger passes his booze bottle to Spic and fingers the white boy LT walking by. I grab the bottle out of the stunned kid's hand. He glares at me as I guzzle the bottle dry in one gulp and step in a fresh honey pot. I drop the bottle and gaze at them with dead eyes until my head falls back.

"Man, I seen that look before, brother. Boy goes into the Major's for a gold star. Comes out on death row."

"You gonna pay us for that booze, LT?" asks laughing Nigger while Spic holds his side.

I stumble to my knees getting out of the barrel. I reach out. The booze bottle falls. My hand reaches out and my eyes beg for help. Their stream shame laughing shoves me to my belly and my face in the piss and shit mud. I begin crawling and learning to like the taste of coward. I rise and fall with each few steps.

"Tell me something," I beg, unable to look at them.

"Sure, you crazy Honkie," giggles one to the other.

"Is the shit insulted?"

Popcorn and hot tea
Shkal mwkolial, mmm t oopa
Ooo doo wanzi, laty binzi dee
Pawkilol rigdon zilly lee
Gilly limme mamma law wa
Limme gilly wa law mamma
Lishy mucka, ZOO don zilly zee
Popcorn and hot tea
Oh...lee...anna
Oh-lee, Oh-lee, anna.
Cross the boy with angel song.
Dead man smiling cold and long.
Hillbilly, Nigger & Spic
Nag, NAG! Koo ooo waloo
Nag, NAG! Koo ooo waaloo
Shilla sham ba we thee
Wah nah walla god boo you
Gika shree ma dat looah jick
'Away' scream, hillbilly, nigger and spic
Virgins ssshhhh di ssshh oftly sshhhh
Um dilly, um dilly, um dilly lam dat
Billy bot hau woo woo f n I dy jol
X riss, ma riss, tor riss quim...
Kila ba—
Kila ba—
Kiiiiiii... laaaaaa... b, b, b, b... ahhhhh
Virgins see the eyes
Virgins feel the lies
Store Bought Teeth
PIKA MUK DUK QUK!
D lala ooo, D LALA OOO
GRUK! Fuj. GRUK n GRUCK MU!
Rah doahla... dooahla m n dit ma
Li, hum li, hum li rah do-ah-LA dit ma.
Ah kee

Ah kee
Jo ah nome, jo ah nome weeth
Blood for store bought teeth
Is My Name Lin Yan
ssshhh do woo, ssh do woo,
f loo wallah fon do woo wa doo!
PIA DAWADA, piadawada, piada—
wada n, n, n yyyyy
wu oppa von ji, kia wa do
do wa doo
do wa doo
Eyes
Koodoo malayless f mon j dalala!
Penk wini mok fer mon, d mon za, d mon za dool
N dol shula p shula, d mon za, d mon za dool
No words
That still I see
Eyes all that's left for me
Eyes disgust all full of pity
Left for me, eyes of we me thee
Never again popcorn boy, hot tea free

Virgins run from lies
Cowards see the eyes.

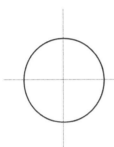

Poets, Pimps, & Poker Players

JULY - OCTOBER 1970

"A hero is just a coward more afraid of doing nothing. Reality is on tomb-stones and in last drinks. Takes guts to know that all you have left to give is fear and failure."

I limp home from the Major's office staggering, drenched in be-wilderment sweat and lost in my emotional tornado of cow-ardice and humiliation. At the stream, my fake appendicitis got rid of the danger to my men, me. I could hide the lie in a fading memory that would grow kinder in time. His demand that I resign turns my white lie solution into shoot the coward revulsion. At the next honey pot burn station, I take my pants covered in piss, shit, coward and toss them in the flames.

I turn and look at the grunts stepping out of a latrine. Fresh from the states surprised replacements stand quietly across from me. The burning drum separates us. My granite stare has them mumbling and pointing in fear. The bolder looking of the two with the ruddy face stares back trying to figure me out. Lurking behind his shoulder, his pasty face bookish buddy thumbs through the Army manual. As the smoky stink fills our lungs, I pass the bold one my whiskey canteen. He drinks and spits it out.

"This rotgut'll turn yer mind to mush."

"You got a truck load?" I ask, with begging eyes.

"You do know you are naked, Lieutenant, don't you?"

"Yup."

"Just checking."

"Are we supposed to salute naked Lieutenants, Harvey? The manual don't say shit about naked," asks pasty face.

"Damn! Don't call me Harvey. It's goofy. No grunt is Harvey. Harv, OK? Jeez. It's like calling the Duke, Jonathan."

I grab pasty face by the scruff of the neck and pull the terrified kid in nose to nose.

"Harvey is a great name for a grunt. Don't ever forget it. You hear me? Harvey now and always. Remember—?"

"Ye... ye... yes, Sir," stutters the kid.

"Why you bein' such a hard ass about such a stupid thing as a name, LT?" demands the brave kid.

"This place hurts forever. Names heal you quicker."

"Meow. He needs expensive booze or cheaper agony."

"Can't burn memories doused with shame," Cat Man sighs as he pets Mees and wanders off.

The grunt holds me up and walks me to my hooch.

"Why weren't you at the stream?"

"Huh? LT, let's get you cleaned up and some sleep."

"No! No sleep. I'll dream—"

"OK! OK. No sleep. I got some good scotch."

"Yah, gimme all the scotch you got, please."

"LT, you killed. How do I deal with that?"

BLAM! Brains.

"Don't look in their eyes!" I yell, blacking out.

"Ah! Here it is, Harvey. You must salute any officer in uniform. Nothing about naked," says the kid, saluting.

"Great, Malcolm. Find the section in the manual about idiot friends who salute naked ass, passed out LTs."

I open my eyes, wonder what day it is, feel a pounding hangover, and see pink-cheeked kids fresh from stateside around me. Feeling my fresh clothes, I look over the faces terrified I'll see someone from the stream and see those Auschwitz eyes again.

"Great orders, LT!" says the kid, slapping my back.

"Huh? What orders?" I ask the smiling gang. I'm with replacements in a chow line.

"Y'all listen to the LT, fellers. Look at that shit eatin' grin," bellows the country boy handing me a tray.

"Where's your store bought teeth, Freddie?"

"Huh? I'm Billy Joe."

"Will forgetting the names make it hurt less?"

"Meow. War kills boys, never old men's memories."

"You say something, LT? How's a grunt get the Major to give him a kick back easy rear job, LT?" winks Spic.

"Kill many Dinks, Lieutenant?" rattles Nigger with acne.

"Sure he did! He got promoted and still has his nuts don't he?" guffaws some Doofus shoving his glasses up.

"Bet y'all itchin' to head back to the bush?"

"Nah. LT's earned kicking back, a rear area WIMP!"

"Weak Incompetent Malingering Pussy!" they all yell.

"I'm not a WIMP!" Standing outside the long sandbag building with a tin roof, I grab one punk's whiskey bottle. Guzzling silences the laughter and I black out.

Clacking typewriters and a droning voice wake me again. What day—who is he I wonder? My new CO in this rear area HQ Company? That's Army speak for hangovers, whores, and fuck you chores. I smack to wet my whiskey dry, cracked lips and puff a breath to sniff how bad I reek. The five-foot nothing Major in front of me has a stern look that says "I'll chew your face off if you screw up."

"I've read the Major's report, Lieutenant."

Names I Can't Remember

"Yes, Sir," I wince back.

"Between this report and the, a-hah, aftershave you are wearing, I don't think an Army career is a wise choice," he says, nearly laughing at his own joke.

My Napoleon in a crisp uniform, stiff manner and West Point broom up his ass wanders to the corner of his anally neat desk. It takes two tries before he can throw a leg over the corner and sit without looking silly. Thumbing through my papers, he looks up at me with a steady gaze.

"The Major has you a coward that should be shot. It doesn't match with your early file. Enlisting for three years these days shows guts. You start a clerk and volunteer for leadership school, airborne, heavy mortar platoon commander school, and infantry OCS. I smell a survivor between the lines. I like survivors. It takes balls to refuse a superior officer demanding you resign."

"How did you know—"

"Information gives little men one damn big stick," he winks. "I don't care what really happened out there. I'm sure the truth is half his revulsion and half your hangovers. You can work in my office as my assistant kissing my ass that loves big wet smackers or get your nuts back leading the commo platoon."

"The commo platoon, Sir."

"Good. My ass is sore. Something tells me my job will be easier if I get your shoulders up and your lips off my ass. Son, I'm five foot one. The gold leaf doesn't make me six six, my balls do."

I snap a crisp salute and head out to command my new commo platoon. Outside his massive sandbag HQ bunker, my backbone and shoulders he lifted a bit, slump. Not seeing my balls anywhere, I empty my whiskey pint to black out.

"Meow. Tell me a single name," Mees hisses, cruelly.

"I can't. I don't remember," I moan.

"Happy you're here, not there?" Cat Man seethes.

"Yes," I say, hesitantly.

"So, who did you save, the men or you?" Mees growls like the Major that demanded I resign.

I bristle but bellow nothing.

"Save me!" BLAM! Brains.

Fuck You, Chicken Shit, and Coward, my private shame at the stream firing squad, pull their triggers.

Cat Man winks and puffs his pipe. "All the answers are here. You're home is poets, pimps, and poker players."

THE POET

"Aarrggh! Jesus Christ!"

"Who the hell are you?" I ask the skinny guy next to me in the officer's latrine.

"James L. Dudley, Lieutenant James L. Dudley."

"L?"

"Mamma was a good Baptist but Daddy was, ssshhh, a New York Jew. Lucifer, her payback for being called a shiksa."

I look at his charming, wide Southern smile. It's the glee of mint juleps before noon, and swallowing the key he used to lock mamma in the attic with bon bons and Dr. Pepper after she signed the new will. The twinkle in his voice is silk and lace.

"Paper please! My asshole's covered with Yankee guts."

I hand him toilet paper silently. His easy manner with a jagged edge and compliment smiles hide insult eyes that dagger my heart.

"Thank you," he says with syrupy sweetness that quiets me. It's that plantation parlor politeness to his boy Nathan a nasty nigger in white only Bubba bar bluntness.

When we look at each other, he offers his hand. When I hesitate, he wipes it on his shirt and we laugh.

"Gonna be a lotta' hours between meals, hangovers, and paper clips clogged with earwax, Douglas."

"How do you know who I am?"

"If y'all gotta' know, go to Dudley.' Money only solves problems when I have it. Information makes me rich even when I'm broke. I'm the Fort Knox of secrets, loan shark of forgiveness and Bible of Bubba BS, Douglas," he laughs with a white toothy grin.

"Jesus, how about an answer instead of a riddle?"

"Y'all wandered by buck neh-kid and drunk. I hauled your sorry ass to the hooch for Lieutenants with panache. Next time, greet your new Platoon Sergeant with an ass kissing bribe not a drunken tirade. If he'd a been sober, even me knowing he wears panties wouldn't a saved yer sorry Yankee ass."

"Thanks. So, what do we do, Jim?"

"Not Jim, OK? James is fine. Most call me Dudley. Let's just say, you are the Yankee. I am the yankor! What we do, Douglas, is stay busy keeping everyone else from figuring out what we're supposed to do. That is the life of a rear area officer. If they ever find out there's nothing to do, it's the bush again. You want that?"

"No."

"Speak up like you got balls, boy!"

"Yah. That does seem to be the issue."

"We don't get many live infantry officers here. Who'd you piss off? Y'all was babbling about eyes and streams?"

My soul whimpers please don't ask.

"OK, a marriage of demons and none of y'alls business. Don't give a damn. We're gonna like one ta other jes' fine. You ah, play cards at all?" he asks, innocently.

"Poker? Seems I did... a long time ago. Three of a kind beats a full house, right?" I respond, dully.

"I do de-clah, a carpetbagger with money in his hand, a smile on his face, and back stabbing bullshit in his black heart. Keep talking, Douglas. Give a Yann-keh 'inuf rope, he'll hang hiz-sef! Pass that lilly white Mason-Dixon paper, Douglas."

"Only four sheets left, Dudley."

"Well, you gave us Reconstruction and niggers with attitude," he says, snatching the paper.

He hands back one square. We laugh.

"How come talking to my guys wasn't this easy, Dud?"

"You wiped asses instead of shitting with them. Your answer is, I'm the first asshole here that's a friend, not a responsibility. I'll jes tuck y'all's guilty coupon away for later redemption. Redemption, damn I'm good. Doc Dudley is in! Whatever Army crap plugs y'all's poon tang, I gots the enema; Plantation Bloody Marys, Louisiana Hot Sauce, bayou lies, and defiance! I'll show you around. So many hangovers, so little time. Dudley to the rescue."

We leave the latrine. Dud points out our comfy compound of bunker offices lost in the mass of this gigantic rear area. Three-ton trucks rumble on dirt roads like elephants looking for water. The hazy blue sky is black with a locust swarm of Dust-off, red crossed choppers screaming by full of bodies for the hospital. Bloody grunts hanging out of the open chopper bays yell like hell bound warriors.

"Give 'em a wave, Douglas. Yours may be the last friendly eyes they see," Dud says waving.

I turn away and stare at the ground.

"What the Sam hill did that Major say to you?"

"How do you know if you're a coward?" I ask, too ashamed to look at choppers going where I should be.

"What's the difference between a hero and a coward? They're the same terrified kid. A hero is just a coward more afraid of doing nothing. What did you do!?"

"None of your damn business!"

Dud walks away, turns, and angrily kicks at the dirt again. "Douglas, that Major have a pencil like this one?"

"Yes."

"All the answers and truths of the universe are in this damn pencil. There's only one thing it can't do."

"What?" I ask, shielding my eyes from the sun.

Dud walks over to me, takes my hand down, and sticks his nose in my face. His smile twinkles.

"Damn pencil can't look in a man's eyes and pull the trigger, or not. Pencil needs an idiot to tell it what to say. Here, reality is on tombstones and in the last drink. Coward is how pencil leaders blame folks when they ain't got the guts to face the same crap. The closest that desk jockey ever got to war is who gets the last steak in an air conditioned chow hall with linen on the tables."

"So that makes him wrong, Dud?"

"No. It makes it too easy to be right. Any idiot can kill with tradition.

It takes guts to know that all you have left to give is fear and failure. It's the nightmare you want to dream again. What's killing like?"

Dud grabs my slumping body and we walk on silently.

The buildings are large sandbag bunkers beefed up with gigantic wood beams. The rectangular bunkhouses roofed in tin are for enlisted men. Officers sleep 6 to a hooch with thick mattresses, private space and air conditioners if you are rich, good at poker, or a good hustler. Dud has one big ass air conditioner. He points out everything that matters; showers, latrines and the bar. The area is half a football field size covered in dirt, weeds, trees, and small hills. His minutes walking tour ends at the Officer's Club.

"Douglas, here we win the war with the first drink and lose it in the last hand of the night. Booze and bad cards fight wars. All grunts do is fire bullets, count bodies, and bury guilt."

"When does it open, Dud?"

"Ah, the hair of the dog committee lines up at the door at eleven. Bloody Mary's are up by eleven O one Zulu sharp! In here is enough rot gut and prime jungle juice to sink the Titanic. Juke box there. Slot Machines there. Conference room there.

"Conference room?"

"The poker table, Bubba. That's where everyone is when the old man can't find us—them."

"Aah. He's in conference, sir?"

"Now you got it, boy. What you buying me?"

"Bar keep, Plantation Bloody Mary's here!"

"Y'all got promise. I'll make you a Bubba yet."

"A Bubba?"

"A Bubba is bourbon, branch, bull shit and don't give a damn what people think. He goes to black tie dinners in a pick-up with a rifle rack, wearing boots and jeans, and has the best flowers for the hostess. He tells jokes that get the broom up the ass folks blushing and laughing. When the shrimp slide by on a silver platter, a Bubba scoops 'em up in a bag, thanks the nigger for the bait, and puts the shrimp fork down after he cleans his ear wax off it with a linen napkin. I'm the plantation version, born with a silver spoon in my mouth. Life was good,

Douglas, 'till the army found out what a whiz I was at counting... beans," he finally blurts out, trembling.

It's my turn to hold him up while his lie beats him down. Dud's far off gaze and quivering lip tell me whatever he does, it has nothing to do with beans.

Recovering, he sips away his own lies and continues. The smile is gone. It's a sad tone of resignation.

"I am lost in the literature of lazy, a true Southern son's state of mind. I am Ferlengetti's Coney Island of the Mind and Brautigan's wave of Watermelon Sugar. Next to me, Hemingway and Brautigan were just drunks and lousy shots."

This irreverent poet makes me smile. Dud is a milky pale skin, slender nothing of a man about five eight with dark auburn hair. Even the skin on his elbows is smooth. To Dud, back breaking work is using a handmade linen napkin just once to pat the sweat from his brow while checking the plantation books. When men rock-n-roll from rear area rocket attacks, Dud waltzes. Gentlemen never rush, and never sweat he says.

I throw back the shots in front of me. Minutes to hours later, I pass out as usual.

"Aaaahhh!" I scream, wiping sweat from my forehead.

"Easy, Douglas, Easy. Barkeep! Another round."

His clean-shaven face I looked at a minute ago has a two-day growth. His clothes are different.

"It's Wednesday, Douglas."

"What's all this money in my pocket?"

"For shooting a moon to the old man on Monday."

Drunks in the dark cool room yowl a drinks up salute. Dud and I re-fight the Civil War.

"You are just pissing fucked that you lost, Dud!"

"Nevah! We withdrew to tactically advantage a gain!"

"Loser!" I belch, ordering another round.

"President Jefferson Davis wouldn't let us win. He wanted peace with honor, not a victory. Lee, The General, couldn't win with dignity, West Point crap, and no blessed bourbon. Grant was a drunk tempting damnation, a winner! His only plan, attack!"

It was time to rest, get some blood flowing in our asses, and go back to our offices to put in an appearance. Dud takes a leak in a ditch. My eyes are fixed on the chopper pad.

"What got you exiled here, Douglas?"

"When you disappear, you're doing what?"

"I'll find out before you will, Douglas."

We shake to seal the bet with bravado and confusing smiles hiding the tension and shame.

"Y'alls' charm is that you have none. Heat stroke shoulda' killed yah. Just what is situational anxiety?"

"How did you know?"

"I know all. There's a why to your little fiasco that I just gotta know. Did it ever occur, Bubba-"

"What – What? Just something I had to do!"

"Exactly! If shot, would they have to carry you?"

"Sure," I say, emptying the beer can I took with me.

"Not every wound bleeds. They shoulda' known."

"Oh-le-anna," I start humming, not listening. "Know what's wrong with that body bag chopper, Dud?"

"No, what?"

"I ain't on it. Oh-le-anna..." I slur, blacking out.

Dud pries my clenched hands off the barbed wire and wraps the spurting gashes as best he can.

"Meow. He doesn't get it."

"No, Mees. Supermen crack before they heal. Let's watch him beat himself up. I love long loathings."

"What the hell is happening, Counselor?"

"I don't know, Doctor. I asked him how he is today."

"Convulsions?! What the— Mr. Bergman!?"

"I didn't save anyone. I fucking chickened out!"

The rain on Dud's tin roof hooch wakes me. Reaching for the booze on the ammo crate, my hangover hand trembles. Where are the cuts and the bandages Dud just put on?

"Better? It's Friday, Douglas."

"Huh?"

"You got that what damn day is it look again."

"Why do Southerners think insults delivered with a smile are flattery? I scowl. "Yankees have feelings? We found them last week after discovering fire. What you call charm, is a stab in the back like Nigger or The General deserted to lead rabble."

Silently, Dud wobbles and serves us both coffees with bourbon from a translucent pot and cups. The afternoon sun passes through them and leaves no shadow.

"Two lumps," I nod. He gives me none.

"The South was honest about slavery. We called 'em dumb niggers. Yankees called 'em Millie and John."

"We never put chains on them."

"No. You made fortunes paying one to capture the other and deliver them to us. You screwed them for fun and left the babies at a church. Southerners raise their bastards."

Sipping whiskey, Dud continues. "Irish maids in crisp crinoline were still slaves. You damn Yankees bought boat tickets. A gentleman has the balls to buy the Niggers outright. Douglas, what is impropah' 'bout a house Nigger doing this or that with a smile and provided a life of gentility they'd a never known? We only hang Niggers. We put darkies in the will, good ones' that is. My darkies were born on crisp linen sheets in the main house, not thrown off ships in chains. Damnation son, mine eat the same food they serve me, what's left that is. And Douglas, NEVAH insult The General"

James is a New-Awlens child of the Deep South at a time when Negroes became blacks but were always Niggers in smoky back rooms of bourbon and branch. To Dud, civil rights means the illegal colored only signs are displayed with pride and a fresh coat of white paint in secret smoky rooms full of white faces.

At half past empty scotch bottle, I wake. When I look up, there's Dud outside hiding behind the hooch door with one of his men. The kid has a cloth scrap over his nose and mouth like a thief's mask. All I can see is his tired anxious eyes. In hushed words, Dud is angrily issuing his instructions and rushing the kid off. All the while, Dud looks left and right, afraid someone will see them talking. He walks back into the hooch and I feign sleep. I rise and fake being startled. He hands me one of two beers from his cooler to oil our gears. Our uneasy stare is full of quivering lips, hurt and suspicion we refuse to share. The words are slow and uneasy.

"So, what do we do?"

"We're doing what Lieutenants in the rear are supposed to, be useless. That's why everything has an officer in charge. They want to know who to blame. When guys get the clap, the hygiene Lieutenant is blamed. When a private blows up his CO with a grenade under the bunk, the grenade count Lieutenant is blamed. I keep everyone from knowing what I am supposed to be doing so I can't be blamed. Everyone sees you slaving at your desk five whole minutes a day signing code reports."

"Cramps my hand. What a bitch."

"Pay attention you sorry Yankee. This is a master class in blame avoidance. State's rights was just a southern dodge to make sure you guilty Northern liberals got blamed for slavery. Now the generals know whose ass to fry if those codes ain't still secret and safe."

"Wanna go salute Napoleon to cover our ass?"

"For a Bureaucratic Medal of Honor with Dull Clusters for dividing X boys into Y amount of mystery meat?"

We stroll out the creaky, ammo crate wood hooch door and squint in the noon glare. The O Club is the only building in the shade of a small stand of half-dead trees. We start shuffling downhill on the dirt path to the O Club at the bottom of our bowl compound.

We laugh and walk arms over shoulders. Entering the club, our drinks are already on the bar by the stools with our ass imprints on them. The first drinks are gone in one glug.

"Back me up!" I yell, remembering the angry Major.

"Calm down, Douglas. Barkeep, pour my angry LT friend a double relaxer with amnesia back!"

"You faked being sick to get out of combat. Resign for the good of the service you coward!" seethes the Major.

"Tell me something else, now!" I yell at Dud.

"How you Yankees won the war?"

"How?" I scream, gulping my drinks.

"You had sharper pencils and cleaner whores!"

THE PIMP

"No money and showing a lousy pair of deuces, you piss in a shot glass, drink it, and bet the trip jacks Captain you'll kiss his ass in front of the old man! The chicken fuck folds!" Sarge laughs so hard he has to hold his side.

"Did I win?" I ask, rubbing my head that feels like it lost a fight with a sledgehammer.

Sarge points at the cash wad in my shirt pocket.

My Platoon Sergeant has this I dare you to catch me glint in his eyes. His chunky build, flush cheeks, immaculate haircut, manicure, gold chains, and pinky ring is the tough guy look. He's the guy that goes to church every Sunday to sell bargains out of a car trunk full of new blood stains and old foul odors. Sarge shuffles endless papers requisitioning everything that always get lost in transit. The only thing known is that Sarge's wallet gets fatter with every lost shipment.

Sarge walks to the beat up metal file cabinet and drapes his arm over the edge. Smoothing down his perfect hair in a cracked and foggy mirror, he speaks softly.

"We drink the best scotch, eat prime steaks, have money to burn, and get fucked by healthy whores."

"For the men huh? You'll wind up with a dishonorable discharge, ten years for grand larceny, or be a Senator!"

"Hard time's for LT mopes that sign their name," he bellows slapping my back. "Give me the officer's gimme gotta get list. Hmmm, soft ice-cream machine, silk slip extra large, and a Jacuzzi. Tell HQ I'll need a shipping approval form for sickly Mom's crate of blankets."

This larcenous, chunky cherub with ruddy cheeks is our HQ chief scrounger. We send him out with a rundown jeep and a list. He comes back with convoy of new trucks loaded with opportunistic acquisitions. His river-rat gunboat score was—inspiring!

We stop at the locked door to Sarge's private storage room. Inside

Names I Can't Remember

is a plush carpet, a brand new air conditioner with two gold stars on it, a fridge, fifteen-year-old bourbon, and cases of state side toilet paper guarded by a private with a loaded rifle.

"Is there anything you haven't stolen?"

"In the bush, guys buy back our own beer from thieving kids. You think all that cash goes for rice not the Viet Cong? Don't bitch just because I'm a better thief. Come to Mamma Yang's, great food, and get your oil changed."

At sundown that night, I hop in a borrowed jeep with Sarge. We leave the base by his private entrance; a hole cut in the tangle of barbed wire behind the latrines.

"Leave that rifle here, Lieutenant."

"Are you nuts? We're going AWOL without weapons?"

"Bingo! With weapons, we're spies. Without, we're just stupid. Wanna' get laid or shot?" he laughs, roaring off.

Dusty and bumpy roads surround the base and lead to Hue by Emerald City, the garbage dump. It's a mile square mountain of rotting stench. I look at the methane haze shroud asphyxiating every gasp for dignity by its munchkin inhabitants. The citizens of Emerald City are orphans of the war with nowhere to live. Every head I try not to see is a knotted oily mass of lice. Each frail frame with its starva-tion-bloated belly hides beneath tattered old army clothes full of grease stains and feces. Each face I look away from is a tombstone to the tinker toy wonder buried in their starving eyes and suspicious glances. I hum nervously to drown the laughs they share playing catch with the dead rat being tossed, ripped, and eaten raw.

They roam this maggot Everest from first light to dusk for scraps of anything to eat or use to build shacks in this city of the ignored. Its nick-name Stumpville is from the kids with stumps for limbs. Old grenades or mines discarded there explode throughout the day and night. As we drive on, blam goes one and then another. The little girl moans, cries out, and bleeds her last. Swarms of kids fight over the fresh garbage dumped by the truck within feet of the dying girl. The kids beat the rats in the battle for one more day without hunger. The rats find an easier meal. They're nibbling on the girl's bloody stumps while she dies in shock too weak to fight or care.

The jeep races down so many bug infested and stinking alleys strewn with garbage and human waste. Driving by gut instinct in the dark, he rumbles the jeep over an arched walking bridge outside a monastery. We guzzle more beer racing by the frail monk nervously selling a monastery icon to a thug with a case of C-rations under his arm. In shadow after shadow, we see the potted plant beauty that once lined the streets, now shards of clay full of urine.

Intricate façade paintings of history or tradition are a tangle of ugly weeds and shot to hell delicate gargoyles. The once bustling market stalls that sold the wares beyond midnight are boarded up or abandoned. Frightened eyes stare as we drive by drinking and ignoring the huddled bodies hidden and sleeping in night black doorways.

Our smiles return pulling up at a run down house on the outskirts of the provincial capitol the Cong had owned months ago. The run down shack was once the grand home of a rich family from the French colonial era beaten ugly by war. The tall wrought iron fence and gate around it is rusty scrap barely hanging onto squeaky hinges. The once smooth stucco walls of white plaster are covered with mold green indifference. Bullet or artillery shell holes, gouges, and craters have been haphazardly filled with cow dung, mud, and straw. As our jeep stops, the rats drinking in the small pond near the entrance scatter from the urine stink water covered in algae scum. The roof is a patchwork of the few expertly crafted ceramic tiles remaining, discarded ammo crate scraps nailed together any which way, and savagely mangled sheets of rippled tin. Windows with jagged slivers of fine leaded glass at the edge are a hodgepodge of scrap wood stamped with Property of the U.S. Army. The dead stumps that were once beautiful trees and cooling shade shrubbery look like the skin and bone arms of children begging for bread. Only a few of the crumbling to dust handcrafted bricks in the driveway remain. Red stains in the dirt are remnants from recent discussions with dissatisfied customers.

Out a creaky door, hanging by a worn out spring come Slit Your Throat, Cut Your Nuts Off, and Mammasan Gave Me This Scar. Sarge shoves his wallet under his balls and hugs them all like long lost uncles and priests. Babbling in pigeon English and pointing to me, hell's bouncers finally smile and wave me inside.

A foul smell throws me back entering a room that looks like a French palace on LSD. It's booze, sweat, cum, and fish head crap steaming on the large table in the middle of the room. This perfume turns the stomach of a needle-marked toothless whore holding her nose and devouring Sarge's cock while her hands search for his wallet. He guzzles booze, slaps her needle marked hips, and laughs.

The unholy three sit on hard ass stone benches around the table. Its elegant cherry wood gloss is gone. Instead of fine linen, it is decorated with knives stuck in its bloodstained and gouged surface. The new owners cackle Vietnamese while chop sticking their way to the bottom of the bowl of fish heads, moldy vegetables, and wallpaper paste rice. They wave me over to join them. My gulp for air answers their I'm not sure what scares me more, their guillotine smiles or the ugly whore squeezing my balls. Rot and beetle nut blackens the only two teeth left in her mouth. Her smile is an opium haze of where am I and she smells like the sores on her cunt.

The one-of-a-kind hand glazed tiles on the walls are full of bullet holes. There are dead rotted potted plants more mulch than style. The leftover from days when this room was full of bone china, triangular sandwiches, and conversation that bubbled more than champagne is a Victorian Victrola. Folk tunes hiss out of its slap dash aluminum foil speaker that once was an ornate floral cone of inlaid ivory and jade.

"Jesus damn Christ! Stop sucking so hard. They're my balls not beetle nut, you fucking cunt!" Sarge yells.

"Fuck in her ass, Sarge-san! Bitch loves it" bellows one of the bouncer pimps. "Try da Tai Stick it's—,"

His voice ends there. The grass cured over opium coals kicks in and his eyes roll back in his head.

Overhead is an ancient ceiling fan moaning and groaning while turning sporadically and cooling nothing. My eyes mist with sadness seeing a gentle past when it cooled a family dressed in white summer silk and lace, sipping lemonade, and relaxing in bright white wicker chairs. The chairs are all frayed bamboo bindings. I sit in one that groans and jerk back up before it crashes into a heap.

"You fuckee suckee me boo-koo dinky dow Roo-ten-ant! You cock so big! Fuck me baby," cackles my toothless sleeping beauty. I wince. It isn't her hand on my nuts that hurts; it's her vise grip on my wallet.

For minutes that seem like days, tits with teeth marks and smelly cunts covered with needle tracks are shoved in my face. A foul breath mouth trying to suck my limp dick hard shakes me out of my red face daze. I run away by drinking myself silly on dreams and dragons in the empty field of weeds out back. The rice jungle juice booze tastes like it came out of a rusty radiator an hour ago.

Seeking privacy that might harden my limp dick, I drag my junkie prom date into the only bedroom I see. This freaks her but I don't understand her chattering. Without the tent like dress, she is very pregnant. There's some nervous and wordless touchy feely. She looks sadly to the side wondering if she'll even be paid for the drunk fingering her smelly pussie because he's afraid to eat it.

The door bursts open. My Sergeant is restraining King Kong, the concierge. It seems I am in his bedroom, the only one, without permission or payment. Sarge convinces him to not use my throat for knife practice. I spend the rest of the night trying to sleep on those slab benches in the main room. For music to lull me to sleep, I have Sarge's moans and groans every hour on the hour and my daydreams of far more tender moments.

"Sugar, here," Silkie sings, raising my weak head to her fat brown nipple stroking my hair and humming. "I loves dem mens when dey needs me." She shushes me, smiles finger to my lips, and leans her breast deeper in my mouth. Silkie dries my tears, feeds me gentle that lets me sleep, and counts my cash that leaves my wallet empty but soul full. Whore and thief, Silkie cared for and needed us.

The cemetery slab of stone wakes me. I wallow in shit hole sorrow; this intersection of hopeless and helpless in a pregnant whore's eyes beaten black and blue.

On the ride back at sunrise in the jeep, I am silent while Sergeant whistles away. "You OK, LT?"

"Just thinking, Sergeant."

"That's for generals, politicians, and idiots. You nearly got us killed taking a pimp's room without asking."

"Pimps for red, white and blue? That simple?" I sigh.

"We got fucked, LT."

"Yah? Just who's the whore in this war, Sarge?"

POKER PLAYERS

"Poker, my dandy drunk Douglas, is any man's windmill when his heart is pure, his damsel fair, his cause just, and his cock a foot long. If you're curious, I took you on sick call for shots after your little trip to Sarge's hooker hell hepatitis emporium two days ago," Dud laughs.

"What happened yesterday?" I ask, clinking his glass.

"Well, when Major Napoleon asks you how his jeep got to Da Nang and who de-flowered the village chief's daughter, a bewildered look is a good choice," he whispers.

Stumbling his way from his stool to behind a slot machine altar, Dud preaches to the O Club converts.

"Hear me brothers, poker is a woman that fucks like a whore, cooks like an angel, keeps her mouth shut, and full of cum she loves swallowing!" he says, doing a jig.

"Amen, brother!"

"I give you cock, cards, and conquest, my Frosted Flake friends! Lies, I say, lies, the very soul of the male ego and dictionary of our lives are born at the poker table. Does any man ever lose at poker?" he yells.

"No, brother," I wail, toasting with a fresh drink.

"Ne-vah! We hold our own, break 'bout even, and the biggest lie, do the best we can with lousy cards all night. In the name of glorious greed, we taunt, tempt, and tease each other into bear traps hidden by the sweet stink of scotch, cigars, and revenge. Poker makes every pimple popper's pony pee-pee a horse hung heavy balls stallion."

I look up and gasp. Every bloodshot eye is staring at me. Dud rushes over and grabs me to stop my shaking.

"No eyes!' I scream again and louder again as he feeds me a drink and bear hugs me to stop the shaking.

"Doctor, he exploded babbling about hating our POW with a clubbed

foot, the locked ward door, choppers on the pad out there, you looking like some gook nun... I don't know. Then he moaned about solving the problem... a wall of pity eyes shame in some stream or something, and jerked like a kid getting shot... I think, Doctor."

"What the hell went wrong in here?"

"Douglas? Where are you going?"

"I gotta... I gotta... go somewhere," I ramble.

Dud falls off his stool and runs out to find me. He finds me by the razor wire at the edge of our compound. Beyond it are the rice paddies of the local village. I am on my hands and knees retching and blubbering. Dud just stands there too stunned to do anything.

"What did you see when they looked at me?"

"Douglas, I don't know. Confusion, wondering what was wrong, maybe feeling sorry for you," he stammers.

My belly heaves for breath as the sweat rains off me like the water in the stream. I raise my weary head, lock gazes with him, and reach out a trembling hand.

"Aarrgghh," I moan in fury and agony.

I saw that look at the stream; the look down and up again gaze of I can't bare to see this but can't leave. It's Dud's droopy look of I pity you mixed with a cold stare that is his fascination seeing me in pain. His face is stiff with fear as his pupils widen with the joy glad it's him not me. His head hanging low barely shaking is I expected more from you. His stream eyes crush me with the killing humiliation you're not a leader, just a weak scared kid like me. His quiet embarrassment pierces me with you failed and you disgust me shame. It's my own self-hate for the lie I told and my giving up. The memory will hurt less as I grow old but the shame of the stream will taste as bitter the day I die. I should have been stronger. I could have tried harder. A leader is never just a man. I'm feeling the truth that crushes boys until they earn the scars of age; every man fails much more than he succeeds. As I puke confusion and fear, Dud feeds me booze so it all goes away and rocks me like a baby.

Coming to, I see Dud dealing cards through the cloud of cigar smoke at the table. My drinks and chips are ready. I smile at Dud.

It is a poker table guys love. It sits in the corner of the bar. The smoky haze of romance and greed swirls around it. The octagon shape sits eight with a recessed chip compartment and glass holder at each seat. It is covered in green felt soured with booze and has a mahogany frame scarred with lies and cigarette burns. The look is finished to perfection with a conical light that swings low over the table and hides lying faces in the shadows. We love games that build the pot. More cards dealt mean bigger pots, more ball-busting tension, and a crapload more booze.

Our regular pot building game, In Between, is simple. Players ante their buck. In sequence, each player is dealt two cards face up. He then bets any portion of or the whole pot that the third card will be numerically between the first two. Aces are called hi or low and ties lose. If it is, he draws his bet from the pot. If it isn't, he adds that to the pot. The game goes on until someone bets pot, wins, and empties the pot. Greedy men gorge horror when the card is turned, the look in a mother's eyes when she can't lift the truck off her child.

The regulars bitch up to the bar to oil their gears and fill up on hundred proof card shark fantasies. Sitting in their regular chairs are bourbon neat branch back Dud, double scotch and water double back me, shot an' beer boilermaker who's-its, macho Budweiser only what's-his-name, Lime Ricky lispy, and the Irish coffee smiler.

One drunk after another bets pot on perfect and near perfect splits of king deuce, or ace high and ace low only to be burned by a matching king, duce or ace. The pot grows and grows to over three thousand dollars, most of it in IOU's. Mine is for eight hundred dollars. The winner is the Irish coffee smiler. The game ends with all promising to make their IOU's good on payday.

The next afternoon, the talk of the whole company is the monster pot won the night before. Three officers from the game last night are at the poker table getting drunk. One is the big winner. They are killing time matching cards for drinks and dollars.

"Douglas, mah friend, that was one mighty fine hand a po-kah last eve-nin, one mighty fine hand."

"When you lost, I was at the bar, James. How much?"

"Douglas, a gentleman has the grace to be a silent winner and the dignity to be a smiling loser. Daddy once told me, son, one day a man will ask you to bet on a fine stallion or a three-legged pig. Last night, a Yankee offered me the chance to bet such a race. Being a gentleman who wants to shoot daddy af-tah readn' the will a might early, I bet the plantation on that beautiful champion stallion. When it happens to you, Douglas, and it will happen, bet the dad blasted pig."

"What happened?"

"You have ne-vah heard such an unholy sound as a beautiful horse screaming with a pig between its hind legs, dangling by his jaw on what that horse valued most. It was the most ungodly gelding I ever heard! What a rollicking bloody ride that pig had"

A Captain in the trio of gamblers taps us on the shoulder. We watch the two drunken Captains at the table matching cards. The big winner from last night is very drunk from celebrating the big win. We watch his sloppy deal from the bottom of the deck. It doesn't prove he cheated last night but it makes us smile and cancels many debts. Sober on his Ides of March, the cheat makes his rounds with a fistful of IOU's. From everyone, he gets a freezer stare minus the cold cash. He never asks why. Our eyes dripping with disgust tell him he was caught. A good thief knows; never shit where you eat.

Dud and I are sidetracked from uncovering each other's secret by another dope inspection memo. The grass is killer and cheap Tai-stick. It's semsimillia; primo grass cured over opium coal beds. It creeps up slow and one-third of a joint is a suicide by giggle. Smoking more than a third of a joint is, well, he was discharged after belly dancing for the general.

Up until now, I turned in every joint confiscated. Since it is my last month, I decide to get stoned once. I need something to kill the coward in me and desire to beg Dud for forgiveness. I keep three joints and head to my hooch. A few drags, nothing. A third of a joint, still standing tall. Anxious, I smoke all three joints massively violating the sacred one-third wait twenty minutes rule.

Dud walks into my hooch and his jaw drops. He laughs at my jelly mass oozing about my bed. Having once sampled the killer weed, he knows my mind is aware but that my body or mouth can do nothing. He sits on the edge of my bunk, tips back his cap, and smiles the smile of the devil having let temptation lure me into a full body cast at Heff's Miss April to August ass fuck freebie festival.

"Leaping tall buildings in a single bound, a tad taller than you figured?" James says, with a straight face.

"Arrrohee wahhhhh," I garble, with hate in my eyes.

"No?" his deadpan continues.

"Bliiiieeoh daaaaaa woooommm!" I blather.

James looks at the three roaches. His evil snicker cracks. "Kryptonite slipped in your shit on a shingle?"

"Naaaaaaowhaahhh blick! Oooooeeeeaaaaaaa," I blubber, until the intense body rush hits me and my eyes roll back.

James gets on his knees beside me and tenderly smiles a mother's smile while stroking my hair. I look deep into those soothing eyes. I would chew his face off if I could.

"You saved a long time for that air conditioner?"

"Yalawoo," I coo in the affirmative.

"When the horse of the century wins the Derby by four lengths, you were strong and didn't bet, did you?"

"Narah," I groan wetly.

"When the stallion pulls away by five in the Preakness, the cash for your sweaty summer, sanity machine is still in your hand?" he says, with syrupy sweetness.

"Mirloooy," I nod, as he mops my bubbling spit.

"Why not a better AC? There you are at the Belmont, six hundred in your greedy little hand, and ready to bet the mighty one to win. It happened, didn't it?"

I nod tearing, as more bubbles form on my lips.

"A stranger sidles up, points to the porker in the race, and whispers in y'all's smart ass Yankee ear. But you bet the steed to win," he sighs, shaking his head and laughing.

I nod affirmative. Our faces crack. Holding the three joints in front of my eyes, he gives me the kiss of death right on the mouth.

"Didn't bet the pig, huh?"

We explode in laughter. Well, James explodes in laughter. I just spray the damn place in spit. James stays with me for hours while my bodily control returns. Then, I show him the losing ticket cased in plastic in my wallet.

"Every man has one of those. It's our shinning moment of supreme stupid when our cock was bigger than our brain."

We laugh uproariously.

"I feel sorry for the card cheat," I weeze.

"For a coward? Why?" Dud asks in shock.

"So cheating makes him a coward?"

"To me it does. If he was bad at cards, he should have asked for help not cheat. Why do you feel sorry for him?"

"Because asking for help is a sign of weakness to the men that depend on him to live."

"Huh? At poker?"

"Because his worst was all he had left to give! If you struggle with the load one mighty time, you fall and never go on. If your faith is stronger than your back, break the load into small parts so you are stronger than it is, and carry it many familiar miles. Faith is a journey, not a destination," I Baha'i sigh.

"Beautiful, Bubba. Who said that?"

"A clean shaven poet with a smile and eagle's wings."

"What is his name?" Dud asks, thinking.

"That's the horror here. Names I can't remember."

Dud sits on the cot next to me. He pokes me in the ribs trying to lighten my mood.

"*Meow. He'll drink away his young crying for them all,*" *Mees purrs in Cat Man's ear.*

"*Or the boy he sacrificed for a hot meal and a soft bed,*" *Cat Man whimpers, drying his eyes.*

The fiery red and gold of the setting sun gives way to the sea blue dark and velvet black of night as our laughter and boozing continues. With each drink and laugh, I yawn. I am not tired. I want Dud to think I am ready to crash. If he buys it and leaves, I will follow him to his real job.

"Douglas? Yo! They got this cute whore at the O Club giving out samples," he jokes, looking for my reaction.

I snort, turn deeper in the pillow, and stifle a laugh with my hidden eyes wide open.

"Johnny Walker Black just in at the club. Stateside Charmin in the crapper," he adds, biting his nails.

Dud's voice is not its usual cotton candy smile. The hurt and anger in the one man that never seems bothered by this piss hole, shocks me. I had to get inside his secret.

I hear his feet shuffle in the dirt as he hides behind the door and waits for me to get up. My lip quivers with concern for a friend so afraid that he works so hard to hide his private agony. As he shuffles off head down and hands in his pockets, I hide in shadows and follow him. He walks in circles around the same shacks repeatedly. My chest heaves for breath and my hands tremble. He drinks courage from a flask. I stare not sure, if anything is wrong. If I rush to help, will I embarrass him? When he flops against the motor pool shed and looks if anyone is following, I gasp and give myself away.

"Save me. BLAM! Brains.

Massive why eyes is all I see.

My jaw drops in my god clarity. He is me at the stream and still I don't rush to help. Is the confusion and bewilderment freezing me what my men felt when I needed them? His eyes flood with the same exhausted desperation. He falls. I look away. Dud rises and stumbles on. Beaten, rage, a fake dream and pride drive him on.

We wander from shadow to shadow fear followed by doubt. At a steel tarmac chopper pad on the most isolated, darkest and foreboding edge of the base, Dud stops. The thunder of unseen choppers fills the air like a chorus of angels moaning a hymn of sorrow. Like a priest at his own wake, Dud covers his mouth with a small white mask and clips his nose.

For hours, I watch Dud and his men off-load choppers. Each body bag is carried slowly to the line of men wearing crosses and purple sashes. Silently, Dud records the names that will destroy so many mothers. When the men of God go for coffee, Dud has his final moment of honor that he has kept private. He opens each bag and gently strokes each faceless face, pile of parts, or single stump. He records each name, puts the papers in his pocket, and leans down.

"I'll remember all your names," he whispers.

Unable to breathe, I stumble away into a darker shadow and search for the guts to run away or cry in his arms.

In darkness of yesterday stands the man with a cat on his shoulders in my stream of madness memories. He tips his floppy leather hat. The smoky curl of the Latakia swirls around the tip of his ornate Meerschaum pipe. Mees purrs and coos at the nape of his neck.

"What happened here?" I beg them.

"Turn around. You'll see the answer," Cat Man moans.

I turn. Dud and I stare at each other with save me stream eyes sharing sympathy and sorrow. It's an endless oration of silence admitting you knew I was here and answering I thought it might help. I help him until the sun rises. On the long walk home, his smile returns, our time to know its OK to love a man.

"Is there a bottle deep enough to drown this year?"

"For a pro like you, maybe," he says, smiling that Mississippi wide Southern smile. "Whatever road you rock, roll, and ride in defiance, I gotta hunch it's gonna' be one bumpy ride, you fucked up Yankee. Do a tired rebel worried about y'alls sorry ass a favor, will yah?"

"Sure. What, you motherfucking hick?"

"Bet the god damned pig!"

"Thanks for the only name, Dud," I say in tears.

We shake and silently share the last smile of the worst and best of the poets, pimps, and poker players.

The counselor's forty-five minute timer rings.

"We have to stop here, thank God," he says, sweating and trembling while I cry crumpled in the corner.

> Road behind is the longer view
> I see smoldered dead coal mountains
> Passion fires ahead where less is new
> Smile n' sorrow memories hug for life

When snowflake friends fall and fade
Wedding a single soul to a loving wife

Cloudy friends withdraw spirit layer by layer
Bless the sunlight poet, pimp and poker player

The poet comes dressed in silk and lace
A charming devil smile on a grinning face.
And story of a stranger's temtpting race
Saw the stallion, such grace and so big
The poet's lesson offered freely to me
In a stranger's race bet the three legged pig

Journeys near and adventure galaxy's far
Pimps will sell you your own home star.
Shake his greedy hand so openly given
The daggers of the loving forever hidden
In gimme gotta get back sugar coated
Summer friends with lists are but pimps demoted

Dreams and dragons will ante, bet, raise, draw
Ageless memories are the gamblers you beat
Smiles too grand are sleeved aces that cheat
Age begs to youth dont't gamble snowflake time
Bet the pot for the coal moments given free
Not diamond smiles a give back responsability

Cloudy friends withdraw spirit layer by layer
Bless the sunlight poet, pimp and poker player

Love you Ma. I owe you everything –
the toughest breod I know and sons.
I'm the handsome old fart with the hair.

What a gaudy life it was and finally meeting
my sister Randie at Tavern on the Green.

Names I Can't Remember

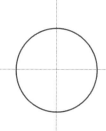

Epilogue

Ding goes the counselor's timer.

"We... have to stop here," the shrink whispers mopping his face drenched by my guilt Hiroshima.

"I have to get out!" I scream, lunging for the door.

"They were sins in your eyes only, Doug," he moans.

"Hell is still hell no matter who lights the match," says Cat Man in the shadows as he puffs his pipe, tips back the brim of his floppy leather hat, and winks.

"I came home to sorrow, silence, and spit. People forget. No soldier wins or loses any war. Countries just tire of fighting. We all fought that war; in jungles, lonely Canadian apartments, on angry campuses, in 4F offices, flashback hospitals, and at graves. We just wore different uniforms. We're born innocent and die so guilty."

"What the hell went wrong?" asks the exhausted shrink.

"Meow. Tell him. You know now, don't you?"

I wink at Cat Man with a satisfied smile, "Not drinking when you need and deserve it. It's the same when we kill too much, care too little, or dream a color future for our black and white efforts. We get lost in arrogance."

Confessions

I detested writing this book. I had to write this book about being a drunk, rotten platoon leader, a punk and utter failure at life. Not until I quit drinking and confronted Vietnam like a man not a cowardly boy could I understand how Vietnam turned me from kid, killer, to confessor.

All these fuckers have been stuck in my heart, life and soul for over thirty-five years and I can't get them the hell out. I am not sure I want to. Killing six people requires company to protect my sanity.

This book was written to beg for forgiveness from my victims, my God and myself. My self-hate is Everestarian for being the one alive. I don't want to die without anyone knowing how life damning guilty I feel for killing "Lin Yan" and the teenagers I met. We Vietnam warriors grew so old so fast giving our youth and blood to a country and history that still turns their backs on the losers they blame. It is such a shame that the lovers of history and peace can't see that no warrior loses any war. A country just loses it will to fight. In the end, we are the same every soldier, protestor, deserter, student and parent. We all fought that war. We just wore different uniforms. Vietnam proved one thing. We get lost in arrogance.

I have survived the hells of my life because I forgot your names. I think knowing them would have carved my heart into pieces, left me drooling in a lock ward forever and crying in sobs overflowing the Amazon. The memory of each and everyone of you has been the soft summer rain in my memory. Your sweet scent and cool feel has brought me private smiles and public tears that I am so proud of. I am a better man because of you all. If you recognize yourself here, contact me. It will be a better finished life looking into your eyes, saying your name, and thanking you for such difficult but great memories.

"Lin Yan," You are the soul and meaning of this book. I do not deserve the life I have for killing you. I will not insult you by asking for forgiveness I do not deserve. I am sorry for being a drunk that day and too many more. I should have known that no kid would or could accuse a nun of being a spy unless he was threatened with death. I could have been wiser, stronger and just sent you home with a swat on the ass after hearing your kid fib. I have lived a life of horror, self-hate and guilt for not being the man and leader I should have been. I will never forgive myself for killing you, watching that ARVN soldier blow your brains out in front of and on my face. I see your hand reaching out to me. I hear your last scream "help me!" I see the fear and agony in your eyes. I hear the shot ... it all haunts me to this day. This book is the closest I can come to giving you any sense of life, begging for forgiveness, saying I am sorry and honoring the bravest, strongest boy I ever met, King of the Coke kids.

The Men of my D Co. 2/327th Plt — I was a miserable leader and failed you horribly. I will never forgive myself for that day at the stream. I had no appendicitis. There was no pain in my gut. I wanted to give up and did like the coward I was. I broke. You brave boys deserved so much better. I am shamed that it was not me. I thank Al Chiola for calling the Medevac chopper that flew me out. If the facts interest you, it turns out I had third degree heat stroke and an emotional breakdown at the same time. The cause was physical exhaustion I brought upon myself for the extra weight I decided to carry and pushing too hard. Neither excuses or forgives my cowardice and utter failure as a leader. I truly got lost in arrogance.

Sister "Nuyen"— Forgive me for my bold and dramatic treatment of you here. Drama will always demand some kind embellishment. I have remembered all my life the quiet truth we shared. Your quiet, plain strength glowed from God's smile on your face. I still see your plump figure in the habit flowing about that barren kitchen in the orphanage. I had imagined your anger when I told you of the accusation. Your calm honesty and spiritual simplicity made me know in an instant that this woman could be no spy. It was all the fib of a child coerced with death threats. Without every trying, you brought the spirit of God to an angry boy's life and made him a better man.

The men of my platoon – A 2/327: My platoon Sergeant – thank you for being the calm and wise big brother E-6 I needed. You were the leader a drunk punk like me could never be. Thank you for saving my life and keeping my head out of my ass, most of the time.

Toothless Freddie – Thank you for saving all our lives at least twice. When I need a Point Man, I'll get the best, you, part hillbilly part bloodhound. I hope all is well with those store bought teeth the Army finally gave you.

The Virgin Corporal – I have remembered all my life the sacred duty we shared. It didn't matter that he was enemy. It was an honor to bring that boy home for a proper burial. It was my honor to have served that purpose with you. If I have remembered it well, I must thank you for protecting us all when we ran out of ammo and were surrounded. Your M-79 fire from all points kept the enemy thinking we could repel them. You deserved more than the Bronze star. Thank you. You've earned all our respect for a lifetime.

Hillbilly, Nigger and Spic – The best, roughest and most honest squad leaders in the Army. Before I knew who you were, you said to me, "The only thing that drops quicker than Hillbillies, Niggers and Spics is 2nd Lieutenants." I thank you for the harsh lessons in no book that saved my life. I wish I could have been a better Lieutenant. I was just so damned afraid, all I could do was get drunk and act like a Patton with pimples. I am sorry.

Doofus – I wish I had the guts back then to talk to you. You and I were the same boy. I felt as goofy and uncoordinated as you seemed to be. I was always afraid around others. I was fat. My nickname was Fudsy for the crew cut my Ma made me wear. In school, the big cool guys stuffed me in a wastebasket and sang the demeaning Fudsy song. The honor and joy of knowing you was a lesson for life you gave me. I felt you knew how goofy or untalented you were but you never gave up. The more people laughed, the harder you tried and trudged on. You did save our lives on the LZ mission. Every time we had to help you we became a stronger unit of men with one purpose to get out alive. Without you, we were frightened children running every wrong way straight into the arms of danger and death. Thank you for

Names I Can't Remember

being the bravest man that day that saved our lives.

Drowned black boy – To you and your mother, I am sorry I did not get to that stream sooner. Forgive me for taking so long to find you in the water. I hate myself for the panic and weakness that made getting you up and out of the water. After so many minutes of breathing into you, I gave up. I'll never know if one more breath would have brought you back to life.

Enemy Kill #1 & Enemy Kill #2 – All my life I have honored and respected you for the brave soldiers you were. I never hated you. I feared being killed by you. I hold you in far higher esteem than the politicians that sent me to kill you in a fucked up war, and my coun-trymen who hated me for killing for them and waiting a lifetime to thank me for the effort, sacrifice and gambling my life.

The Baha'i – You have made me a better man. The peace and strength of spirit in you has taught me that I can fight without violence, I can win without another's defeat and that a standing firm with quiet smile is the mightiest weapon. Every day I remember the strongest man ever that beat an entire Army with a quiet "no."

Thank you Lt. James L. Dudley for the one and only name I do remember. I still see that Southern charm and toothy white smile. You made my horror bearable with your grace, laughter and not judging me. I think I remember your name because your life was the only one not resting atop the silver bar on my weak shoulders.

Marion Shelton – I am sorry I was not wise enough to see the weary in you, read the signs better and be a better friend that could talk you out of what you did. Knowing you was a great honor of my life. I marveled at how quiet, private and meek you seemed but were the David among an army of Goliaths for Charles and every POW. I loved your impishness, bawdy sense of humor and plain talk that cut to the heart of the issue. A weary country gave up on your husband and left him counting heartbeats and wondering when. You are the strongest person I ever met.

PERSONAL DATA	1. LAST NAME-FIRST NAME-MIDDLE NAME BERGMAN, DOUGLAS RONALD	2. SERVICE NUMBER 05361793	3. SOCIAL SECURITY NUMBER

PERSONAL DATA

4. DEPARTMENT, COMPONENT AND BRANCH OR CLASS	5a. GRADE, RATE OR RANK	5b. PAY GRADE	6. DATE OF RANK		
ARMY USAR INF	1LT	O-2	DAY 15	MONTH Mar	YEAR 70

7. U.S. CITIZEN	8. PLACE OF BIRTH (City and State or Country)	9. DATE OF BIRTH		
☒ YES ☐ NO	Minneapolis, Minnesota	DAY 16	MONTH Jun	YEAR 49

SELECTIVE SERVICE DATA

10a. SELECTIVE SERVICE NUMBER	10b. SELECTIVE SERVICE LOCAL BOARD NUMBER, CITY, COUNTY, STATE AND ZIP CODE	DATE INDUCTED		
11 102 49 1131	LB #102, Des Plaines, Illinois	DAY NA	MONTH	YEAR

TRANSFER OR DISCHARGE DATA

11a. TYPE OF TRANSFER OR DISCHARGE	11b. STATION OR INSTALLATION AT WHICH EFFECTED			
Relieved from Active Duty	Fort Sheridan, Illinois			

c. REASON AND AUTHORITY	d. EFFECTIVE DATE		
Ch 3 REG XXVII AR 635-100 SPN 611.Completion of Hospitalization	DAY 16	MONTH Dec	YEAR 70

12. LAST DUTY ASSIGNMENT AND MAJOR COMMAND	13a. CHARACTER OF SERVICE	13b. TYPE OF CERTIFICATE ISSUED
HHC 101st Avn Gp 101st Abn Div USARPAC	HONORABLE	None

14. DISTRICT, AREA COMMAND OR CORPS TO WHICH RESERVIST TRANSFERRED	15. REENLISTMENT CODE
USAR Control Group (Annual Tng) USAAC, St. Louis, MO 63132	

16. TERMINAL DATE OF RESERVE/UMT&S OBLIGATION			17. CURRENT ACTIVE SERVICE OTHER THAN BY INDUCTION		a. SOURCE OF ENTRY:	b. TERM OF SERVICE (Years)	c. DATE OF ENTRY		
DAY 28	MONTH Feb	YEAR 74	☐ ENLISTED (First Enlistment) ☐ ENLISTED (Prior Service) ☐ REENLISTED ☐ OTHER Commissioned			NA	DAY 15	MONTH Mar	YEAR 69

18. PRIOR REGULAR ENLISTMENTS	19. GRADE, RATE OR RANK AT TIME OF ENTRY INTO CURRENT ACTIVE SVC	20. PLACE OF ENTRY INTO CURRENT ACTIVE SERVICE (City and State)
NA	2LT	Fort Benning, Georgia

SERVICE DATA

21. HOME OF RECORD AT TIME OF ENTRY INTO ACTIVE SERVICE (Street, RFD, City, County, State and ZIP Code)	22. STATEMENT OF SERVICE	YEARS	MONTHS	DAYS
2467 Peter Road Des Plaines (Cook) Illinois	a. CREDITABLE FOR BASIC PAY PURPOSES (1) NET SERVICE THIS PERIOD	1	9	2
	(2) OTHER SERVICE	1	0	16
23a. SPECIALTY NUMBER & TITLE	(3) TOTAL (Line (1) plus Line (2))	2	9	18
71542	b. TOTAL ACTIVE SERVICE	2	9	18
Parachutist	23b. RELATED CIVILIAN OCCUPATION AND D.O.T. NUMBER NA	c. FOREIGN AND/OR SEA SERVICE USARV	0	11	0

24. DECORATIONS, MEDALS, BADGES, COMMENDATIONS, CITATIONS AND CAMPAIGN RIBBONS AWARDED OR AUTHORIZED
Parachutist Badge   Combat Infantrymen Badge Vietnam Service Medal   Vietnam Campaign Medal Air Medal

25. EDUCATION AND TRAINING COMPLETED
USA Infantry School - Infantry Mortar Platoon Officer Course

VA AND IMP. SERVICE DATA

26a. NON-PAY PERIODS TIME LOST (Preceding Two Years)	b. DAYS ACCRUED LEAVE PAID	27a. INSURANCE IN FORCE (NSLI or USGLI)	b. AMOUNT OF ALLOTMENT	c. MONTH ALLOTMENT DISCONTINUED
NA	25	☐ YES ☒ NO	NA	NA

	28. VA CLAIM NUMBER	29. SERVICEMEN'S GROUP LIFE INSURANCE COVERAGE	
	c. NA	☐ $10,000 ☐ $5,000 ☒ None $15,000	

REMARKS

30. REMARKS
4 Years High School
Blood Group "O"
Item 5a: Temporary 1LT AUS appointed 15 Mar 70
          Permanent 2LT USAR appointed 15 Mar 69
Item 22c: Vietnam - 21 Nov 69 thru 6 Nov 70.

AUTHENTICATION

31. PERMANENT ADDRESS FOR MAILING PURPOSES AFTER TRANSFER OR DISCHARGE (Street, RFD, City, County, State and ZIP Code)	32. SIGNATURE OF PERSON BEING TRANSFERRED OR DISCHARGED
922½ Market Street DeKalb (DeKalb) Illinois 60115	*Douglas R. Bergman*
33. TYPED NAME, GRADE AND TITLE OF AUTHORIZING OFFICER	34. SIGNATURE OF OFFICER AUTHORIZED TO SIGN
D. J. BAUER, 1LT, Asst. Adjutant	*DJBauer*

DD FORM 214 1 JUL 66	PREVIOUS EDITIONS OF THIS FORM ARE OBSOLETE EFFECTIVE 1 JAN 67.	☆ GPO: 1969-351-112	ARMED FORCES OF THE UNITED STATES REPORT OF TRANSFER OR DISCHARGE	2

Names I Can't Remember

BERGMAN, DOUGLAS RONALD
05361793

Copy for...

1. NAME *(Last, first, middle)* **AND SERVICE NUMBER** | | **2. GRADE** 1LT | **3. COMPONENT** USAR AUS | **4. DATE OF BIRTH** 16Jun49 | **5. RACE** CAU | **6. DATE OF CURRENT TOUR** 15Mar69 | **7. RELIGION** Not Stated | **8. BRANCH** BASIC Inf / CONTRA Inf

9. 27 MAY 70	MILITARY OCCUPATIONAL SPECIALTIES			15.	RATINGS, SPECIALTIES AND DESIGNATIONS		
CODE	**TITLE**	**DATE**	**QUALIFYING AUTHORITY**	**TYPE**		**DATE**	**AUTHORITY**
1542	Inf Unit Comd	15Mar69	Hq TCB USAIS	Parachutist		15Mar69	SO204HQTSB21Aug68
(P) 71542	Parachutist	15Mar69	Hq TCB USAIS				
1543	Hvy Unit Inf Comdr	15Oct69	Hq USAIS				

16.	CIVILIAN EDUCATION AND MILITARY SCHOOLING			
SCHOOL	**MAJOR OR COURSE**	**DURAT.**	**COMP.**	**Y**
Des Plaines, Ill (HS)	Academic	4Yrs	Yes	
Ft Leonard Wood, Mo	Clerk	8Wks	Yes	
Ft Benning, Ga	Basic Airborne	3Wks	Yes	
USA Inf Sch	Inf Off Cand	23Wks	Yes	
USA Inf Sch	IMPOC (1543)	5wks	yes	

10. ASSIGNMENT LIMITATIONS

11. INVESTIGATIONS AND CLEARANCES NAC 1Apr68 DOD NACC Secret
SPH Compl 29Feb68

CHANGES	12.	APPOINTMENTS		DATE OF	
	GRADE	**TYPE**	**APPOINTMENT**	**ELIGIBILITY**	**RANK**
	2LT	USAR	15Mar69		15Mar69
	2LT	AUS	15Mar69		15Mar69
	1LT	AUS	15Mar70		15Mar70

17.	FOREIGN SERVICE				MONTHS
FROM	**THROUGH**	**OVERSEA COMMAND**	**PCS**	**TDY**	**T**
21Nov69	6Nov70	USARPAC-VN	11		

13.	SERVICE AGREEMENT	14.	PHYSICAL STATUS						
TYPE	**TERMINATES**		**P**	**U**	**L**	**H**	**E**	**S**	**DATE**
ORY 07	14Mar71		1	1	1	1	1	1	

HEIGHT 5'11" WEIGHT 180

DA FORM 66 1 NOV 64   PREVIOUS EDITIONS OF THIS FORM AND DA FORM 66WS, 1 JUL 47, ARE OBSOLETE   **OFFICER QUALIFICATION RECORD**

18.		RECORD OF ASSIGNMENTS			
EFFECTIVE DATE	**MOS**	**DUTIES PERFORMED**	**ORGANIZATION AND STATION OR THEATER**	**NON-DUTY DAYS**	**TYPE OF REPORT**
Enl Svc:	29Feb68-14Mar69 SP5 (E5) (Inf)				
15Mar69		Commissioned INF-USAR fr Inf OCS			
15Mar69	0001	Dy Unasg	HHC,TSB(3A-3151-01)FtBngGa	4	None
19Mar69	72110	Asst Adj (4thStuBn)	HHC,4thStuBn,TSB,FtBngGa	0	None
1Apr69	72110	Adjutant (4thStuBn)	HHC,4thStuBn,TSB(3A-3151-01)FtBngGa	0	None
23Jun69	71542	Asst XO	42dCo,4thStuBn,TSB(3A-3151-01)FtBngGa	0	None
2Jul69	71542	XO	42dCo,4thStuBn,TSB(3A-3151-01)FtBngGa	15	None
28Sep69	0001	Casual (TDY Ft.Benning)	Enroute to USARPAC	5	None
7Sep69	0006	Stu O (IMPOC #2-70)	42dCo 4thStuBn TSB(3A-3151-01) Ft Bng GA	0	None
15Oct69	0008	Casual	Enr to USA RPAC-Vietnam	0	None
25Nov69	0001	Casual	Det#3101AdminCo101AbnDiv(Ambl)USARPAC-VN	13	None
8Dec69	0001	DtyUnsg	HHC2Bn327Inf101AbnDiv(Ambl)USARPAC-VN	2	None
10Dec69	1542	PltLdr(Cinsgcy)	CoA2Bn327Inf101AbnDiv(Ambl)USARPAC-VN	0	67-6
20Jan70	1542	Plt Ldr(Cinsgcy)	CoA2Bn327Inf101AbnDiv(Ambl)USARPAC-VN	0	67-6
1Feb70	4010	Asst S-4 (Cinsgcy)	HHC 2Bn327Inf101AbnDiv(Ambl)USARPAC,RVN	0	67-6
24Apr70	1542	PltLdr(Cinsgcy)	CoE2Bn327In101AbnDiv(Ambl)USARPAC-RVN	0	67-6
16May70	1542	PltLdr(Cinsgcy)	CoE2Bn327In101AbnDiv(Ambl)USARPAC-RVN	0	67-6
24May70	1542	PltLdr	(Cinsgcy)	CoD2Bn327thInf101AbnDiv(Ambl)USARPAC-RVN	0	None
15Jun70	1010	CommPltLdr	(Cinsgcy)	HHC101stAbnBp101stAbnDiv(Ambl)USARPAC-RVN	0	67-6
6Nov70	0003	Patient	Great Lakes NavalHospital	40	None
16Dec70		REFRAD Para 45 SO 263 Hq Ft Sheridan, IL dtd 16 Dec 70			

2

21.	AWARDS AND DECORATIONS			24.		DETAILS		
TYPE	AUTHORITY	ISSUED	BRANCH	FROM	AUTHORITY	THROUGH	AUTHORITY	
NDSM	AR 672-5-1	NO						
GCMDL	GO16HQTCBUSAIS12Feb69	no						
Prcht Badge	SO204HQTSB21Aug68	Yes						
VSM	AR672-5-1	yes						
CTB	GO48HQ1CAVDiv17Feb70	yes	25.	BIRTHPLACE AND CITIZENSHIP			26. MARITAL STATUS	
RVNCM	AR672-5-1	yes		PLACE OF BIRTH	CITIZEN OF	Single		
Ar Medal	GO 1041 7 HQ Div Ru 369		OFFICER	Minneapolis, Minn	US			

						27. DEPENDENTS	
	SPOUSE			SPOUSE	CHILDREN	OTHE	
	FATHER	Chicago, Ill	US	0	0	0	
	MOTHER	Chikid, Minn	US				

28. MAIN CIVILIAN OCCUPATION	TITLE AND INDUSTRY		DOT CODE	MONTHS EMPLOYE
	Actor		150.048	24
DUTIES PERFORMED	Stage Acting and Singing			

PRINCIPAL EMPLOYER	Minneapolis, Minn			
29. SECOND BEST CIVILIAN OCCUPATION	TITLE AND INDUSTRY		DOT CODE	MONTHS EMPLOYE
DUTIES PERFORMED				

22.	CAMPAIGNS	
DESIGNATION	AUTHORITY	
X Unassigned	DA MSG 16155 JAN70	
Unnamed		

PRINCIPAL EMPLOYER				
30.	AVOCATIONS	31. SPORTS (Specify)	AMAT.	PROF. CI
	Guitar	(1) Skying Skiing	X	I
	Writing	(2) Golf	X	
	Speaking	(3)		
32.	LANGUAGES (Specify)	INTER. TRANS. UNDERSTAND SPEAK READ WRITE		
	(1)			
	(2)			
	(3)			

33. REMARKS 2485

BPED 29Feb68 PPN S7 15Mar69
SSN 11-102-49-1131 IR#102 Des Plaines (Cook) Ill 60017
CBR instr compl 7Mar69
Code of Conduct: 2Nov68; Mil Justice Tng: 7Feb69

33.	QUALIFICATION IN ARMS			
WEAPON	COURSE	QUAL.	SCORE	DATE
Rifle (m-16)	SS	48	r10c768	
Rifle (m-16)	exp	2/	26Dec69	

Battle Indoc: 11Mar69; "DORE Administered 13Mar69"
RVN Tng: 14 MAR69   Elig Prcht #3
Geneva Conv; 21Nov68

ALAT-1 22 6Mar68   Used 12 s Naval Hosp Blakes I

34. SIGNATURE OF OFFICER (Name, grade, branch and date)	35. DATE OF ANNUAL AUDI
Douglas R Bugman 2LT INF 19Mar69	

*I*f you enjoyed this book and would like to pass one on to someone else, please check with your local bookstore, online bookseller, or use this form:

Name _____

Address_____

City _____State_____ Zip_____

Please send me:

___ copies of *Names I Can't Remember* at $14.99 $_____
    (Soft cover edition)

___hard cover, certified first printing at $99.95 $_____

___Signed hard cover, certified first printing at $249.95 $_____

    New York residents please add sales tax $_____

Shipping*: $4.00 for the first copy and $2.00
for each additional copy $_____

Total enclosed $_____

Send order to:
    The Warrior Group
    47–28 Francis Lewis Blvd.
    Bayside, NY 11361-3046
or visit our website at www.namesicantremember.com
or e-mail to warriorbooks@aol.com
718-224-8246

For more than 5 copies, please contact the publisher for multiple copy rates.
*International shipping costs extra. If shipping to a destination outside the United States, please contact the publisher for rates.

The Cover

It is four pieces of typing paper from a nurses' station taped together. The paint is watercolor from the Psych Ward activity and therapy box. As the Post Traumatic Stress Disorder began oozing out of me, making winged warrior sculptures with massive erections out of chicken bones, this picture of inner shame and self-hate just exploded out of me one day.

"We" Lost!

No warrior loses any war. Countries loose their will to fight. It hurts you so much when he cries alone. I wish I knew what made him this way. *Why you should read this book.*

I am tired of hating myself. *Why I wrote this book...*

You love him and would die for him, but have you ever thanked him and said, "Welcome home?" You have to feel and mean it. If you don't, he'll know – he'll see it in your eyes and it will hurt worse than if you never said it at all. *What I want you to do because of this book.*

When your husband, father, uncle, mother or aunt suddenly stops talking, stares off, begins to cry, won't let you touch them, can't talk and just wanders off, they were remembering what happened in this book and how much it hurt, made them laugh or cry. Not the wars and how they took hill three zero nothing but what changed that teenager you used to know, how lost and cant get back that he/she feels. This book is how I changed from an arrogant angry punk drunk to an arrogant angry drunk punk finally realizing that a blows apart bodies and there were fifty pimple poppers that live or die depending on what I decided. This book is how boys become scared men at war. Funny thing is, I never stopped being that little boy. War demands you act like a man weather you are one or not.

The guilt and self-hate from my Vietnam failures has broken me. I wrote this book because I need to scream it out and have someone listen and care. There is so much I can't forgive myself for. I doubt I ever will. In the beginning, that I could be such a damnable drunk and allow myself to be in charge of other men's lives is an offense that should get me shot at sunrise. I was drunk on and in command. More often, I was more worried about my own sorry ass or next drink than the welfare of my men. I am supposed to be better, smarter and able to rise above the stupidity around me and solve the problems at hand. But the beginning is not the heart of my horror.

The devil ghost of my life is "Lin Yan", the young boy that accused a nun and had his brains blown out in front of and on my face. Every day, those eyes crying out and begging me to save him at the instant of his death accuse me. They remind me that I was supposed to spot his obvious kid lie, swat him on the ass and send him back to his home or the orphanage. That I still don't know if he had a family or was one of the orphanage kids is an insult to his memory. I am taking a copy of this book back to that village to start my guilt bleeding, to try and learn his real name and beg any living family for forgiveness.

The day at the stream with the men of D company was my last cowardly act. I deliberately faked an appendicitis attack because I knew the company commander would have to call a chopper to get me out so he could continue his mission. I chose to cowardly dessert my men in combat because I was physically exhausted and emotionally broken. Every day of my life I see their eyes piercing me as I take that last look up before collapsing. The image in my mind is that of the heaving and blood snorting bull, his neck muscle carved to mushy flesh raising his head one last time to the sun just before the matador plunges the blade into his heart. The glory of God's sky is lost in the hell of the crowd yelling for his slaughter in the name of bravery. The eyes of that crowd are the eyes I still see that day at the stream.

In these pages, you learn what lead to my decision and you may go oh well... Let us be clear about one thing, my decision to fake the attack was the clear and calculating mind of the coward I was at that moment. There is absolutely no other explanation, excuse, or mitigation. It was and remains pure cowardice. In the end, I was a drunk, stupid and incompetent coward leading your sons in combat. In these pages you learn who and what selected me to lead.

I am exhausted by the loneliness and isolation my anger and guilt has rammed down my life. I am tired of being the strong survivor rescuing all when I can barely stand stumbling through the rest of my life looking for a lap to collapse in and cry myself to sleep. What happens when the big man falls? I know. You look away embarrassed. So shove all that sensitive man crap up your ass. I am trying to scatter my hate and anger to the wind. I want God to like me more than I like myself. My intellect and ego wants to type about some global meaning, ultimate truth and understanding about the war from the inside of one who fought it. Bullshit. I haven't the slightest idea what the war was or meant. I was a scared shitless, incompetent and drunk twenty year old trusted with the lives of fifty other men. That we are not all dead is poof of the existence of God. I wrote this book to admit that I killed "Lin Yan", Enemy #1, Enemy #2, soldier at stream, and Marion Shelton. My weapons were bullets, Claymore mines, artillery, stupidity, alcoholism, narcissism, fear, and cowardice. I should have been shot by a firing squad of spineless deserters.

Once upon a time, the media was a weapon of war. It was slow or censored. It could turn cluster fuck massive confusion into a massive victory, convert a blood and guts defeat into an offensive redeployment, or just ignore the red soaked sand and sea of Omaha Beach for decades. Even though the list of the dead and Mathew Brady pictures from the Civil War brought home sadness and horror, few read and fewer read the papers that had the distant and detached news. Now, the media is a weapon of peace. Its even an election vote net. Corporate controlled media gives us vanilla to chocolate views of all the current disagreements with laughable different slants and political frames. News used to be facts. Now its focused information embellished by speculation to improve the numbers. The sad part is that the loss of national will for the Vietnam War was probably created buy politicians who got more votes selling giving up, walking away and brilliantly calling it all declaring peace and going home. If anything, Vietnam may be the first war lost because we finally saw what war is. A crusty WWII vet put it best, "Hell. If they'da had God damn cameras and Walter Cronkite at Omaha Beach, they'd be havin' sauerkraut and Oktoberfest in Paris and London every damn year now!"

The Vietnam War was arrogance on indifference overdrive mania that made a self-absorbed drunk like me an officer. The demand for meat grinder lieutenants was so high, an incompetent like me could suck up the glory myth, sleep through enough classes and pass enough tests to be branded qualified to be responsible for other boy's lives. That ought to tell you how fucked up any war is. It is strange how so much energy is focused on the soldiers. For the Vietnam War there were so many armies. So many ran north to live lives of quiet desperation, loneliness and fear in Canadian cold-water flats fearing every knock at the door. Would they ever get a coded letter from the states? Battalions bashed their brains out in books that were Greek to them and paid others for papers and test taking to maintain student deferments. Legions picked up the weapons of words, violent protest and bloody rebellion throughout the land. That strategy still makes me laugh and cry. Mothers stoically packed goody boxes for overseas then ran into the bathroom, slammed the door, turned on the faucet and cried. Fathers, well, they did what men always do; nod a bit, purse their lips, pinch there eyes, cough and walk away without saying anything to organize the garage he just cleaned yesterday. A million men and women served in-country in the Vietnam War, about 3 million in the Asian theatre and I am told 7 million for the era. I think 200 million fought that war. We share the same defeat and regret at graves throughout the land.

It was the day when I marched down the Canyon of Heroes and was proud for the first time in fifteen years. It was the day when angry soldiers and a worn out country made peace with each other and cried together. I am talking about the first Vietnam War welcome home parade here in New York. The crowds were thin but loud. The soldiers were pot-bellied but double time marched anyway. I will never forget the girl ten floors up in an office over the Brooklyn Bridge. Her tits are a life memory for every nineteen year old with grey hair that day.

The oddest thing about the 85 (?) parade is that it happened at all. There was no PR, flyers, announcements on the evening news, or dedications from the steps of Gracie Mansion. With no fanfare of any kind, word began circulating on the smoke signal vets word of mouth wire that some idiot was organizing a march of Nam vets over the Brooklyn Bridge and through the Canyon of Heroes. Gossip flew. Had a permit been acquired? Yes. The city approved? Fuck! Did you here anything from your cop uncle? Damn! They were gunna stop traffic and let it happen!? Holy fucking shit! This could be real! And the steam slowly built. Citizens and groups got the word. Word leaked that offices were gathering ticker tape and confetti. There wasn't one damn vet of us that didn't wonder if we'd get applause or have to wipe spit off our face again.

I went to Kaufmans and got an original issue jungle shirt. I decorated it with my 1st Lieutenant bars, Infantry crossed rifles, Combat Infantry Badge, Airborne wings and 101st Airborne patch. All the time I was terrified. I was afraid I would be disgraced meeting someone from my platoon. I had to go. The only way to bury the demon was meet him in the graveyard. By God I wanted and deserved the same fucking moment Patton and his legions got in the Canyon.

With zero organized effort, 25,000 tubby punks like me showed up that day and started a national craze. At 6AM we wandered up from the subway holes and from around corners in that Brooklyn Park. We all eyed each other warily looking for familiar eyes to avoid or rush to and start crying while hanging on in desperation. Silently, crude signs made from scrap paper and torn boxes went up. This unit here and that unit there. Marching over the bridge that day, the harmonies of every marching song were as pure as our memories let them be. Like aging angels we sang to glorify and compete with one another. We double time marched into Manhattan and through the canyon damning our bouncing bellies and weezing breath. THIS was the moment of our lives. These cheers were ours. It was our welcome home 15 years late and we wanted to see every screaming face with tears in their eyes through our teary eyes.

I wrote this book to try and understand me. I needed to puke out the life changing memories of these simple, human and touching boys. Their simple acts of humanity, bravery, honesty and giving made me what I am. I am amazed how their seemingly tiny acts of individuality can affect and change people; a spiritual kid who wouldn't shave, a boy who just wanted his store bought teeth, one so inept he saved us all and on and on. War is an intimate thing. A kid shivering in a muddy hole at Khe San or swimming in an ocean of red at Omaha Beach never talks about the great campaigns of the war and their global implications. We tell you about the smile we shared with the guy dieing in our arms, if we ever get the guts to tell you any of it before we die.

And then there is the blood on what I call the blam brains page. It is real. It is mine. It is the least I could do for the boy I killed. To understand why I did this, I must say that I am a guilt driven whore. I owe that blood to "Lin Yan". That I bleed and suffer in some small measure for a lifetime is good and proper. That I am a whore to my literary career on the exotic isle of obscurity must be put first in line. It is meant to shock you. It is meant to get you to question my sanity. It is meant to be a damn rude and brilliant marketing ploy. What other limited, first printing, numbered, and flatsigned books can claim to have the blood of the author on one page? Maybe I'll get lucky with a foolish idea. Maybe some crumbling copy will be found eons from now and I will be cloned from the DNA. What a kick in the ass that would be. With my luck, a rumor will start that it is blood from the night I committed suicide.

In bringing this book to the light of day, I will share with you the death of a painting in my mind. Until you read this, I saw me as a boxer, muscled, oiled, trained and dressed for the championship bout. I have been invited into the arena, allowed to walk half way down the isle in the dark. While the warriors in the ring beat beach other bloody to the hoots and hollers of the bloodthirsty crown, I am stopped by a rope. I can go no farther. For a lifetime, I trained my writing talent for the one moment to get in a ring for the chance to get my brains beat out by my audience and critics. Until this moment, I was never allowed that literary warriors' destiny; the chance for a bloody victory or an honorable death. There seemed no room anymore for pissed off scribes in this era of cookie cutter crap literary mania. Drop me a line and I send you a picture of my scars and tell you who won the fight. At least the picture in my mind is dead.

The Vietnam War taught us vets one thing. With teary eyes and wobbly voices, we greet each other with, "Welcome home." It is the one thing we craved from you but never got back then. It is the gift we give to each other, the respect that is ours to share. To me, it reflects the painful truths of the warrior spirit that every soldier learns in time. We are disposable. You need, cherish, and glory us when the blood must be spilled. When the victory is won or the loss forgotten, so are we so instantly that it hurts. The reason is simple. We remind you of your weakest and most bloodthirsty moments. Thus, we must be forgotten quickly lest you remember the ugly you asked from us. Every warrior sadly learns that glory is in a dying wind until the next angry fire blazes. Warriors also learn how forgetful history is and how fickle honor and bravery are. Did you know it was McArthur who shot at and burned out the WWI bonus marchers? Governments and their soldiers are blamed for the rivers of blood in history. The sad reality is that more life has been lost under the banners of the one true god than any army of warriors for it is the warrior that knows the only best victory is the last one – walking off the battlefield.

In the end, you will love or hate the book as you will. I ask you but one thing. The next time you see any veteran, thank him with a smile, a handshake and a heartfelt, "Welcome home!"

Names I Can't Remember

Do you Know Now?

Eternity will always speak of war as the gigantic clashes of national and spiritual will that devastate nations and shape the future. It is sad that each historian is not forced to live a war before he writes it.

Soldiers and survivors who live, breathe, feel, and suffer a war, remember the passion, smell, sight, tastes, fear and closeness of it all. War is so very tiny and so very shallow breath, boiling blood, and racing heart intimate.

It is the letter to mom you were afraid to mail, the buddy dying in your arms that you smile and lie for, and the first sex to the moon and back you two will never have.

Worst of all is a life of gray and wrinkled days remembering; how hard you cried lying to mom in those letters, what that dying buddy begged just before he died, and that a life of sweaty sex never matched the passion you only dream of or the fatal orgasm of the war you would readily live again in an instant.

You never read about that pain in the history books of war. It's simple. History but remembers war from a distance. It takes the broken hearts and lives of boys to fight them. Mankind's ideas are so very dangerous. To prove righteousness or best, nations will forever ask warrior boys to dominate and take revenge in bloody rampages that leaders and old men were afraid to face ever or again for beliefs and fears they refused to give up to solve the grief with peace.

Some truths are simple horrors. Given the same outcome, that I come home alive and with all my body parts, wounded mind and spit at aside: I would live Vietnam again in an instant. Were my brother to say he was off to war, I would lock him in a dungeon and swallow the key. Vietnam was my war so deeply a part of my soul. Yes. We get lost in arrogance.